SEA KAYAKING IN NOVA SCOTIA

SEA KAYAKING
IN NOVA SCOTIA
A GUIDE TO PADDLING ROUTES
ALONG THE COAST OF NOVA SCOTIA

SCOTT CUNNINGHAM

NIMBUS
PUBLISHING

Nimbus Publishing Limited
PO Box 9301, Station A
Halifax, NS B3K 5N5
902 (455-4286)

Design: Terri Strickland, Halifax
Photos: Scott Cunningham; back cover photo by Peter Oickle
Printed and bound in Canada

Canadian Cataloguing in Publication Data

Cunningham, Scott.
Sea kayaking in Nova Scotia
ISBN 1-55109-317-0
1. Sea kayaking — Nova Scotia — Guidebooks.   2. Nova Scotia — Guidebooks.   I. Title.
GV788.5.C86 2000   797.1'224'09716   C00-950151-7

Canadä

Nimbus Publishing acknowledges financial support for our publishing activities from the Government of Canada through the Book Publishing Industry Development Program (BPIDP), and the Canada Council.

In memory of Ralph MacDougall,
a paddling companion, and a friend.

Contents

ACKNOWLEDGEMENTS

The information in this paddling guide has evolved from over 20 years of exploring Nova Scotia's coastal waters in canoe and kayak, but the summer of 1980 marks an important beginning. During three eventful months, Paul Potter and I circumnavigated the province of Nova Scotia in an open canoe. It was a trip that changed the course of my life. I am indebted to Paul for his companionship and his patience during our journey of more than 2,500 km (1,550 mi.). We are both grateful to those who supported us in our adventure: John Abbass (Econocolor), the Canadian Forces Base Shearwater, the Canadian Coast Guard, Norma Johnson (Campers World), Maritime Tel & Tel, the media (especially Kevin Trudel of CHNS and Chuck Bridges of C-100), Deryk Oland (Moosehead Breweries), Terry Siefried (Leckies), Greg Smiley (the Trail Shop), and our parents and friends—especially Penny Stoker, who was our contact and resupplier throughout the trip.

Special thanks go to my paddling buddies who have made exploring the nooks and crannies of our rugged coastline so enjoyable, and to the people of Nova Scotia who have truly lived up to their reputation for warmth and hospitality. Whether it was a fisherman giving us lobster or haddock, a lighthouse keeper offering us shelter from a storm, or coastal residents welcoming us into their homes, I have been exposed to remarkable friendliness, which I will not soon forget.

For this current revision I would also like to acknowledge Gerry Gladwin, Ken d'Entremont, Dave Etter, Terrance Fortune, and Jeff Norman for their additional suggestions and information. The improved maps are thanks to the generous support of the NS Geomatics Centre (Curt Speight and Tom Somers) and the NS Sport and Recreation Council (Ted Scrutton).

PREFACE TO
THE SECOND EDITION

Since the publication of the first edition of *Sea Kayaking in Nova Scotia* there has been an unprecedented growth in sea kayaking in eastern Canada. No longer is the sight of a vehicle carrying a kayak and its paddler to the coastline a rare event. On some waters (such as Halifax Harbour and Mahone Bay) these sleek, colourful craft are now a frequent part of the everyday summertime scene. Accompanying this trend are the stores and outfitters that cater to the sport, with hardly a region in the province where you can't buy or rent a sea kayak, take a course, or go on a guided tour.

The media have also observed this phenomenon, reports and articles appearing with increasing frequency on TV and radio, and in newspapers and magazines. Glossy ads, promoting products that have nothing to do with sea kayaking, use kayaks as props to suggest a dynamic, healthy lifestyle. Your next door neighbour, who once thought you were crazy to take that "tippy craft" out onto the "dangerous" ocean, is now asking to come along. A sport that once languished in obscurity has blossomed.

This burgeoning interest has had mixed results. From a personal perspective, I sometimes bemoan that I have to share what was once my private little world with others. However, I helped create this change when I wrote the first edition of this guide. More generally, this popularity has created some conflict with other users in some coastal areas reminding us that a special effort is required to accommodate the various coastal water activities and interests. The current project to create a coastal water trail from Lunenburg to Halifax has highlighted these concerns.

However these are just growing pains in a new sport finding its way, and with 7,000 kilometres of coastline we have a lot of nooks and crannies to explore. Sea kayaking has introduced many to the unique natural environment with which our province abounds, and is at the forefront of a new awareness of outdoor recreation, which includes bicycling, hiking, and climbing. It has also has attracted tourists to the region, providing an interesting summertime livelihood for an increasing number of folks (myself included). And it has created an important awareness of the intrinsic value of our coastal region, and of the necessity of preserving this legacy for the future.

In this second edition, I have attempted to improve upon the original version and include new information that has become available. I have updated and enlarged the appendices and included many new photographs and enhanced maps. I have also expanded the guide to include five new routes. With these revisions, this guide should be an indispensable aid to sea kayaking in Nova Scotia for some years to come.

COASTAL PADDLING ROUTES
OF NOVA SCOTIA

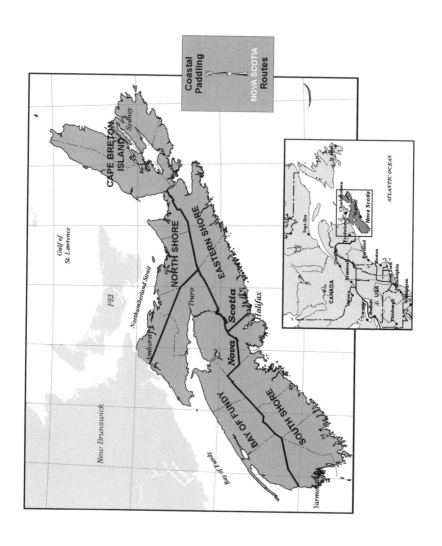

Introduction

Prior to 1980, I had little meaningful contact with Nova Scotia's coastal waters, although I had spent the better part of my life in this, my native, province. I had lounged around the occasional beach in summer, visited Peggy's Cove with the tourists, taken a sailing course on the Northwest Arm, and even crossed to Prince Edward Island on the ferry. But that hardly led to a significant understanding of the Maritimes' heritage. All that changed on June 16, 1980, when, after hugs from the family and a few swigs of champagne, Paul Potter, Bert (his dog), and I left from Halifax's Historic Properties on a voyage that was to take us around the province—in a canoe.

During the next three months, I paddled over 2,500 km (1,552 mi.) along a winding route of inlets, islands, headlands, and harbours where the only constant was the unknown. Life leapt from one unpredictable event to another, leading my intellect and emotions through regions I had seldom explored before.

We were battered by violent squalls one day and caressed by moonbeams dancing off ebony waters the next. Local fishermen greeted us with lobster and scallops; lighthouse keepers entertained us with stories (and rum); and we camped on isolated islands with only the seals, sea birds, and the incessant lapping of the waves for company. I viewed some of the most spectacular scenery in North America as few have a chance to see it.

My journey took me to the very essence of our past, into the reality of our present—and it changed my life. I left my job in central Canada and returned to live in my home province, along the rugged Atlantic coast.

Twenty years have now passed since my circumnavigation. I still spend most of my summer—and earn my modest income—plying the coastline of this and other Atlantic provinces, but coastal paddling in eastern Canada is only now becoming known. Perceptions have only gradually changed a little towards an activity once seen by many as either inherently foolish, devoid of interest, or both. Why risk your life along miles of monotonous shoreline when lakes and rivers (not to mention the warm water) lie just outside the back door? This sentiment was unfortunate, for although there are some risks (see Safety Considerations), these can be recognized and mitigated with experience and good judgement. Happily, attitudes are changing and more of us are finding a measure of escape and fulfillment in discovering what has been in front of our eyes, but beyond our vision, for so long—and the rewards for this adventurous spirit are endless.

The coastline displays a biological and geological diversity distinct from that of the interior. Its unique life forms have evolved complex mechanisms to cope with the great stresses inherent in a harsh environment. Every organism has adapted to its position on the shore, and specific zones have developed between low and high water. The salt spray even creeps inland to cover the trees with moisture-loving lichens. On the barren offshore islands, sea birds and seals embrace a rugged existence in return for protection from humans and other predators, while the sheltered, warmer waters of the salt marshes nurture an enormous biological productivity, ultimately responsible for many of our commercial fish species. And unlike the inland realm, with its dearth of wild edibles, native food abounds along the coast, and with some dexterity and effort you can still live off the land.

Swept clean by the sea, the underlying geology in this stark landscape regains a prominence lost inland to the vegetation. The colour, form, and texture of rock and sand tell the earth's history, a story laid bare by eons of incessant erosion. And it is a story still being told. Headlands become beaches, beaches become marshes, and marshes become dry land. Sand bars can appear then disappear overnight, and elderly dunes can be routed in a single storm. But the bedrock remains, immovable, resisting the ocean's onslaught as do enormous granite boulders, often erratically positioned, attesting to the ice sheet that once covered much of the continent.

Then, there is our own past. Who knows what your wanderings will find along a coastline enshrouded in human history: perhaps some of the treasure, guns, or shipwrecks lost at sea; perhaps arrowheads from a Mi'kmaq site; or perhaps some strange engravings like ancient Phoenician script or Norse runes! The early North American inhabitants lived by the sea for it provided their livelihood and was their highway.

Today, hidden graveyards, abandoned settlements, and overgrown fields lie undisturbed and forgotten, along with those who built them. Rusting iron and rotting wood attest to our maritime past. But for those who aren't biologists or who can't be seduced by tales of buried gold, there remains the simple romance of the deserted island, far from the bustle of everyday living. This is our last wilderness.

And don't forget those utilitarian advantages of coastal paddling routes! Seldom will you have to portage through dense spruce woods on trails scarcely wider than the boat or over sphagnum bogs, knee-deep in anaerobic ooze. Your route won't dry up in midsummer, stranding your fully loaded canoe on a bed of wet rocks, and the bugs, although sometimes present, never reach the epic proportions of the inland waterways. The sea breezes blow them, and your cares, far away. You might have to bring your drinking water along with you, but that is a minor inconvenience, for this is a journey into a new realm of experience. I paid my dues on the lakes and rivers and now return to them only in late season, under fall colours and cool nights. Otherwise, it's the mystique of Nova Scotia's saltwater shores.

As its title suggests, this book is intended as a guide, and with that in mind, I describe specific paddling areas. It is not an exhaustive description of our coastline. Rather, it is an attempt to offer aspiring or experienced paddlers some information that I have acquired in my notes over the years. Sections of this book include routes along the Eastern Shore and the South Shore, the Bay of Fundy, around Cape Breton Island, and along the North Shore. This is not a treatise on sea kayaking or coastal canoeing either. There are many such works already available, especially on sea kayaking, (see the Appendices), although you won't learn as much from reading a book as you will from doing the activity. Seek out and travel with an experienced paddler or take an introductory course to learn the basics. Join a paddling club or an outfitters' association, which often have guidelines to encourage safe paddling. Gradually move on from there. Don't take needless or foolish risks. Coastal paddling can be practised safely, but I must emphasize that there are certain dangers inherent with taking a small craft on the ocean; these should be understood and respected. In the following section on safety considerations, I include a few important generalities on coastal paddling conditions, especially as they relate to Nova Scotia waters.

DISCLAIMER

The information contained in these route descriptions has been compiled from years of paddling the coastal waters in canoe and kayak, and every effort has been made to ensure accuracy.

However, the author assumes no responsibility for errors or omissions. This is especially true when it comes to safety. Coastal paddling is not without some risk. Weather and water conditions can change quickly, and it is up to each paddler to learn the proper skills and make prudent judgements. The ultimate responsibility for safety lies solely with the individual.

SAFETY CONSIDERATIONS

"You have got to be crazy!" How many times did I have to explain my apparent insanity to incredulous friends when, in 1980, I announced my plans to paddle an open canoe around the entire province of Nova Scotia—on the ocean! For some, it seemed merely a waste of time, for others, though, it appeared to border on the suicidal. However, it was neither. I had no intention of leaving this earth prematurely, and after three months, 2,500 km (1,552 mi.), and an extraordinary summer, my paddling partner, his dog, and I returned to Halifax—our departure point—tanned, fit, and unscathed.

Although taking a canoe or kayak on the ocean has some risks, their potential can be recognized and reduced. With the proper equipment, the necessary skill, and an understanding of the limitations of both, paddling coastal waters can be a safe and enjoyable experience.

In analyzing the safety issue, you should consider three factors: your equipment, your technical ability, and your knowledge of coastal conditions. The equipment list will vary depending on where, when, and with whom you will be paddling; there is plenty of room for personal preferences and idiosyncrasies. However, certain items (such as your craft) are fundamental and require special attention.

Kayaks come in all shapes and sizes; some of the differences are trivial, some are not. The choice of a particular design will depend on the type of paddling you wish to do (e.g., open water where tracking is important versus shallow, rocky shores where manoeuvrability is an asset), durability, stability, availability, and price. Floatation is required and bulkheads with hatches are now the norm. The kayak should have deck lines with fore and aft toggles, which help during rescues and carries, and at least one extra paddle per group should be firmly attached and accessible. Rudders are very useful in doubles but optional in singles. With canoes a good deal of freeboard is recommended to add an extra margin of safety. I use a 5.6 m (18 ft.) aluminum model to which I can attach a spray deck when I anticipate rough water, but I have also used many other types.

Flares should be considered, along with a VHF radio or EPIRB, especially in remote regions. Recent advances in telecommunications have also brought us cellular phones and GPS receivers. Soon satellite phone service will become affordable and eliminate the last barrier to 24-hour coverage anywhere in the world—a technological achievement bringing mixed blessing, to be sure. Include a map and compass and know how to use both, as well as repair and first aid kits. Pack fresh water (many islands have none), food, and a means for making a hot drink. Wear a wet or dry suit if the water is cold and if you plan to travel offshore. Also a good waterproof paddling jacket, poggies (specialized mitts for use with kayak paddles), and nonslip footwear are recommended. Store extra clothing and a bivouac sack (or tent and sleeping bag). Of course, bring a life vest—and wear it. An itemized list of suggested equipment is given in the Appendix.

If you have the funds, all the equipment your fantasy trip requires can be bought. Developing your ability and acquiring knowledge of the marine waters is another matter. The notion that you can buy experience (and, hence, safety) with certain equipment is a pervasive and dangerous misconception. The best equipment will not help much if your skills and knowledge are inadequate. Of the mishaps that have occurred on the west coast and, more recently here, almost all have been due to major errors in judgement, usually combined with inadequate paddling skills. Very few accidents have been due solely to inappropriate equipment. Inexperienced paddlers often overestimate their ability and underestimate possible problems, and the ocean can be quite unforgiving. Therefore, before venturing into unsheltered waters, you should first master the basic paddling strokes, be able to brace effectively, and be capable of a self-rescue should the need arise.

A flawless eskimo roll is the first and best means of rescue after a capsize (in a kayak) and the only method to be relied upon if travelling alone. With a group there are several acceptable assisted rescues. Learn and practise these in a swimming pool or lake with the help of an experienced friend or through a course. Then practise them in the colder ocean, since that is where you will actually have to use them in an emergency. Learn to launch and land in a moderate surf and to control your craft in strong tail or beam winds.

Understand your paddling environment. This is essential, without which no amount of high tech equipment or fancy paddling strokes will protect you. It is in this domain that coastal paddling differs most from inland touring. Much will be common sense but much is also novel and will have to be learned gradually. The coastline is a high-energy, dynamic world where the land, sea, and air often meet in confusing and complicated fashion, although these constituents are sometimes easily understood when examined separately (see Related Reading).

Unique to the coastal environment is, of course, the sea. Its single most important feature for paddlers in eastern Canada is its temperature, which can be very cold. Books have been written on hypothermia and what it can do to an immersed body. Suffice it to say that it can be deadly. Be particularly wary from April to July, when a warm, calm day can breed a false sense of security, just when the water is the coldest. As the summer season progresses, the temperature increases. Along the North Shore and in sheltered inlets it can even become rather warm, over 18°C (65°F). On the other hand, in the Bay of Fundy, the upwelling keeps the water cool in the outer reaches. Whether you should sport a wet or dry suit will depend upon several variables, including the degree of personal risk you are willing to accept.

Current strength and tidal range vary considerably in Nova Scotia, and they are discussed in the introduction to each region. They seldom pose a problem, except in the Bay of Fundy or when opposing wind produces standing waves and erratic currents around headlands or through narrow channels. Waves are usually a permanent feature of the seascape and can result from either local winds or a distant offshore storm. They can be short, steep, and cresting or barely discernible, long sequence swells. Sometimes they arrive from different directions, meet and cancel out or reinforce one another. They are of particular concern in shallow areas where they can break unexpectedly over an underwater shoal. Cliffs pose a special problem as they will reflect incoming waves back out to sea, sometimes creating extremely turbulent conditions. Always be conscious of what the water is doing, from where the waves are coming and to where they are travelling.

Keep an eye on the weather too, especially when it is unsettled. Don't rely on the forecast. It is frequently wrong and even a correct one won't tell you if or when that isolated rain squall is going to pass just over your head. This is less of an issue when you are meandering among an island archipelago, a mere five or ten minutes from a safe landing, but it is crucial during open-water crossings. Fair-weather sea breezes can pick up in the afternoons to a good clip (over 20 knots), and in some areas you might have to restrict your paddling to the morning hours. Choose your campsite judiciously or you may be blown away or washed out. Beware of fog. It is common in Atlantic Canada, especially early in the year when warm, moist, continental air condenses over the cold, coastal waters. That thick bank lying harmlessly offshore for days could suddenly move in and blanket you and the entire coastline in a cloud so dense that you will scarcely see beyond the bow of your boat.

Bring good charts or maps during your trips and make a habit of relating them to what you are actually seeing. They are a great source of information, especially on topographical features like islands, shoals, headlands, beaches, and cliffs. The soundings on marine charts are of more use to larger craft but will help you anticipate where you might encounter currents or breaking seas. Navigational aids will indicate where larger vessels should be heading and thus where will be the usual dangers of marine traffic.

Learn to adjust to how the depth of field plays tricks with your mind. On a clear day, the far away objects will appear much closer than they actually are, much the same effect as in the Arctic. Haze and fog have the reverse effect. Time your speed under different conditions so that you may estimate your progress, especially if you have to travel in fog. Much more can be said about coastal conditions, and I recommend past issues of *Sea Kayaker* magazine or *The Fundamentals of Kayak Navigation* by David Burch.

Finally, good judgement is what links your equipment, skills, and knowledge for a safe paddling trip. Without good judgement you won't be long in getting yourself into trouble. It is important that you realistically assess your level of expertise and whether it is sufficient for your particular destination. It is far more important to avoid a potentially dangerous situation altogether than to rely on a technique that may fail you just when you need it the most. Ultimately, you are no match for the sea. There is much to learn about the ocean, how it interacts with the shore and the boat, and this will come only with time.

Be wary of the "rules of thumb," such as never paddle alone and always wear your life vest. Although I agree with most of them most of the time, they may supplant independent thinking and give a false sense of security. Situations tend to develop that require immediate and creative solutions. Anticipate problems before they arise and prepare for the unexpected. Leave a trip plan with family or friends, but alter it if conditions dictate. Carry safety equipment, but don't let it lull you into complacency about your security. A life vest, radio, and flares won't help you much if you capsize offshore in the foggy Atlantic in springtime and can't get back into the kayak. Proper judgement comes with an understanding of the coastal environment—and lots of experience.

The foregoing was just to point out potential problems that can arise in a paddling environment, which may be unfamiliar. The reality is that, after twenty years of paddling all sorts of craft on the ocean under variable conditions, I have yet to have a major mishap. That may indeed happen someday, but I feel safer in my kayak than in a car where a split-second miscalculation by someone else could lead to tragedy. Most problems that do arise are those familiar to all wilderness travellers, such as sprains, splinters, minor cuts, and sunburn. Out of concern for major events, don't ignore these more likely possibilities. Tread lightly over the seaweed-covered rocks, watch for nails in the driftwood, and protect yourself from the elements.

ETHICS

Many of us seek the freedom and isolation that coastal paddling offers in an increasingly populated world. Fortunately, Nova Scotia shores can still fulfil these expectations and have thus far escaped the bureaucratic tentacles of regulators only too willing to extend their influence into another sphere. For the most part, we are able to paddle where, when, and how we please. In the past, I have been somewhat selfish in exercising this privilege and have belatedly come to the realization that I, too, am responsible for my actions and am part of our collective impact on the natural world. We must act accordingly.

This concern, of course, is for the state of the environment, and in these days of increased environmental awareness, it would be difficult to find someone now who wouldn't at least acknowledge its importance. The problem lies in dealing with the specifics. What should be done to minimize the impact of our actions on the environment? What exactly are one's responsibilities? Discussions on these matters can (and sometimes do) take up the better part of the evening chatter around a campfire. In the end, they often don't lead to complete agreement on the problems or the solutions. However, even asking yourself questions can put you on the right path towards awareness. Issues about the environment and our responsibilities towards it are not always clear, especially in a society that stresses consumption without regard for its ultimate local or global consequences.

A realistic perspective on how to live responsibly on the planet and in our own communities is often only reached after much analysis of one's own goals and expectations. I have yet to reach total enlightenment myself, but I stumble along, sticking with some views and tossing out others, never satisfying all the difficult questions. I tend to avoid slogans and blind adherence to rules (much as with safety concerns), however well-intentioned and useful they may be in some circumstances.

As a biologist, I have come to realize that very little occurs exactly as textbook examples suggest or popular myth dictates. Variety and diversity are the norm; the ecosystem is much more complex than we imagine and often throws little wrenches into our pat theories. We must adapt to specific situations; behaviour appropriate in one location may be totally inappropriate in another.

I recall an incident of fanatical environmentalism at summer camp when leading an extended paddling trip. We were canoeing along the Northumberland Strait, not far from Pictou, and stopped to camp for the night. We prepared and ate supper, after which one of the kids brushed his teeth, washing with a glass of fresh water that he subsequently spit into the strait. Noticing this, another counsellor reprimanded him harshly for polluting the environment. The poor kid couldn't grasp what he was doing wrong; neither could I. Aside from the etiquette of spitting within sight of the camp (which, I suppose, some would take offence to), the actions of that camper in no way harmed the environment. The natural absorbing capacity of the coastal waters is immeasurably greater. And what was more, this misguided indignation overlooked the odorous smoke plume of a nearby pulp mill, a structure that would pollute more in one hour than this child could in a lifetime of effort. No wonder he was confused and less than impressed with that example of environmental rhetoric.

Keep an open mind. What is appropriate in the wilds of

Canada may not be acceptable in the White Mountains or a city park, and what the Eastern Shore will tolerate may differ considerably from the Arctic coastline. You don't help the environment by forsaking a campfire if you drive a hundred kilometres to the put in, with a boat stuffed with high tech gadgets and processed food, all of which consume considerable energy in their making. In fact, you only perpetuate a smug contradiction, while the reality of your actual impact grinds on. That said, be gentle with our shoreline. If your passing leaves too great a mark, you damage the experience for yourself and for others.

Our coastal environment is reasonably forgiving, but not limitlessly so. Camping is permitted on crown land. Technically, on private land, the owner's permission should be obtained, but this is often impractical or impossible, since many islands are owned by nonresidents. Be considerate. Years ago during, my circumnavigation, and for many years since I would launch most anywhere and camp wherever. No one ever harassed me. If near a dwelling I would ask permission (whether to launch or to camp) and it was always gladly given. I still have little problem since I have gained the experience of when and where and how. However, some areas are now being used more frequently by paddlers and not everyone cleans up like I think I do. Mess caused by motor boater is also sometimes attributed to kayakers. Occasionally some animosity has arisen and landowners, who didn't care much before on the rare occasion when someone launched from their land, are now annoyed by cars blocking their access and people assuming the right to transit their land. In my first edition of *Sea Kayaking in Nova Scotia* I was at times unwittingly guilty of encouraging some of this and therefore have made a special effort in this edition to be sensitive to landowners' concerns. Ask if in doubt. We still enjoy the friendly, open mentality that makes this province so attractive to visitors and, within reason, you will find people accommodating.

I pack out most of what I bring in (although I'll probably leave that extra leaf of lettuce to compost under the seaweed on the beach) and leave a tidy campsite. If making a campfire, use dead wood. It burns better, and there is usually plenty on the beach. Douse and clean up when you are through. I have returned to some sites after a year and found, to my pleasure, no obvious traces of a previous visitation. Occasionally, in a well-travelled location, I establish a fixed campsite, if only to make sure others will use this one area and avoid a myriad of fire rings. As for toilet etiquette, be discreet. Choose a concealed spot in the woods, well away from the camp and off any trail, and when done, cover with a layer of twigs and needles. Better still, use the zone below high water and cover with a beach rock. Above all, be realistic, and be open to change.

ROUTE FORMAT ⟵

Nova Scotia's more than 7,500 km (4,657 mi.) of coastline would extend to Europe and back if it were unravelled, and it would be impertinent to suggest I have canoed or kayaked it all. Thankfully, many islands, bays, and inlets are left for me to explore. However, during my over twenty years of coastal tripping, I have paddled along much of our shoreline. The following routes, while not exhaustive, do represent the best areas that I have found around Nova Scotia. The routes are somewhat artificial in the sense that there is often no natural boundary separating one from the next. Some directly abut on another, and an extended trip overlapping several is certainly possible; I do it all the time. However, for the purposes of this guide, such arbitrary divisions are necessary and each description can be used independent of the others. I have also attempted to make the route descriptions concise, while including sufficient information to make the trips both safe and enjoyable. They are structured under the following divisions.

DEPARTURE/ARRIVAL POINTS

In some cases, these are the only practical places for putting in and taking out, but usually they are chosen from several possible options. Your own time constraints or weather conditions may dictate otherwise, especially when returning from a trip. Study your maps/charts carefully, prior to departure, to determine alternate landing places. This will seldom be a problem along the Eastern Shore but can be critical in the Bay of Fundy or off the Cape Breton Highlands. It is wise to leave your vehicle where it can be observed by local residents. Ask if you may park in a private yard. You will seldom be refused, and it will ensure added security for your vehicle. In the course of making this request, you might also obtain useful information about the area as well as having someone to notify the authorities if you should fail to return on time.

Note: Since publication of the first edition of this guide I have had to alter several suggested departure points. In some cases this was because the launch site was on private land. In others, a public wharf has been sold by our government (part of the current policy of the federal government to divest itself such structures) to a private individual. Sometimes the local community has taken over responsibility for the port and a modest charge is levied (often even on kayaks). However, don't feel restricted by the suggestions given in this guide as there are many others. Just be sure to always ask for permission and it will usually be granted. We still have a remarkably free access to our coastline of which many south of the border can only feel envy.

TRIP LENGTH

I give distance estimates in kilometres but prefer to talk in time—an afternoon, a day, or several days. These subjective assessments have come from numerous trips with a variety of groups. Your own speed will depend on your experience with paddling, your goals (to relax and explore or to "go for distance"), and the weather and sea conditions. Again, always keep in mind an "escape route" should you need to abort a trip prematurely.

MAPS AND CHARTS

Once I took a trip without any map. Several times I had only a highway map. However, I highly recommend either a topographical map or a marine chart. Both can be obtained at major camping or marine supply stores or directly from the printer. (Refer to Appendix for sources.) Either one is sufficient for the coastal paddler. During my circumnavigation, I used topographical maps exclusively (when I had them) as they were the most inexpensive at the time, and I already had a considerable number from my hiking and inland canoeing days. They contain useful information on coastal roads and other landmarks, which helped in planning for resupplies. Marine charts contain much more information on the coastal waters—although a lot of it isn't relevant to the paddler—and they often came in larger scales. Recently, many of these detailed charts have been discontinued. As well, they are more expensive per unit area. Be sure to purchase the booklet defining the terms and symbols along with the chart, otherwise much of it will be meaningless. I note the scale in parentheses, along with the chart number.

Regardless of whether you take a map or chart, make sure you know how to use it along with your compass. The line drawings in this guide are done to scale, faithfully represent the general features, and indicate the main points of interest. However, they are not meant to be used for navigational purposes as they omit much detail and they should be used in conjunction with a topographical map or chart. The suggested route, indicated by a broken line, is merely one possibility, subject to change, depending on sea conditions, time constraints, or your own preferences.

ROUTE DESCRIPTIONS

These are general remarks, meant to convey an overall feel for the area. Specifics are given in Points of Interest.

SAFETY CONSIDERATIONS

In addition to the general safety concerns inherent in coastal paddling, each route contains certain areas where special caution is recommended. These remarks are important and should be heeded.

POINTS OF INTEREST

Along with safety considerations, this is the most useful section to the individual routes. Special areas of interest are highlighted that you might overlook if you are not familiar with the area. They include such things as seabird colonies, seal rookeries, shellfish beds, unusual or spectacular geological formations, remnants of early human habitation, vistas, and lighthouses. As far as I have been able to ascertain, the campsites that I indicate are on public land. They are not the only ones, or necessarily always the best, and there are others on neighbouring private islands. Use your discretion.

COASTAL PADDLING ROUTES
OF THE EASTERN SHORE

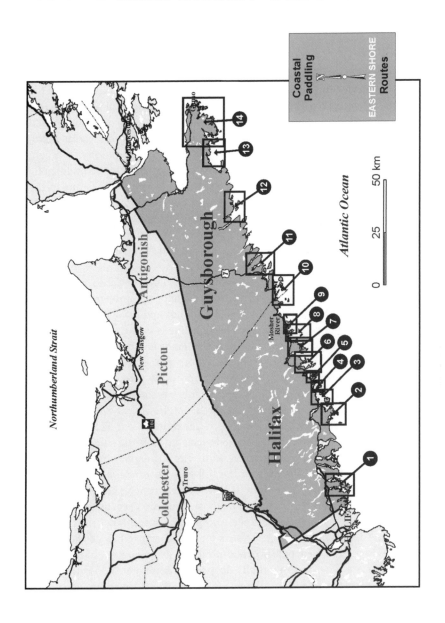

INTRODUCTION

The fog had just moved in and shrouded our island campsite on
the Eastern Shore in a thick mist. The silence was absolute. I
made my way under the lichen-covered spruce in search of mush-
rooms for the evening meal, anxious to return to the warmth of
the fire. My gaze wandered over the moss-carpeted forest floor to
what, at first, seemed only to be one of those uniquely positioned
stones left by the retreating glaciers. I took little notice. This
scoured coastline is littered with such remnants of our geological
past. Then another stone caught my attention, and another—all
three in an unnatural alignment. Curious, I edged towards them,
unable to suppress the feeling of unease rising in my stomach.
Suddenly, the explanation dawned on me: I was in the middle of a
graveyard! Inscriptions on the markers and depressions in the
earth removed any doubts. Other observations I had made now
fell into place—the pile of rocks, the large hole in the ground, and
the well-spaced trees with the developed understory branches,
unusual for this type of forest. We had made camp in an abandoned settlement.

The Eastern Shore extends from Halifax to Canso, along Nova
Scotia's Atlantic coast. The direct distance is approximately 250 km
(155 mi.), but if you follow all the inlets and bays, it easily exceeds
three times that distance. The coastline is very irregular, interrupted by numerous harbours and headlands and highlighted by a narrow band of offshore islands. Faults, perpendicular to the shore,
have created the deepest harbours in the province, Halifax and
Country Harbours, along with numerous smaller coves where tiny
fishing communities are sheltered. Salt marshes have developed in
a few shallow inlets, especially Chezzetcook and Petpeswick, but
for the most part only exposed rock confronts the ocean.

This is a young coast, and when the glaciers scoured the
region they took most of the soil with them, depositing it far out
to sea. What little there is now comes from sediment carried in
rivers and from erosion of loose drumlins scattered along the
shore. Weathering of rock to replace the soil takes much longer
than the ten thousand years that have elapsed since the last ice
age. The bedrock is predominantly greywacke (quartzite) and
slate. These were initially deep-water sediments deposited on the
eastern side of the Atlantic off Africa, transformed under extreme

heat and pressure, and thrust up against North America during continental drifting, millions of years ago. Igneous material later pushed up through this metamorphic cover to form the granite outcrops at the eastern extremity around Canso.

It is the island archipelago that especially distinguishes the Eastern Shore and what makes the region such a pleasure for the paddler. Nowhere else in the province will you find the number and variety of shoals, islets, and islands as along this neglected coast. A few are large, hundreds of acres in size, but most are more modest, and some barely rise above the surface at high tide. Some are tree covered while others have acid bogs and scrub bush. The smallest are mere lichen-draped rocks, fringed with seaweed. Collectively they offer many sheltered routes and protection from a capricious ocean. These days, none are permanently inhabited and only a scattering of cottages and camps interrupt a wilderness trail. You will be sharing them with only the seals and sea birds.

A harsh maritime climate coupled with the lack of any significant top soil has resulted in an impoverished vegetative cover. In some places this is entirely absent or restricted to the lichens and hardy shrubs, which can find a hold among the crevices.

Lighthouses have guided mariners among the offshore islands and shoals of the rugged Eastern Shore for generations. Today, those that remain have all been automated.

Elsewhere a forest of dense spruce creeps up to the water's edge, stunted and deformed by the omnipresent salt air. This is not farming country. However, the coastal waters are clear and clean, and the littoral vegetation blossoms. Molluscs, crustaceans, and fish that have not yet been caught by offshore trawlers thrive in the nutrient rich, cool sea. You will occasionally spot a porpoise or a whale (rarely, though, for their feeding grounds are elsewhere). The main attractions are the sea bird colonies and the seals. Gulls, guillemots, petrels, terns, and cormorants nest on the islands along with Eider Ducks, Ospreys, and occasionally, Bald Eagles. Recently Gannets have become more frequent summer visitors, offering impressive aerial displays as they dive headlong into the water to catch fish. Harbour and Grey Seals are common, and it is an unusual trip where you won't find them basking on the shoals. Deer live on the forested islands, sometimes year-round and sometimes only during the summer, swimming out and back. Bears are absent, though, so you need not take any special precautions about your campsite in that regard.

The ocean moderates the temperatures considerably. During the winter, the little snow that falls is often interspersed with rain, and thaws are frequent—still it is not pleasant kayaking weather! Summers are much warmer, although the temperatures are several degrees cooler than inland readings, averaging 21°C (70°F) in the daytime and 15°C (60°F) at night. A sweater and hat will be needed by the campfire later in the season. The water temperature seldom reaches comfortable bathing levels, let alone allows an extended immersion due to a capsize. An exception is the protected, shallow inlet. Until July it is particularly cold and sometimes not much above freezing. By September it ranges from 13°C to 20°C (55°F to 68°F).

Expect plenty of fog from May to July (even later in some years) as warm, moist continental air condenses over the ocean. The Eastern Shore experiences slightly more fog than the South Shore and considerably more than along the Northumberland Strait. Prevailing winds are from the southwest, and storms, when they occur, are usually short. As in other places, the topography influences local weather conditions, but rapid and dramatic changes, such as catabolic winds and twisters, are very rare. Beware, however, of the funneling effect around headlands.

The tidal range is only about 1 m to 2 m (4 ft. to 8 ft.) and the currents are negligible (under 1 knot), except for a few narrow channels or around headlands. The outflow from the rivers is insignificant since the drainage basins are small and the summers relatively dry. Large swells will occur in areas exposed to the open ocean, but inside the island belt these are usually attenuated. On a windy day, you will experience a chop that is often at an angle to the swell(s). Special attention should be given to shoals (of which there are many). Even on a calm day, a seemingly innocuous swell can break unexpectedly over these rocky areas.

Of particular interest is the history of the Eastern Shore. Human habitation goes back several thousand years, when natives travelled along it in birch bark canoes. They have left their mark in names such as Musquodoboit Harbour, Mushaboom, Necum Teuch, and Canso. On some islands you might find a shellfish midden, the garbage dump of these early inhabitants. The first European to have recorded his visit was Champlain during one of his voyages to map the coast. Fishermen soon followed and made use of the many islands and sheltered coves to salt and dry their catches. Some remained throughout the year and supplemented fishing with a little subsistence farming. Small settlements arose along the shore, taking advantage of the rich inshore grounds. Dozens of fish plants, shipyards, and lobster canneries opened.

Canso was the largest of these communities, and in the early 1700s hundreds of vessels called annually at the port. By the early part of the twentieth century, economic conditions were changing. The interior of the province had opened up and road transportation became practical. People moved to the urban centres and the coastal population began to decline. By the end of the Second World War, there were few permanent residents left on the islands. Today there are none. The recent crisis to befall the Atlantic fishery has only hastened a long-established trend. Most of the islands, once private, have reverted to public ownership and the remainder are seldom used. This is slowly changing but rare are the no-trespassing signs. Except in lobster season (mid-April to mid-June), you will seldom encounter another craft on these waters. Even the lighthouses, operated manually until the '80s, have all been automated. What was once a reasonably prosperous shore is slowly reverting to wilderness. Even the two largest towns have less than one thousand residents.

1

PORTERS LAKE TO CHEZZETCOOK

DEPARTURE POINT:

Sandy Point

Route 107 to Exit 20. Take gravel road immediately north of exit to parking lot by the lake, approximately 20 km (12 mi.), from Dartmouth.

Porter's Lake Provincial Park

Route 107 to Exit 19. Follow Lawrencetown Road south to park (approximately 24 km, 15 mi, from Dartmouth)

ARRIVAL POINT:

East Chezzetcook government wharf. Alternatively, at high tide you can take out about anywhere that a road meets the inlet.

TRIP LENGTH:

Day-long or weekend, 26 km (16 mi.) from Sandy Point.

CHARTS AND MAPS:

Topographical Maps: 11/D/11
Marine Charts: Taylors Head to Shut-in Island (#4236; 60,000)

ROUTE DESCRIPTION:

Only a few miles from Halifax, this accessible coastal route is an intriguing combination of freshwater lake, open ocean and sheltered inlet. Except for a couple of kilometres separating the northern sections, this could be a circular route. The topography is characterised by numerous hills of loose glacial debris called drumlins, which can be observed as rapidly eroding headlands on the exposed coast. The irregularity of this relatively young coastline is gradually evening out with the abundant local sediments produced from these drumlins. Spits and barrier beaches connecting islands and promontories isolate ponds and protect the shallow estuary of Chezzetcook Inlet, allowing extensive salt marshes to develop. The route is lined mainly with coniferous woods, interspersed with open fields and houses. The cottages of Porters Lake give way to the fishing shanties of Three Fathom Harbour, then the Acadian community of Grand Desert and West Chezzetcook. The area is rapidly developing as a bedroom

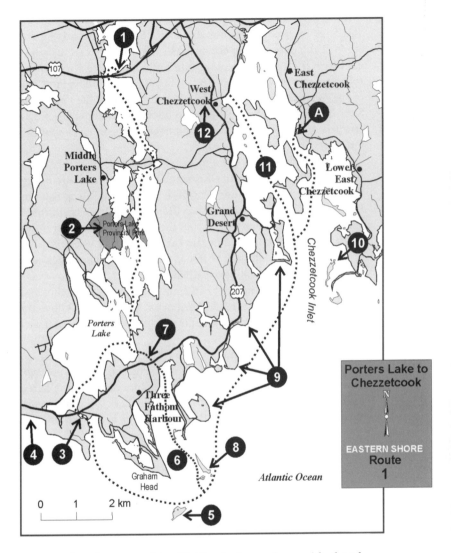

community of metropolitan Halifax but remains an ideal paddling locale.

SAFETY CONSIDERATIONS:

My first encounter with this section Nova Scotia's Atlantic coastline was on the second day of our circumnavigation of the province in 1980, when with a complacency bred by inexperience and encouraged by the idyllic conditions, we decided on a shortcut between Graham Head and Shut-in Island. As we reached the passage, the ocean swells that had seemed insignificant earlier steepened rapidly, and within minutes we were on roller coaster waves of 5 m (18 ft.), higher than the length of our canoe. We beat a hasty retreat and headed around the outside of Shut-in Island. We has just learned about the shallowing effect, the first of many lessons we would have that summer about the interaction of ocean and coast.

Use caution along the exposed coastal section of this route from the Rocky Run into Chezzetcook Inlet. There are many shoals, particularly around Shut-in Island and in Three Fathom Harbour. The narrow entrance to Chezzetcook Inlet will funnel and steepen any ocean swells, and there can be a fair current as the tidal water enters and exits the inlet. Time your passage through Chezzetcook Inlet with consideration of these tides, and make sure that you will have sufficient water under your boat for the entire journey. The inlet can empty surprisingly quickly and leave you stranded on a muddy bed of eel grass up to a kilometre from shore in some places. Paddling against the current can also exhaust you.

With the ebb of the tide Chezzetcook Inlet becomes a plain of salt marsh and eel grass flats.

Pay particular attention to Rocky Run, especially at low tide. Scout carefully before paddling through, and if in doubt, portage. The other option at high tide is to paddle into the ocean at Three Fathom Harbour via the canal (7). In Porters Lake, your main concern on warm, sunny days will be the power boats, which may

not be on the lookout for small kayaks or canoes. If conditions (or experience) prevent you from venturing onto the open coastline, you still have the option of exploring either Porters Lake or Chezzetcook Inlet on a day outing.

POINTS OF INTEREST:

1. Sandy Point

This is where Highway 107 crosses Porters Lake, cars often line the edge in summer as their occupants take advantage of the adjacent warm water and sandy beach. Eventually, after repeated attempts to prohibit this often hazardous unofficial parking, the government created a parking lot. This is a good departure point.

2. Porters Lake Provincial Park

This is an alternative launching spot, especially for those who plan to get an early start by camping the night before. The park, however, is closed between September 5 and June 10. (These dates may change from year to year.)

3. Rocky Run

The passage where Porters Lake empties into the ocean requires caution. After paddling under the highway bridge you will encounter the remains of a railway trestle. About one hour prior to high tide, the current begins flowing into the lake. It can be strong enough to prevent your passing through, in which case you will have to portage over the bank and into the basin on the other side. At high water, the current stops and then reverses direction as the tide ebbs. The water level drops considerably over the next six hours, eventually becoming a forceful stream. You should stop and scout before attempting to run the narrow gaps between the pilings. Again, if in doubt, you can portage. There is another channel where the basin empties into the ocean and where you may also encounter turbulence, especially if surf is present.

Rocky Run was originally less influenced by tidal waters. However, when the second Halifax Harbour bridge, the MacKay, was being built in 1970, gravel was removed from the area of Rocky Run for use in the construction. Thus weakened, with subsequent storms the sea broke through into the lake, widening the current outlet.

4. Lawrencetown Beach Provincial Park

This popular beach, located between two drumlin headlands, has lifeguards on duty, changing facilities, and toilets. It is often washed by ocean breakers, inviting paddlers with surfing experience.

5. Shut-in Island

This small, flat, and treeless outpost was once connected to the mainland. The original name might have been Chetigne Island, and it has been suggested that this was the name taken by a man who came to the island during the early days of Acadian settlement, fleeing from a murder that he had committed in the United States. He lived as a hermit on the rocky island and pretended to be mute. Perhaps he was the one who built a stone house, the only remains of which are an obscure depression in the ground that is covered with stones. The only residents these days are the gulls, which dominate the area during nesting season.

6. Three Fathom Harbour

This protected harbour is flanked by two narrow headlands and guarded by shoals. The entrance can be treacherous in rough conditions. A number of quaint fishing shanties line the eastern side.

7. Canal

This narrow passage was created in the early 1900s to allow boats to pass from Porters Lake to Three Fathom Harbour. Like many other similar channels, this one gradually lost its usefulness as a transportation venue and has fell into disrepair, although at high tide you can still pass easily through with canoe or kayak.

8. Wedge Island

My first campsite during our circumnavigation in 1980 was on this tiny outcrop. Technically, it is not an island any more since a breakwater connects it to the mainland.

9. Drumlin Headlands

These eroding cliffs of glacial debris are uncommon along the eastern shore—Clam Harbour is the only other stretch with any significant number—but are a major topological feature east of Halifax. They supply much of the sediment that ends up forming the barrier beaches and salt marshes so characteristic of this region. The rapidity of the erosion process was demonstrated recently when several coffins, presumably dating from early Acadian settlement, were found protruding from the top of the slopes.

10. Fishermans Beach

This narrow spit of cobblestone and sand forms the eastern entrance to Chezzetcook Inlet. At its tip are several fishing shanties. A few are still used during lobster season (mid-April to mid-June), others are in various stages of deterioration, some are mere stone foundations where the storm tides rearranged the spit. Years ago this would have been a site of continual activity; these days you will seldom encounter anyone. It is a memorable campsite.

11. Chezzetcook Inlet

While Porters Lake indicates the location of a fault in the bedrock, Chezzetcook Inlet, like Petpeswick Inlet and Musquodoboit Harbour further down the shore), is a drowned river estuary. The name is derived from a Mi'kmaq expression meaning "running water that divides into many channels," a fitting description for the effect of the tides. The inlet is very shallow due to the accumulation of abundant local sediments, and at low tide it is exposed for much of its area with only a couple of channels allowing access (refer to a map or marine chart). Eel grass beds are extensive, and salt marsh is interlaced with numerous passageways. Three of the islands are forested drumlins. Roasts Hay Island has a sand beach with a good campsite and is beside the channel (thus accessible even at low tide).

12. West Chezzetcook

This area, along with Grand Desert, was settled by Acadian families who had been imprisoned during the Acadian Expulsion and made their way here following their release in 1763. Although it is the closest Acadian settlement to Halifax and is well separated from the major Acadian centres in Nova Scotia, such as Chéticamp, St. Mary's Bay, and Pubnico, it retained its language and culture until the middle of the twentieth century. Unfortunately, their linguistic isolation, along with increased mobility since the 1950s, has taken its toll and most of the younger generation no longer speaks French. An impressive parish church—a symbol of this earlier period—dominates the hillside overlooking the inlet.

2

LITTLE HARBOUR

DEPARTURE POINT:
Little Harbour Government Wharf
Route 7 to Lake Charlotte. Turn right at Clam Harbour exit (Weber's store), follow signs to Little Harbour, approximately 70 km (43 mi.) from Dartmouth, and park on the road by the wharf. Do not block driveways or entrances to the buildings. There is ample room in clear view of nearby houses.

ARRIVAL POINT:
Route 2A: Same as the departure point.
Route 2B: Owls Harbour Government Wharf
Although you can return to Little Harbour after exploring the area covered by Route 2B, brisk prevailing southwest winds may make this difficult.

TRIP LENGTH:
Routes 2A, 19 km (12 mi.), and 2B, 10 km (6 mi.), can both be completed during a day trip or extended for a leisurely weekend. Route 2A should be reserved for calm weather, especially the section to Long and Egg Islands. The Clam Harbour loop is only open during the six hours bracketing the high tide. At other times it is a mud flat.

CHARTS AND MAPS:
Topographical maps: 11/D/10
Marine chart: Taylors Head to Shut-in Island (#4236; 60,000)

ROUTE DESCRIPTION:
The jagged shoreline and numerous islands of these two routes offer plenty for the coastal paddler. Sea birds nest on several small, exposed islands, which are some of Halifax's closest sea bird viewing spots. Black-backed and Herring Gulls, Double-breasted Cormorants, and the Common Eider have colonies here. Migratory sea ducks feed on the abundant eel grass in the shallow waters. Contrasts abound: rocky islands and sand beaches; muddy tidal water and clear turquoise lagoons; deep coastal inlets and a meandering channel through a salt marsh. Definitely a must.

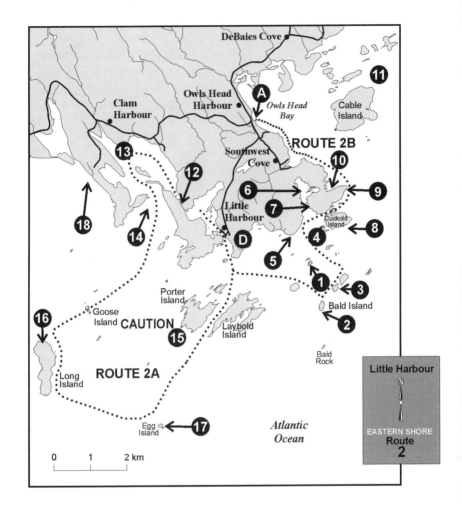

SAFETY CONSIDERATIONS:

A glance at the provincial road map will show how this area juts out into the Atlantic further than any other headland along the Eastern Shore. This position can have a dramatic effect on the local climate. It may be sunny and calm in Halifax but windy and/or foggy in Little Harbour. This variation of climate should be considered when choosing clothing for the trip. Often, Route 2A will present too much of a risk for the group. Don't venture out to the more exposed islands with inexperienced paddlers. These open areas are shallow, with numerous shoals, and if the wind should pick up it can become hazardous. Several years ago, when the remnants of a hurricane passed offshore, I was stranded for a couple of days. If you keep among the inner islands and remain sheltered from the ocean swells, you should have little problem returning to the mainland, even if the wind picks up.

POINTS OF INTEREST:

1. Cut Leg Island

This was a once a cormorant colony, thriving as recently as 1982. Now, all that remains are the dead spruce trees killed by the birds' excrement.

2. Bald Island

This former cormorant colony has also relocated although Common Eiders still nest here.

3. Laney Island

Impressive bedrock outcrops form the southern side.

4. Seal Rocks

Exposed, barren islets are often just the place sought by nesting, or resting, cormorants.

At low tide these long, parallel ridges separated by channels of water are particularly indicative of what happened here over 400 million years ago, when the continents collided, folding the earth's crust. This is shallow and sheltered water and on a sunny day takes on the appearance of a tropical lagoon.

5. The Sand Bar

Sand beaches are usually found in sheltered coves, but this one

has accumulated on a headland. The section with alternating beach and rock ridges are particularly striking. Recently, I discovered a road being built inland, and a sign that the isolation of this shore may soon end.

6. Long Cove
Warm salt water is a rarity along the Atlantic coast except in protected, shallow basins where the temperature can become quite warm by late summer. The muddy shoreline is the ideal habitat for soft-shelled clams.

7. An abandoned homestead
Foundations, ruins, and regenerating field are well hidden in the woods.

8. Cuckold Island
Barren ridge with great view of the surrounding islands. The passage between Cockold and the mainland is "dry" at low water.

9. Owls Head
Automatic light (powered by solar cells) beside remains of the former lighthouse. Excellent view of Ship Harbour and Nichol, Borgles, and Tangier Islands.

10. Heron Point
Good examples of sand volcanoes and Swiss cheese erosion patterns (due to preferential erosion of iron pyrite, of fools gold, and crystals) in the slate outcrops.

11. Cable Island
Sheltered sand beach on the east shore. The exposed bedrock ridge to the east offers a view and plenty of blueberries in season. Black Guillemots on the tiny islet (Shag Rock) off the south side.

12. The Drain
This winding channel, bordered by a large salt marsh, connects Clam Harbour with Little Harbour and is passable at midtide.

13. Clam Harbour
A large mud flat at low water, an ideal time to dig for clams.

14. Harbour Point
The junction of ocean and harbour can be a very turbulent area, especially when the entrance is narrow and the flow significant. Special caution is needed when tide/current is running against the wind.

15. Porters Island
The ragged shores of this large public island offer numerous camping options. The sheltered, shallow waters on the northern side

have extensive eel grass beds and are often visited by sea ducks.

16. Long Island
Sheltered beach with a good campsite on northern tip.

17. Egg Island
Large light tower amid ruins of former lighthouse. Very exposed.

18. Clam Harbour Beach
Supervised provincial day park. This is a possible departure point when the sea is calm or a good beach for surfing practise when there is a swell.

Murphy Cove  3

DEPARTURE POINT:
Murphy Cove Government Wharf
Route 7 to Murphy Cove, approximately 75 km (47 mi.) from
Dartmouth. A private campground is available for those who want
to ensure an early departure. General store nearby.

ARRIVAL POINT:
Same as the departure point.

TRIP LENGTH:
Weekend, 17 km (11 mi.).

CHARTS AND MAPS:
Topographical maps: 11/D/10,15
Marine chart: Ship Harbour and Approaches (#4236; 30,000)

ROUTE DESCRIPTION:
The coastal waters off Murphy Cove are among the most attractive saltwater paddling areas in the province and only an hour's
drive from Halifax. For a time, it was under consideration as the
marine adjunct to Kejimkujik National Park, but a botched proposal and local opposition ended that idea. Now "developers" have
purchased one of the largest islands and plan to build a resort.
Things are still quiet for now, and the wilderness experience continues to exist. The offshore islands offer considerable diversity
along with shelter from the open sea. Several day-long excursions

*Idyllic sandy
coves can
still find a
haven along
this rugged
coast.*

as well as overnight trips are possible and camping sites are plentiful. Large sand beaches, protected lagoons, seal and sea bird colonies, Ospreys, deer, early homestead foundations, and lighthouse ruins are only a few of the attractions—an ideal starting ground for the coastal paddler.

SAFETY CONSIDERATIONS:

Although the small inner islands and the eastern shoreline of Wolfes Island (Nichol on some maps) are protected from the prevailing southwesterly winds, the passage from the end of Wolfes Island (6) to Borgles Island (Charles Island on some maps) requires caution. It is exposed and relatively shallow. A visit to Friar Island (7) should be contemplated only in calm weather. Avoid rounding Outer Island (9) if your are not an experienced paddler.

POINTS OF INTEREST:

1. Murphy's Campground
Modest facilities with great view and hospitality. Camp prior to long trip or use as a base for day outings.

2. Ship Rock
A sheer, vertical section of a fold in the earth's crust, formed over 400 million years ago, when the continents of Africa and North America collided. The name derives from its shape, reminiscent of a schooner sail. It is also one of the best rock climbs along the province's Atlantic coast.

3. Wolfes Point
An automatic light atop a small metal tower among the foundations of two earlier lighthouses. Good campsite with an excellent view. If you follow the northern shoreline of this large island, west from here, you will encounter small islets tops with impressive glacial erratics, a reminder of the power of the moving ice sheet.

4. Long Creek
This narrow inlet was once a base for lobster fishermen. The decaying remains of old fishing camps line the shores. Some have been renovated into summer cabins. In the upper reaches, the water warms up enough in late season for a pleasant swim—a rare commodity in these parts. Bring a mask and snorkel, for the bottom is covered with mussels, seaweed, and sea anemones.

5. Harbour Island
In amongst these tiny islets in the shallow water you can study

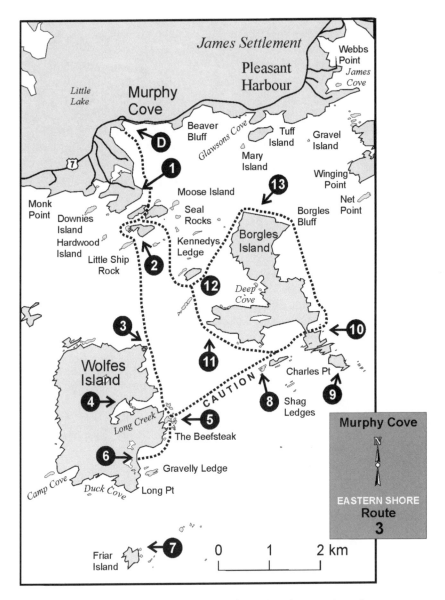

James Settlement

Webbs Point

James Cove

Pleasant Harbour

Little Lake

Murphy Cove

Beaver Bluff

Glawsons Cove

Tuff Island

Gravel Island

Mary Island

Winging Point

Monk Point

Moose Island

Net Point

Downies Island

Seal Rocks

Borgles Bluff

Hardwood Island

Kennedys Ledge

Borgles Island

Little Ship Rock

Deep Cove

Wolfes Island

Long Creek

CAUTION

Charles Pt

Shag Ledges

The Beefsteak

Gravelly Ledge

Camp Cove

Duck Cove

Long Pt

Friar Island

Murphy Cove

N

EASTERN SHORE Route 3

0   1   2 km

the marine plant and animal life in safety. Good examples of glacial erratics and striations.

6. Sandy Cove

One of the most impressive crescent sand beaches on any of the Eastern Shore islands. It has become popular with the local crowd

The wilderness islands are home to several sea birds species, including these Great Black-backed Gull chicks.

during summer holiday weekends, but during the week it is seldom visited. A sheltered camping site is situated in the wooded area between the two ponds.

7. Friar Island

The more isolated the island, the more likely it is to have a sea bird colony. Several species nest here, but it lies exposed and should be visited only by experienced paddlers, in calm weather.

8. Monahan Island

Only a few stunted spruce still cling to this exposed island, and the western point holds a large Osprey nest.

9. Outer Island

In the spring and early summer, Eider Ducks and gulls nest among the large mats of crowberries. Recently, many of the cormorants, which had been nesting on a similarly named island off Tangier Island, have moved to the interior of this islet.

10. Middle Island

Borgles Island is linked to Middle Island by a narrow sand bar, which is sometimes submerged at high tide. Two beautiful crescent sand beaches are opposite one another.

11. Tuckers Head

Great view from atop the sea cliffs.

12. Long Island

Harbour Seals often bask on the exposed shoals among these islands.

13. Borgles Island

This private island has been slated for a resort development but little has happened since the mid 1980s, when a log home and a road were built. Remains of several homesteads along the north shoreline lie among the regenerating woods, once open fields. The locals tell of a fox farm in the early 1900s owned by a German, who spied on the convoy assemblies in Halifax during the First World War.

4 TANGIER HARBOUR

DEPARTURE POINT:
Tangier Government Wharf
Route 7 to Tangier, approximately 85 km (53 mi.) from Dartmouth. Right at Coopers Road (1 km from the post office) and 2 km (1.6 mi.) to the wharf.

ARRIVAL POINT:
Same as the departure point.
Trip Length: Day-long or weekend, 17 km (11 mi.).

CHARTS AND MAPS:
Topographical map: 11/D/15
Marine chart: Taylors Head to Shut-in Island (#4236; 60,000)

ROUTE DESCRIPTION:
The waters between Murphy Cove and Tangier Harbour are known as Shoal Bay, and as the name implies, it is a shallow basin with numerous reefs, islets, and islands. These create diversity as well as some protection from the open sea. It is close to Halifax but offers a degree of the seclusion common to more remote areas. All the islands in the Tangier grouping are crown owned and have a variety of exceptional campsites. Several interesting day-long and weekend excursions are possible and you can put in or take out at many different spots, other than the one mentioned, since the coastal highway runs almost parallel to the shoreline. Beautiful sand beaches, protected lagoons, seal and sea bird colonies, and hidden homestead remnants will make this a charming and fascinating paddle route. Mussel beds and clam flats can add to the evening meal. Although not yet inundated with paddling visitors, this has become one of the more popular locations. Take special care with campsites.

SAFETY CONSIDERATIONS:
Tangier Harbour is well sheltered from the prevailing southwesterlies. Even with a change in weather, you should have little trouble returning to the departure point. If necessary, you can follow the protected shore and land at Popes Harbour. The water is shallow

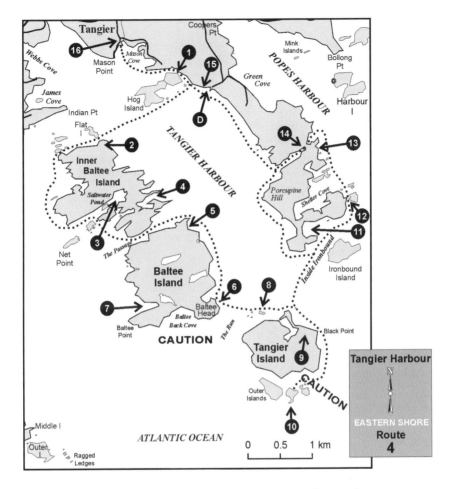

Map labels:
Tangier, Coopers Pt, Mink Islands, Bollong Pt, Webbs Cove, Mason Point, Mason Cove, Green Cove, POPES HARBOUR, James Cove, Hog Island, Harbour I, Indian Pt, Flat I, TANGIER HARBOUR, Inner Baltee Island, Saltwater Pond, Porcupine Hill, Shelter Cove, Net Point, The Passage, Baltee Island, Inside Ironbound, Ironbound Island, Baltee Head, Baltee Back Cove, Baltee Point, CAUTION, The Run, Black Point, Tangier Island, Outer Islands, Middle I, Outer I, ATLANTIC OCEAN, Ragged Ledges

Scale: 0   0.5   1 km

Tangier Harbour
N
EASTERN SHORE
Route
4

and there are countless shoals, great for seals but treacherous for large boats. You will encounter few vessels, except in lobster season (mid-April to mid-June). The exposed areas can be transformed from a quiet sea into a frothy maze of whitecaps in very little time. Of particular concern are the areas beyond Baltee, Tangier, and East Ironbound Islands, which should be avoided by the inexperienced paddler.

POINTS OF INTEREST:

1.   Hog Island

Collect some wild mussels for the evening meal. At very low water the channel is impassable.

2. Jeans Field Point

An early homestead is overgrown with white spruce where remains of a root cellar and stone wall are clearly evident. Note the cone-shaped trees at the water's edge, an indication that they originated on an open field where they had space to fully develop the lower branches. A glance at the mainland fields shows this process currently under way.

3. Saltwater Pond

This sheltered cove is a good stopover for migrating ducks. I have seen deer browsing at the water's edge. As with most offshore islands their trails crisscross the woods.

4. Inlet

The ocean prods deep into Inner Baltee, almost slicing it in two. A small sand beach juts into the upper reaches beside a developing salt marsh.

5. Outer Baltee

At very low water the passage between the Baltees is shallow (even for canoes and kayaks) and is, at times, impassable. At the eastern entrance a small crescent-shaped sand beach offers an ideal campsite. Behind the beach, along the passage, is a soft-shelled clam bed, and in deeper water are the quahogs. A long-standing Osprey nest sits atop one of the shoreline trees south of the beach.

6. Baltee Head

The remnants of another homestead lie atop a bluff of bayberry, blueberries, and blackberries. An interesting hike west along the sea cliffs offers a spectacular show when a heavy sea breaks against the shore. The dead bleached trees are from a forest fire purposely set years ago to enhance blueberry growth. Large glacial erratics are scattered about the treeless barrens, and ridges of greywacke and slate dominate the landscape.

7. Western Cove

This offers a protected sand beach and campsite during an easterly blow. A high sea, breaking on the barren bedrock ledges of Baltee Point, puts on a great show.

8. Tangier Shoal

Keep a lookout for Harbour Seals around these shoals and islets. Terns also nest here.

9. Tangier Island

The island and then the village got their names from a ship that foundered on the outer shoals in the 1700s. The first settlers along this shore arrived about 1790 and the foundations of the original homestead are still visible at the edge of the open field. This is a good campsite for a large group. The saltwater lagoon is a nesting and feeding spot for sea birds, and the deep pool at the entrance becomes a warm swimming spot when, during low tide, the trapped water heats up. It also has a clam bed.

10. Outer Island

This former cormorant colony is a good example of how devastating the guano can be to wood. Most of the trees are now dead. The birds, nesting each year until 1994, have moved to a healthier forest on the outer island of Route 3. Note: The channel leading into the lagoon is chaotic in rough weather (even from the southwest) and should be avoided at such times. Hike around from the campsite instead.

The isolated islands and islets of Shoal Bay offer the inquisitive paddler a maze of sheltered routes.

11. Sandy Cove

With its classic crescent beach and turquoise waters, this cove suggests a tropical lagoon on a warm summer day. A must! It is a sharp contrast to the rocky southern shoreline with the tidepools—an excellent place to examine the intertidal plants and animals. This headland is owned by Friends of Nature and protected from development.

12. Bulls Gut

In the cliff flanking the pocket sand beach is a vertical section with rock fragments embedded in a matrix. These are known as the "Tangier Dykes," and thought to be parts of the bottom of the earth's crust that have been broken off and transported by molten lava upward through fissures. The mixture solidified before reaching the surface and subsequent erosion and uplifting has exposed it. This is among the oldest rock on earth.

13. Glacial striations

The cliffs display clear horizontal gouges produced by the rock-embedded ice sheets from over twelve thousand years ago.

14. Carryover Cove

As the name implies, this once served as a portage, but at high tide you can ease a kayak or canoe through. At low tide you will be lugging your craft 75 m (246 ft.) over salt marsh and mud.

15. Abriels Fish Plant

Usually fresh fish and lobster (during season), always frozen fish available. Lobsters can also be obtained at Ferguson's pound a few miles west, and smoked fish—salmon, mackerel, and trout—at Willi Krauch's in Tangier.

16. Coastal Adventures

This major sea kayaking outfitting business is located on Mason Point Road where you can rent equipment, or take a course or tour. They also have a paddling shop and the Paddler's Retreat Bed & Breakfast.

Popes Harbour ⟋⟍ 5

DEPARTURE POINT:
Popes Harbour
Route 7 to Popes Harbour, approximately 90 km (56 mi.) from Dartmouth. Put in near the private wharf at the only spot where the main road touches the water. General store 2 km (1.5 mi.) west.

ARRIVAL POINT:
Same as the departure point.

TRIP LENGTH:
Day-long or weekend; Route 5A 12 km (7 mi.) and Route 5B 16 km (10 mi.).

CHARTS AND MAPS:
Topographical map: 11/D/15
Marine chart: Taylors Head to Shut-in Island (#4236; 60,000)

ROUTE DESCRIPTION:
This route explores two of the larger Eastern Shore islands. Gerard Island has numerous remnants of previous habitation— some fairly recent—with stone walls, foundations, regenerating fields, and hidden roads, all of which tell a story of the past. It is still divided among several private landowners, but to date, there are no summer homes or cottages. Phoenix Island is more rugged and had only one homestead. Today it is public land and there are several good campsites. Wildlife is abundant. White-tailed deer trails crisscross both islands, and Harbour Seals congregate in the protected basin (the Bawleen). Gulls, terns, eiders, Ospreys, and even a Bald Eagle nest in the area. This is a great place to hike as well as paddle. Don't miss it!

SAFETY CONSIDERATIONS:
The waters around Gerard Head (3) are open to the ocean; there-fore, they are potentially dangerous during a southwesterly flow. The steep, submerged cliffs at Gerard Head reflect the incoming waves to produce chaotic conditions in rough weather, with swells sometimes coming from several different directions. The southern

tip of Phoenix Island borders shallow water and is also exposed. This segment, Route 5B, should be reserved for calm conditions. The portage through the centre of Gerard Island offers access into the Bawleen (a protected area for the novice). Prepare for mud and slippery seaweed on the north end when portaging at low tide.

POINTS OF INTEREST:

1. Gerard Island

The early Europeans often settled the Eastern Shore islands where remnants of their homesteads and grave markers can be found hidden in the forests.

Hidden among the trees are the remains of a former settlement. Fields, foundations, and stone walls cover several acres of what was once one of the larger communities along this shore in the 1800s. Traces of the road that linked the two ends of the island are still evident. Scattered about the woods are several species of introduced plants (e.g., rhubarb and lilac) resisting, for a time, the advancing native flora. The last inhabitants left the island in the 1940s.

2. Harbour Island

This site of an abandoned lobster cannery has an intact seawall along the northern shore. A large foundation, a well, and an open field are all that remain of the original house, which was transported on a raft to the mainland in the 1940s.

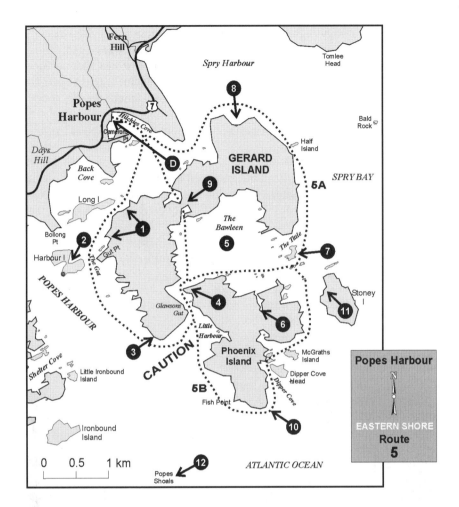

3. Gerard Head

This area should be rounded with caution in rough seas (refer to Safety Considerations). Use the portage into the Bawleen if necessary.

4. Glawsons Point

The remains of a stone wharf, well, and root cellar border a good campsite (particularly when the bugs are absent).

5. The Bawleen

The name derives from the baleen, or whalebone, present in a certain group of whales. The baleen whales use a comblike structure of the same name to filter their food from the water. Here, the large lagoon has two narrow, shallow entrances through which only small boats may pass. Harbour Seals are usually plentiful, sometimes numbering in the dozens. The best time to view them is at low tide, when they have hauled out onto the exposed shoals. Terns and Eiders nest on some of the small islets.

6. Goose Marsh
A shallow inlet with a large salt marsh, which is unusual for the offshore islands.

7. Cap Island
Covered mostly by dune grass and beach pea with a small cap of spruce. This islet is a nesting site for the Common Eider (and plenty of mosquitos).

8. Gerard Island (East)
As recently as 1985 I was able to climb the stairs to the second floor of the last standing house on Gerard Island and look out over Spry Harbour. Today it is no more than a pile of prostrate boards, and the abandoned fields are giving way to white spruce. In the woods, on the hill to the southwest, are the remnants of several more homesteads.

9. The Portage
This well-marked, short portage has been used for over a century and offers easy access (at mid to high tide) to the Bawleen when rounding the island is inadvisable.

10. Popes Head
This crowberry-matted promontory gives a panoramic view of the neighbouring coastal islands. It can be reached by hiking from a sheltered cove to the northeast.

11. Stoney Island
One of the few sandy beaches in this group of islands faces the Bawleen. Near the exposed southern tip is the wreck of a steel barge.

12. Popes Shoals
Scarcely breathing air at high water this small group of rocks are a popular haul out for seals and a resting spot for sea birds and their fragrant guano. These should be visited only on calm days.

Mushaboom Harbour 6

DEPARTURE POINT:
Taylors Head Provincial Park
Route 7 to Spry Bay, approximately 95 km (59 mi.) from
Dartmouth. Turn right at park entrance and follow gravel road to
parking lot at the beach, 5 km (3 mi.). Note: This is a day park and
is closed from 9:00 P.M. to 9:00 A.M. (Steel gate at the entrance.)
Camping isn't permitted, so advise the park staff of your inten-
tions for an overnight coastal paddle. You can leave your vehicle.
Toilet facilities are available, and there is now drinking water
available.
A launch spot in Mushaboom (D')
Continue a few kilometres beyond Taylors Head and take the turn
off to Mushaboom. Follow the gravel road to Malagash Island
where you can put in at several spots bordering the water.

ARRIVAL POINT:
Same as the departure points.

TRIP LENGTH:
Day-long or weekend, 13 km (8 mi.).

CHARTS AND MAPS:
Topographical map: 11/D/15
Marine chart: Barren Island to Taylors Head (#4235; 60,000)

ROUTE DESCRIPTION:
Taylors Head is one of the more conspicuous headlands of the
Eastern Shore and presents a potential barrier to an extended trip,
often necessitating a portage. Its large crescent beach is exceptional, fronting a sheltered bay of blue and turquoise waters. The
wind, if present at all, is usually light due to the long peninsula,
which blocks the prevailing southwesterlies. A park trail leads
from the beach, runs along the shoreline and through the woods
to the barren tip. In rough weather, the ocean puts on a good
show here with the seas breaking over shoals and pounding
against the cliffs. The islands are grouped close together and the
route is relatively short, which allows plenty of time for poking
about. Keep in mind, though, that a return to the main beach may

involve slugging against a headwind and require more time than initially anticipated. Sea birds (cormorants and gulls) nest in the area, and with the abundance of shoals, you will have a good chance of spotting seals. Some of the islands are privately owned and there are a few cabins, but these are seldom occupied. There are also a couple of excellent campsites.

SAFETY CONSIDERATIONS:

The inexperienced paddler should remain within the island grouping. Don't venture outside Psyche or Guilford, and certainly don't round Taylors Head itself, except in very calm conditions. The seas are shallow in this area and it takes little wind to whip them into an unpredictable maze of whitecaps. Even within the harbour, exercise more caution on a windy day.

POINTS OF INTEREST:

1. Taylors Head Beach

Layers of slate and grewacke create a fascinating texture in the exposed cliffs.

After Clam Harbour, this is the largest sand beach along this section of our coastline. During the season, even on warm summer days, it is seldom crowded. However, the water is a bit chilly!

2. Taylors Head

This barren headland, covered with crowberry mats, offers an extraordinary view of the ocean and the surrounding islands. A trail leads out from the beach. This can be a dangerous area to paddle!

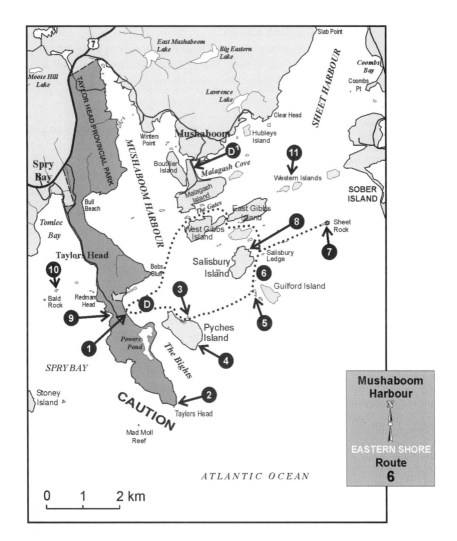

3. Psyche Rock

A protected sand beach is adjacent a tiny freshwater pond and a large Osprey nest. Camping is not permitted.

4. Pyches Island

Excellent examples of sand volcanoes are present in the exposed bedrock on the southeast shoreline. Also good examples of alternating greywacke and slate, and their differential erosion, on the eastern and western shorelines.

5. Little Guilford Islands

This large cormorant colony (Double-crested and Great) clearly illustrates the effect of these sea birds on the trees. Some are now barely stumps in the shallow soil. In many cases, the birds nest on the bare rock.

6. Guilford Passage

Spotted with shoals, this shallow area often has seals and sea ducks.

7. Sheet Rock

An excellent example of crustal folding, this slate bedrock is accessible only on the inner side. An automatic light tower dominates the harbour.

8. Salisbury Island

An abandoned log cabin overlooks the water atop a steep bluff.

9. The Portage

This wide portage links Spry Bay with Mushaboom Harbour. It can be used on extended coastal trips when conditions prevent rounding Taylors Head, which is often the case.

10. Leslie Island: Here, a cormorant colony is in the final stage of its cycle. The trees have been killed, and all that remain are the rotted stumps. The birds nest on the ground.

11. Western Isles: These large platforms of smooth, gently inclining bedrock, topped with a spruce wood (and plenty of gulls in nesting season), provide excellent examples of glacial striations and erratics.

Sober Island ⟶

7

Departure Point:
Sheet Harbour Passage
Route 7 to Sheet Harbour (Watt Section), approximately 115 km (72 mi.) from Dartmouth. Continue right towards Sober Island and put in by the bridge.

Arrival Point:
Return to departure point or continue on to Beaver Harbour.

Trip Length:
Weekend, 15 km (9 mi.); Beaver Harbour 19 km (12 mi.).

Charts and Maps:
Topographical Maps: 11/D/16
Marine Charts: Barren Island to Taylors Head (#4235; 60,000)

Route Description:
When booze was being smuggled into Canada in massive amounts during the Prohibition era, myth has it that the only thing found sober on this island was the island itself. An apocryphal story perhaps, but indicative of the isolated nature of Nova Scotia's Atlantic coastline. Smuggling still occurs throughout the region, and large caches of drugs have been confiscated in recent years, however, none yet on Sober Island, as far as I have heard.

Sober Island has been linked to the mainland via a bridge for several decades, and it has been inhabited since the early days of European settlement. It is the largest island along the Eastern Shore, and along with more modest adjacent islands, offers an interesting paddle with diverse scenery: several bedrock islands contrast with eroding drumlins (unusual for this part of the shore); exposed shoals welcome Harbour and Grey Seals; a large rusting shipwreck is strewn along the rocks; a shallow cove covers eel grass beds with large quantities of blue mussels; and a massive, steep cobblestone beach traps a large pond. There are several good camping sites.

Safety Considerations:
Much of this route can be explored in relative shelter but be cautious if paddling around the southern tip of Sober Island. This

area is shallow, particularly around MacDonalds Shoals and MacDonalds Rock, and will be churned up considerably with onshore swells or winds.

POINTS OF INTEREST:

1. Sheet Harbour

At the end of a deep inlet, this charming community—the largest between Musquodoboit Harbour and Canso, but still with under 900 inhabitants—is a major service centre on the Eastern Shore with grocery stores, restaurants, accommodation, a hardware shore, a post office, and a hospital.

2. Sheet Harbour Passage

A narrow channel separates Sober Island from the mainland and was often used in early days as a protected coastal passage into Sheet Harbour, thus avoiding a more perilous voyage around the southern tip of the island. Although a route exists at all tide levels for canoes and kayaks, large sections become exposed eel grass beds at low water. Several small islets occupy the passage, and a tiny one is home to a Common Tern colony.

3. Sober Island Pond

Noted as Saltwater Pond on earlier charts, this large basin almost cuts Sober Island in two. It was probably open to the ocean until sediments blocked off the entrance(s). Back Beach, on its western end, is an impressive cobblestone barrier where it is rarely possible to land. The slope is steep, and the ocean swells are persistent.

4. Sheet Rock

A light tower surmounts this steep, treeless islet. Foundations of an earlier keeper's house are still apparent. Landing is possible on the north side only during calm weather. The designation "sheet" is perhaps due to the enormous slabs of bedrock that characterize much of the landscape. It has also been suggested that it refers to the long sheltered harbour that is sometimes as smooth as a sheet of glass.

5. The Flats

This shallow, protected basin has a sand and mud bottom, which is covered by eel grass and shellfish. It is sprinkled with several tiny islets. At very low tides, the flats are inaccessible, even by canoe or kayak.

6. Fishery Island

This tiny outpost is draped in mats of crowberry along with a few ragged spruce. On the south side, remains of a freighter are

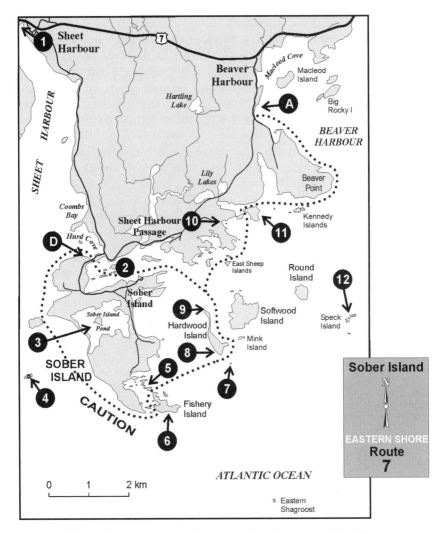

scattered about the shore. Some fragments have been tossed well onto land, indicating the power of Atlantic storms.

7. Hardwood Island Reef

These small shoals are frequently used by seals for hauling out and sunning during low tide. In the evenings, an eerie cacophony of grunts and growls permeate the surroundings.

8. Hardwood Island

Hardwood Island extends in a north-south axis, unlike most other Eastern Shore islands, which are parallel to the mainland—

since it is the result of glacial deposition, not of bedrock folding. If there was a hardwood forest here at one time, it was cut down by early settlers. A large foundation in the middle is all that remains. Now, the island is mostly cleared field with some regenerating white spruce. The south tip is an actively eroding drumlin, and except in the driest of summers, freshwater springs seep from the slope. It offers a superb view of the Bay of Islands—a great campsite.

During the last Ice Age large boulders were often carried great distances and dropped in unusual positions.

The sheltered eastern shoreline is lush with coastal vegetation: sea beach senecio, sea beach sandwort, sea side parsley, beach mustard, and sapphire, orach, sea milkwort, and silverweed. It is one of the few islands that has abundant ragweed, which is not native to the area, and dewberries (related to the raspberry) in season.

9. Sand Point
This small, circular point is home to noisy colony of terns.
10. Hydroponic Greenhouses
On a shore where farming is impossible or impractical due to the rocky soil and short growing season, a prosperous greenhouse operation provides high-quality tomatoes and English cucumbers for the Nova Scotia market.

11. Campbell Island

Hidden among the woods are the foundations of an early homestead. Sheltered campsite.

12. Speck Island

These islets are barely exposed at high water and the original trees have been killed by the cormorants, which now nest on the ground. Other inhabitants include Herring and Black-backed Gulls and Eider Ducks. Expect also to find seals.

8

BAY OF ISLANDS (PORT DUFFERIN)

DEPARTURE POINT:

Factory Cove

Route 7 to Port Dufferin, approximately 125 km (77 mi.) from Dartmouth. Turn right shortly after bridge and follow to the wharf at Factory Cove, 2 km (1 mi.). Motel and general store in the village. Alternative departure at Beaver Harbour.

ARRIVAL POINT:

Same as the departure point, or the arrival point in East Quoddy (refer to Route 9).

TRIP LENGTH:

Two days, 23 km (14 mi.).

CHARTS AND MAPS:

Topographical map: 11/D/16
Marine chart: Barren Island to Taylors Head (#4235; 60,000)

ROUTE DESCRIPTION:

I first explored this neglected paradise in 1975, when I assisted a friend in a field study of Leach's Storm-Petrels (sparrow-size birds that nest in burrows and feed on plankton far offshore). This was my introduction to our coastal islands. It seemed worlds removed from the inland waterways and planted the seed for my eventual circumnavigation. The Bay of Islands is appropriately named. It has one of the largest concentrations of islands, islets, and shoals along the entire coastline and was known to explorers as early as Champlain. Fishermen built shanties and lobster trap depots on some islands, but permanent settlers never arrived. It was far too rugged and inhospitable, and the isolation contrasts sharply with Shoal Bay and Popes Harbour. The tiny remote islands attract the sea birds. Some of the outer islands have been designated sanctuaries, and camping isn't permitted during breeding season (until August 15).

SAFETY CONSIDERATIONS:

Due to large areas of shallow, open water your planned route will

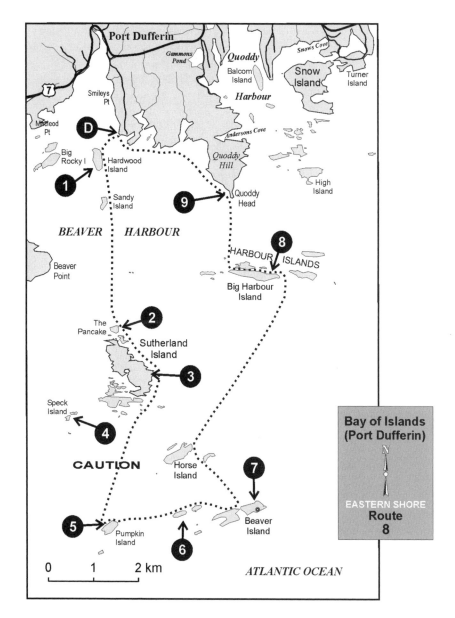

often have to be revised. A wind from any direction can quickly whip up the sea. Pumpkin and Beaver Islands are particularly exposed and should be avoided by inexperienced paddlers. In a case of poor weather and sea conditions, the inner islands of

Route 9 [Bay of Islands (East Quoddy)] will offer an alternative trip. Unlike many of the previous routes, good campsites are at a premium, especially for a larger group, so look for a spot early to avoid an uncomfortable improvisation.

POINTS OF INTEREST:

1. Hardwood Island

The hardwoods were cut down a long time ago, and spruce and fir have taken over. This island is a drumlin, meaning "a pile of loose debris dropped by a glacier," and the southern cliff face is rapidly eroding. Most of the other islands in this group are bedrock outcrops.

2. The Pancake

This low, flat islet was once home to a large cormorant colony. Only a tight stand of bleached stumps remain.

3. Sutherland Island

The very ragged shoreline with thick, wiry spruce growing up to its edge, renders those quaint little coves inhospitable to the camper. Several hunting cabins are tucked into the woods. The

Lunchtime!

tight cluster of islets and coves on the southwest shore contrast with the exposed nature of most of this route.

4. Speck Island

Scarcely more than a large rock, this islet also has a small cormorant colony. Large numbers of Grey and Harbour Seals usually occupy this area.

5. Pumpkin Island

If the weather will permit, this grass-covered, relatively high island gives a great view of the entire bay. But it is surrounded by cliffs and shoals and is only accessible from the southwest cove, the side which is usually exposed to the weather. This is home to one of the largest Leach's Storm-Petrel colonies on the Eastern Shore. This tiny sea bird (about the size of a sparrow) nests in burrows and travels at night. It feeds on plankton far out to sea. Their eerie calls and erratic, batlike flight during a misty night can be disquieting to the uninitiated.

6. Brother Islands

Another cormorant colony, this one well past its prime. The guano has long since killed the trees, which also have been succumbing to the elements. Only a few stumps are left and the remaining birds will soon depart for another isle.

7. Beaver Island

No beavers on this island. It was named after a prominent family on the mainland and one of the early lighthouse keepers. The tower remains but the keeper left in the mid 1980s. A good campsite.

8. Big Harbour Island

A narrow channel with smooth, steep walls that separate two islands. A good illustration of crustal folding from millions of years ago.

9. Quoddy Head

A double-crescent cobblestone tombolo—a bar that connects one island with other land—links this small point to the mainland.

Bay of Islands
(East Quoddy)

Departure Point:
East Quoddy
Route 7 to East Quoddy, approximately 130 km (81 mi.) from
Dartmouth. Follow gravel road 1 km (0.6 mi.) to the Aitken Point.
Launch at beach by the causeway. Parking available.

Arrival Point:
Same as the departure point.

Trip Length:
Day-long (excluding Bird Islands) or weekend, 18 km (11 mi.).

Charts and Maps:
Topographical map: 11/D/16
Marine chart: Barren Island to Taylors Head (#4235; 60,000)

Route Description:
This route offers a relaxing weekend paddle where, except for the
digression to the Bird Islands, you remain close to the mainland
and relatively sheltered from the southwest wind. This is an alternative trip when weather/sea conditions render the previous
Route 8 too risky. The larger islands close to shore were settled,
and among the mixture of cleared and regenerated fields are the
remnants of this former habitation. There are a few cabins in
varying stages of decomposition, and lobster fishermen still store
their traps on some of the islands. Campsites are plentiful. I particularly recall tenting on the fragrant crowberry mats of Black
Duck Island overlooking the bay, when the bioluminescent plankton sparkled in the dark night, a counterpoint to the stars. The
outer islands are the domain of sea birds and seals, and camping
is prohibited until after the end of breeding season (August 15).

Safety Considerations:
Small islands that are close together suggest shallow water and
hidden shoals, hence, trouble in rough seas. Among the inner cir-
cle of islands, you are seldom far from shelter, but special care
must be observed when approaching the Bird Islands. These are

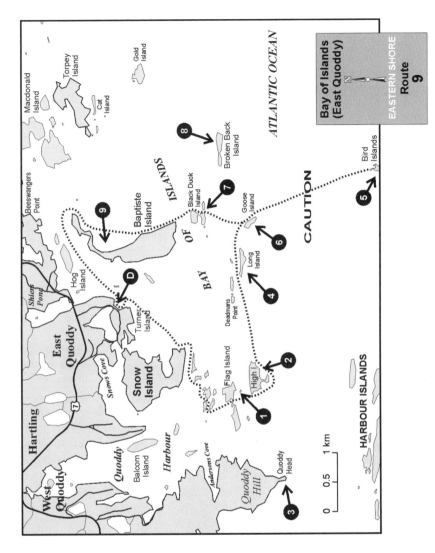

totally exposed and surrounded by numerous submerged reefs. Venture out only if you are an experienced paddler, and only then, in calm conditions.

POINTS OF INTEREST:

1. Flag Island
The exposed flat plates of greywacke at the west end of this island offer some excellent examples of glacial striations, caused

by the enormous pressure of the ice sheet dragging debris over the surface.

2. High Island

This good campsite has a view of the outer islands. The spot offers a sheltered landing regardless of wind direction.

3. Quoddy Head

A cobblestone tombolo connects this small island to the mainland.

4. Long Island

This narrow island with its steep, smooth sides running parallel to the mainland is typical of many along the Eastern Shore and particularly in the Bay of Islands. They are the eroded relics of ancient crustal folding, which occurred as the North American plate crushed into the African plate, over 350 million years ago. A cormorant colony clings to the southeast corner. Eider Ducks nest among the raspberry bushes.

5. Bird Islands

These four treeless islands are so close that you can almost jump from one to the other at low tide. Their small size and isolation offer sea birds a protected nesting area. Black-backed and Herring

A paddler pulls up beside salmon pens to get a closer look; aquaculture has become a booming business in Atlantic Canada.

Gulls, Eider Ducks, terns, and Leach's Storm-Petrels breed here. Camping is not permitted.

6. Goose Island

No geese are here, rather a noisy (and smelly) gull colony, and one very large Osprey nest.

7. Black Duck Island

One island at low water becomes three at high. A large tidepool doubles as a bathtub on a sunny day. An idyllic camping site sits above the south cliff. The shallow water bounded by Long, Goose, and Black Duck Islands usually have Harbour Seals.

8. Brokenback Island

Two tree-covered humps are connected by a low saddle of smooth bedrock-hence, the name. Osprey nest here and it is also one of Nova Scotia's few breeding sites for the Fox Sparrow. IBP Proposed Ecological Site.

9. Baptiste Island

Until recently a cleared field, with root cellars and stone piles, overlooked a crescent cobblestone beach. Now, a private home savours the exceptional view. This has become an increasingly popular trend along our Atlantic Coast.

10

ECUM SECUM

DEPARTURE POINT:
Ecum Secum Government Wharf
Route 7, approximately 165 km (102 mi.) from Dartmouth. Several houses nearby where you can ask to leave your car.

ARRIVAL POINT:
Same as the departure point, or Marie Joseph Government Wharf.

TRIP LENGTH:
Two days, 35 km (22 mi.).

CHARTS AND MAPS:
Topographical map: 11/D/16
Marine Charts: Ecum Secum (#4235; 30,000)

ROUTE DESCRIPTION:
I emerged from two days of chilling fog in June 1980, when I entered these waters for the first time. It was a welcome relief, and the brilliant blues and greens that were etched in my mind still warm my memories. With a stiff wind at our backs, we glided effortlessly through narrow passages and around broken shoals and islands on the way to Liscomb. I have since returned many times and it has become one of my favourite coastal areas. This Eastern Shore route contains an interesting mixture of islands, large and small. Of special note are Goose and Barren Islands that unlike most other coastal islands of comparable size are mainly treeless. The interiors have large sections of acid bog, good habitat for pitcher plants, sundew, and some heaths but little else. The White Islands are part of the Eastern Shore Islands Wildlife Management Area.

SAFETY CONSIDERATIONS:
The White Islands are well offshore. Visit them only when the sea is calm. It wasn't until several years ago that I had my first chance to explore these outposts and to wander over the large tongue of bedrock which makes up the western end. My previous attempts were thwarted by bad weather.

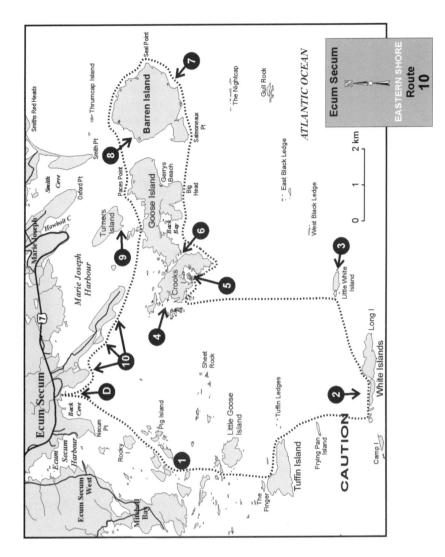

POINTS OF INTEREST:

1. Shoals, Islets, and Islands

Bunched together in shallow water with fringes of salt marsh and eel grass. These numerous outcrops provide plenty of nooks and crannies to explore. Root cellars and foundations are found on some of the islands and there are some sheltered campsites. Rams, Pig, Jacks, and Rocky are public.

2. The White Islands

An interrupted chain of greywacke bedrock parallels the coast. The middle section is sheer rock, the eastern part forested. This is a sea bird sanctuary, and the Department of Natural Resources have a primitive cabin on the eastern section of Big White.

Once part of ancient Africa, this huge slab of bedrock now forms the western extremity of the White Islands.

Landing/camping isn't permitted until August 15, when breeding season is over. Camp Island, the westernmost of this group, has one of the few breeding colonies of the Grey Seal in Nova Scotia. The others are Sable Island and the Basque Islands along the eastern coast of Cape Breton and Hay Island off Scatarie. This animal is a carrier of the cod worm, and mainly because of this and their growing numbers (and fondness for fish), they are less than beloved by fishermen.

3. Little White Island

Until recently it was forested, but cormorants nested and killed the trees with their excrement. Only a few bleached stumps remain among the chickweed; the cormorants now breed on the ground along with the Eider Ducks. This is the only location in Nova Scotia for Scurvy grass.

4. Frenchmans Cove

Here you will find a field returning to forest, a root cellar, and foundations.

5. Crooks Island

The rising sea level is encroaching upon a large peat bog, several metres thick. It shows clearly that this area was once a freshwater bog.

6. Goose Gutter

At low water this passage is navigable in canoe or kayak. The narrow channel is carpeted with eel grass and is a good resting area for migratory waterfowl.

7. Barren Island

The wreck of a large wooden fishing boat is scattered above the beach.

8. Barren Island

This is one of the largest sand beaches on the Eastern Shore islands.

9. Turners Island

Partially overgrown homesteads with walls and foundations shelter a campsite, but the bugs can be a problem.

10. Hapes Point

A prime example of drumlin cliffs are being eroded by the sea.

LISCOMB ISLAND

DEPARTURE POINT:
Little Liscomb Government Wharf
Route 7, approximately l75 km (109 mi.) from Dartmouth, past Liscomb. Gravel road 2.5 km (1.5 mi.) to Little Liscomb.

ARRIVAL POINT:
Same as the departure point. Consider leaving a car at Sonora, 30 km (19 mi.) from Liscomb, since strong southwest winds can make the return trip from the shipwreck difficult.

TRIP LENGTH:
Day-long to two days, 15 km (9 mi.).

CHARTS AND MAPS:
Topographical map: 11/F/4
Marine Chart: Country Island to Barren Island (#4234; 60,000)

ROUTE DESCRIPTION:
This route includes highlights seldom encountered elsewhere in the province, and it is a trip well worth the long drive from Halifax. During the weekend paddle, you may come across a boulder engraved with Captain Kidd's name; a pit where someone has attempted to uncover his treasure; a small graveyard lost deep in the woods; a large light tower; and perhaps the largest exposed shipwreck in the province. (You can actually paddle into the hold of the ship.)

SAFETY CONSIDERATIONS:
Between Liscomb Island and Steering Reef, hidden shoals and an exposed ocean dictate caution. It is quite possible that after the long drive from Halifax you may find this section too rough for a safe paddle, even via the passage inside Tobacco Island. Personal experience has taught me that this harbour can become very hazardous for a small craft; the wreck, impressive as it is, will still be there another weekend. Of particular concern are the offshore breezes, which can be accentuated by the long fetches of coastal inlets, such as Gegogan Harbour. A large sea with cresting waves can develop in a short time. The string of shoals stretching east

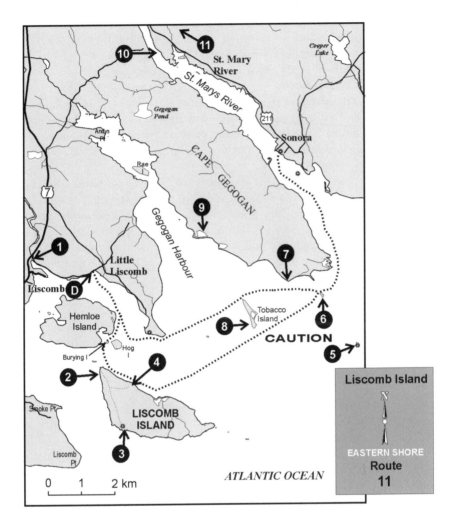

Liscomb Island

N

EASTERN SHORE
**Route
11**

0 1 2 km

ATLANTIC OCEAN

from the tip of Liscomb Island add to the potential for danger. If in doubt, you can reach the wreck from Sonora (sheltered from the southwesterlies) or spend the weekend exploring Liscomb Island.

POINTS OF INTEREST:

1. Stone engravings

Kidd's name, a date, and an arrow pointing to Liscomb Island are chiselled onto this boulder beside Gaspereau Brook. The growth of lichens attests to some age, but whether they originated with the infamous pirate is doubtful. To find the boulder, look for a path leading to the brook, a short distance (0.5 km or 0.3 mi.) down the Little Liscomb Road. There are no signs. It is on a small point where the brook enters the salt water.

2. Graveyard

It is located in the woods south of the wharf and is difficult to find. At one time the island was cleared and settled by several families. The last inhabitants (two lighthouse keepers) moved off several years ago and the forest is continuing to erase early traces.

3. Light tower

A long, winding dirt road leads across the island to the light station. The classical tower is one of the tallest on the coast. The lighthouse keepers' houses were well built, with hardwood floors and several bedrooms each. I spent an enjoyable night with the keepers, and their rum, during my 1980 circumnavigation. After automation, they were destroyed by vandalism. All that remain now are the concrete foundations.

4. Money pit

Legend has it that Kidd's treasure was buried on this spot. Nothing has been found and only a dilapidated cabin and a few pits remain. Reach it by taking the now overgrown trail marked on the topographical map or, more easily, by following the coastline and landing north of the small pond.

5. Wedge Island

Steep cliffs and shoals make this eroding drumlin an inhospitable place during a storm. A great view from the top should be savoured only in a calm sea.

6. The _Fury_

The remains of this large, rusting liberty ship rests firmly skewered atop a sharp reef. Driven ashore during a hurricane in 1965, it is slowly succumbing to the sea. Recently, the bow section has broken away. When I passed this way in 1980, you could paddle through the gaping holes in the hull and wander about the holds and the huge boilers, and even climb up to the deck. This once impressive hulk would be a major tourist attraction if it were more accessible, but it can't even be seen from the highway. To reach it by land means a hike of a few hours.

7. Byrne Head

Sheep are sometimes pastured in this large field, cleared for an early homestead.

8. Tobacco Island

No tobacco plants but plenty of sea birds. This island has been designated an ecological reserve under the International Biological Program and is one of the few breeding sites in Nova Scotia of the Fox Sparrow. Camping is prohibited.

9. The Big Sand

This magnificent white sand beach, backed by a tiny pond, is one of several in Gegogan Harbour. Most are make great campsites and are on pubic lands. This one can be reached only by water or a long hike through the woods.

10. St. Marys River

One of the major rivers along the Eastern Shore, begins its journey well inland and ends in a long tidal reach before emptying into the open sea at Sonora. In the past, it has been known for its excellent salmon sport fishery. In recent years, though, there has been a dramatic decline in returning stock—a phenomenon reflected in the other east coast salmon rivers. If water conditions on the open coast aren't appropriate, this stretch of 12 km (7 mi.), from Sherbrooke to Sonora, is an alternative trip. In this case, be sure to paddle in the direction of the wind.

11. Sherbrooke

This picturesque village is nestled in the St. Marys River valley at the limit of the tidal influence. Much of it has been restored into a living museum, which realistically reflects life on the shore between 1860 and 1890. Over 30 buildings are now open. The restoration is well worth a visit. Sherbrooke also has accommodations, restaurants, and food stores.

The Fury *rests atop a shoal near Liscomb Island. Driven ashore by a hurricane, it is gradually succumbing to the elements.*

DEPARTURE POINT:
Drumhead Harbour
Route 7 to Sherbrooke, approximately 190 km (118 mi.) from Dartmouth. Follow Route 211 and then Route 316 to Drumhead, an additional 45 km (28 mi.). You may have to pay a $5 launch fee.

Note: The cable ferry at Country Harbour runs continuously during the summer. However, on the off season it leaves from the Port Bickerton side only on the half hour. You may wish to coordinate your arrival.

ARRIVAL POINT:
Same as departure point or the Coddles Harbour wharf.

TRIP LENGTH:
Day-long to overnight, 16 km (10 mi.). Plan on two full days when leaving from Halifax/Dartmouth.

CHARTS AND MAPS:
Topographical map: 11/F/4
Marine chart: Berry Head to Country Island (#4283; 25,000)

ROUTE DESCRIPTION:
This is the only significant island group between Liscomb and Whitehead. They are low lying, relatively large, and close to one another and to the mainland. Two islands, Harbour and Coddles, are forest covered, Country Island has been cleared, and the largest, Goose Island, has a mixture of woods, bog, and heath. They all have saltwater ponds but no fresh water. There are plenty of landing sites with sheltered sand and cobblestone beaches. None of the islands have been settled, but they have been used as fishing bases during the summer and at least one has been used for grazing sheep. Goose Island has a cabin on it.

In 1999, the pipeline carrying the Sable Island natural gas came ashore between Drumhead and Goldboro. After the initial purification (at a large plant out of sight a few kilometres over the hill) it gas will flow a far as New England. Except for a new wharf there is little to suggest the presence of a major gas project and the area retains its wilderness character.

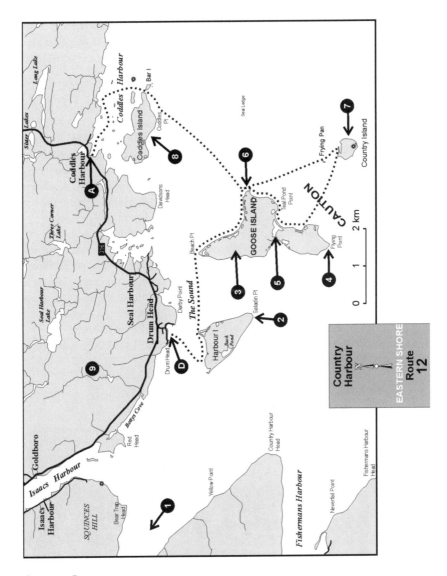

Safety Considerations:

Although the water around the islands is certainly sufficient for the draft of a canoe or kayak, it is shallow, particularly to the east of and between Goose and Country Islands. Ocean swells being pushed through the channel between the islands will break over the shoals and create a confusing maze of whitecaps leading to Country Island. Normal afternoon sea breezes are sufficient to render this stretch treacherous, so govern yourself accordingly; there have been more than a couple of wrecks in these waters. Marine charts are particularly useful here.

POINTS OF INTEREST:

1. Country Harbour

One of the longest and deepest harbours along Nova Scotia's Atlantic coast (second only to Halifax) was settled in 1783 by Loyalists from the Carolinas (mainly soldiers and their families) and prospered for a while on the fishery. Work has since been scarce, and the population decreasing. There has been a recent temporary, construction boom due to the natural gas project.

2. Saladin Point

Here ended of one of the bloodiest mutinies in Nova Scotia history in 1844. The barque Saladin crashed upon the rocks of Harbour Island Point with only six drunken sailors remaining out of a group of fourteen. The others had been butchered and thrown overboard. The surviving sailors were captured and taken to Halifax, where they were found guilty and hung on the Commons. Some believe that the silver bars the Saladin was carrying remain buried under the breakers.

3. Cormorant colony

A large wooded area of Goose Island is gradually dying from the excrement of this sea bird colony.

The exposed bedrock shoreline often makes it difficult to find a good landing spot.

4. Flying Point

In the spring of 1988, the tall ship Merker foundered on the rocks while attempting to enter Country Harbour. The remains of the wooden hulk are scattered along the shoreline.

5. Goose Island

According to a local tale, a large troop ship foundered in this cove shortly after the fall of Louisbourg. It was carrying a large number of French prisoners and a detachment of British troops. Although there was no loss of life they had to wait several days to be found and rescued. In the meantime, the British had the muskets thrown into the pond to prevent the French getting hold of them and taking over. A later attempt to drain the pond and recover the guns failed when the sea water flooded through the porous cobblestone.

6. Sheep Pen Point

As the name implies, sheep were grazed on this island. When it was time for shearing, the people from the nearby mainland communities would gather and drive the animals into holding pens on this point. The island served as a communal pasture.

7. Country Island

The light station was automated in 1986, although the houses still remain. The island was originally forested but all the spruce were cut down by the early lighthouse keepers. It appears that large birch once covered the island, for if you find areas where the sparse soil has been uplifted by storms, sheets of birch bark have been preserved underneath. A mammoth tooth has also been recovered. The island has a tern colony (Roseate, Arctic, Common), which varies in size from year to year. This is public land but don't camp during nesting season.

8. Coddles Island

Another tale tells of a treasure find on this island. Years ago, a foreign ship arrived and hired several locals to help dig a pit. Unfinished by the evening, they were sent home with booze for a break. When they returned, the pit was deeper, planks were strewn around, and the mysterious ship was nowhere to be seen. The passage between the mainland is very shallow at low tide.

9. Sable Natural Gas Plant

Country Harbour is the landfall of Nova Scotia's offshore natural gas. After an initial fractionation at this large facility, the gas is piped to market.

Torbay (The Sugar Islands)

DEPARTURE POINT:
Port Felix Wharf
Route 7 to Sherbrooke, then Route 211 to Isaac's Harbour, and Route 316 to Port Felix. Turn at Fred Davids Road shortly before the church. Total distance 275 km (171 mi.). And alternative departure point is from Charlos Cove. However, since there is 4 km (mi.) crossing this should be reserved for calm weather.

ARRIVAL POINT:
Same as the departure point.

TRIP LENGTH:
Day-long or overnight, 15 km (9 mi.).

CHARTS AND MAPS:
Topographical map: 11/F/3
Marine chart: Whitehead Island to Berry Head (#4282; 25,000)

ROUTE DESCRIPTION:
The Sugar Islands are the earliest documented European fishing station in Nova Scotia. During his 1607 journey from Port Royal to Canso, Samuel de Champlain stopped here and was entertained by Capt. Savelette, a Basque fisherman (and one of the pioneers of the dry fishery) who had been active in these waters every summer since 1565. Not far way (Larry's River) was the landfall for the first transatlantic cable reaching continental North America. Today this compact grouping of islands, islets, and shoals, both forested and barren, are uninhabited and are easily accessible for a day-long sea kayaking journey. Numerous seabirds nest (including Cormorants, gulls, and Eiders) and large numbers of seals are always present. This is public land with some excellent campsites. The Sugar Islands offer an alternate destination if weather or time doesn't allow for the longer Whitehead-Canso route.

SAFETY CONSIDERATIONS:
Although the Sugar Islands are grouped close together, not far from the mainland (all within 3 km), they are surrounded by shallow

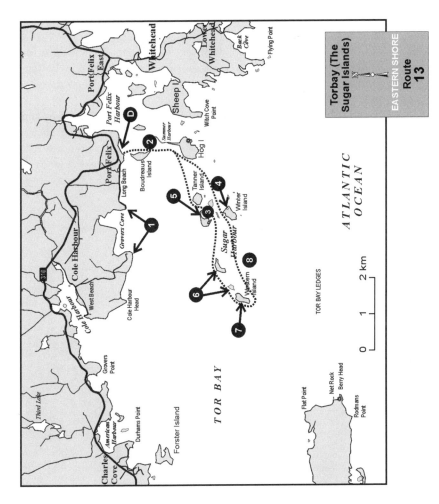

water and numerous shoals. This will result in broken seas when
the offshore swells roll in. On the north side of the group and within the lagoon bounded by Winter, Cahoon, and Tanner Islands you
will be sheltered.

POINTS OF INTEREST:

1. Drumlin Headlands

Several hills of glacial debris are eroding into the sea and providing the sediment that forms the many beaches in this otherwise
rocky landscape. Dominating one hill is the church at Port Felix,
which serves as a landmark at a long distance.

2. Inner Islands

Rapid erosion is apparent at Mattee and Patate (French slang for potato) Islands and the long spit of Hog Island is flanked with toppled trees and bordered at low tide by a field of glacial erratics.

3. Lagoon

This shallow, sheltered basin is a paddling gem. Once inside you are protected from the roughest weather. The surrounding islands have a bedrock base with a coating of glacial till and are forest covered. They have several fine sand beaches and eel grass beds cover much of the bottom. Shoals are strewn throughout, often topped with a Harbour Seal.

Grey seals will haul out on the shoals at low water.

4. Winter Island

The northern tip of this island is a large promontory of flat cobbles of grewacke.

5. Eastern tip of Cahoon Island

This is a gentle sandspit covered in dune grass. Magnificent beach.

6. Larrys Island and Passage Island

These bedrock islands are significantly more exposed, although you can land on the northern side. The tree cover has long since gone (probably due to cormorant nesting years ago), highlighting the large number of granite erratics. In spring this is a large gull colony.

7. Western Island

Recent topo maps still indicate a forest cover in the interior. However, only a few scattered spruce remain. The rest have succumbed to the guano from a large cormorant colony. Significant areas are covered with raspberry bushes, which seem to be resistant to the bird droppings.

8. Ledges

This area has one of the largest congregations of seals on the Atlantic coast. Seldom will you sight less than a hundred, hauled out on the rocks or bobbing up and down around the kayaks.

WHITEHEAD TO CANSO

DEPARTURE POINT:
Whitehead
Route 7 to Sherbrooke, approximately 190 km (118 mi.) from Dartmouth. Follow Route 211 to Isaac's Harbour, then Route 316 to Whitehead, total distance 280 km (174 mi.). Put in beside the canal.

ARRIVAL POINT:
Canso Harbour
This route involves ferrying a car a further 25 km (15 mi.) to the destination. There are several landing spots on the Canso waterfront.

TRIP LENGTH:
Due to the long drive from Metro—a total of nine to twelve hours return, including the car shuttles—allow a full three days, 35 km (22 mi.).

CHARTS AND MAPS:
Topographical maps: 11/F/3,6,7
Marine charts: Whitehead-Berry Head (#4282; 25,000); Canso Harbour (#4280; 37,000)

ROUTE DESCRIPTION:
Because of its distance from Halifax, this route will probably be one of the last along the Eastern Shore that a coastal paddler will visit. However, it is well worth the long drive. The section of coastal highway from Sherbrooke to Whitehead is one of the most scenic in the province and is seldom travelled by either tourists or Nova Scotians. In many ways, its rugged beauty is reminiscent of remote shores in Newfoundland. The topography consists of rugged granite bedrock (most of the rest of this shore is metamorphic rock, either greywacke or slate), much like the Peggy's Cove barrens, without the people. Trees are scarce and stunted, and there are numerous shallow lakes and bogs. Glacial erratics are perched in various unusual places and positions; it seems as if it was only recently that the ice sheet scoured the region. The islands, some no larger than a house, hug the highly indented shoreline, often coalescing at low tide. This is coastal paddling at

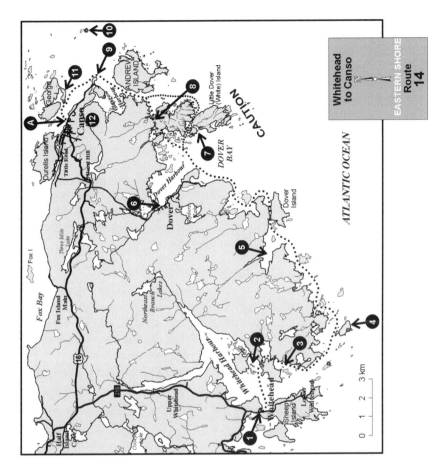

its most enjoyable with hidden coves, narrow channels, and something different around each corner. Most of this route borders
public land (one of the provinces protected areas) and there are
numerous campsites.

SAFETY CONSIDERATIONS:

The beauty of isolation has its price, and there are few places
around the province where you will be farther from a road than in
Wine Cove, halfway between Whitehead and Dover. It's a long,
arduous trek on rough terrain, if anything should happen to you
or your craft. During my circumnavigation, we were stormbound
for three days and couldn't reach anyone, even with our radio.
The islands will help shelter you from the open sea, but the water

is very shallow. Shoals are numerous and waves can break unexpectedly over seemingly deep water. Be especially prudent during periods of heavy swell and avoid skirting the outer tips of islands such as Dover, Little Dover, and Andrews. The portage near Canso was used for boats larger than canoes and kayaks, with good reason.

POINTS OF INTEREST

1. Boat canal

In the days of sail a trip around Whitehead could be treacherous in rough weather. To avoid this route, a boat canal was constructed to link Port Felix Harbour with Whitehead Harbour. Today it is seldom used and in disrepair, but at mid- to high tide there is still plenty of room for canoes and kayaks.

2. The Basin

Shelters a large mussel aquaculture site.

3. Yankee Cove

Named for the New Englanders who, in the 1800s, came up during the season to fish. The foundations of several early homesteads can be found in the fields along the shoreline. The keen observer will note the boundary between the greywacke and the granite intrusions that makes up most of the Canso headland. Blocks of grey parent rock can be found surrounded by the whitish granite.

Carried by the ancient glaciers a long way from its "home," this boulder of greywacke sits atop a platform of granite.

4. Whitehead Island

The only easy landing spot is on the north tip but it is an enjoyable trek over the huge granite slabs to the lighthouse. The station has been automated, but the keepers' houses are still there, although slowly succumbing to the elements.

5. Port Howe

This remote and sheltered harbour is one of best anchorages along the Atlantic coast (others include Country Harbour and Halifax). Both sailboats and freighters have found refuge here during storms.

6. Dover

This small fishing community is the only take out spot between Whitehead and Canso.

7. Little Dover Island

The early settlers in this region built in False Cove. This name was a modification of its first inhabitant, Falt, who lived in the area in 1821.

8. Portage Cove

Still used by the locals, this short carry avoids the shoals around Little Dover Island.

9. Glasgow Head

Early transatlantic cables were brought ashore at Canso since this is the closest point on mainland North America to Europe. Glasgow Head was the site of one of the receiving stations. Satellite transmission has rendered the cables obsolete, although some continue to be maintained in case of emergency.

10. Cranberry Island

This exposed lighthouse has been recently automated.

11. Grassy Island

A National Historic Site where excavations examine one of the earliest permanent European settlements in North America. A boat shuttles tourists to and from Canso.

12. Canso

On the extreme eastern tip of Nova Scotia, this town is the oldest continually inhabited fishing community in the country. Today, depleted fish stocks have created a crisis in many small coastal communities, and Canso faces an uncertain future.

Our Atlantic coastline is dotted with countless off-shore islands. Some are just barren bedrock, while others have thick forest reaching to the water's edge.

COASTAL PADDLING ROUTES
OF THE SOUTH SHORE

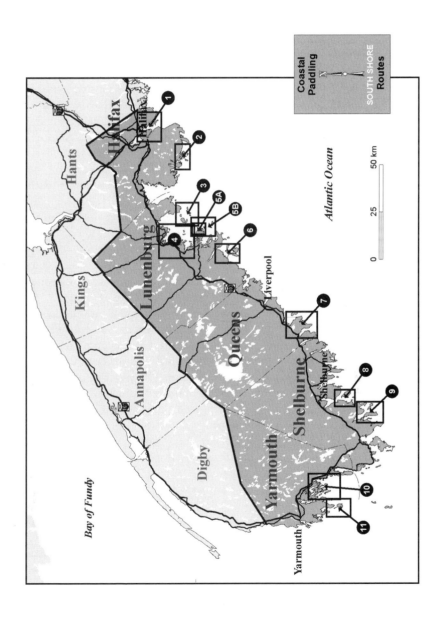

INTRODUCTION

The sheltered cove seemed strangely quiet as we tethered our canoe to the wharf. The thick fog, so typical of this ragged coastline, blanketed the islands and obscured the mainland in the distance. The calm water was disturbed only by the gentle rocking of our craft. High above our heads, lobster traps were stacked in neat piles on the weather-beaten planks, awaiting another season, while the solitary light at the end of the wharf struggled to penetrate the mist. We had passed through Yarmouth Harbour shortly before leaving behind the tides and currents of the Bay of Fundy, and were once again entering the island domain of the Atlantic. We had reached the South Shore.

In need of fresh water—always a scarce commodity on the rocky outposts—we docked at this small fishing community to fill up our jugs. Perhaps the hospitality that had greeted us around the coast would here, too, result in a coffee and a piece of pie (if not a full course meal and a hot bath). Any supplement to our dwindling rations would be welcome.

As we made our way towards the nearest house, several startled sheep scattered over the rock strewn hillside and disappeared over the ridge. We knocked several times at the porch door, but there was no answer. "Anyone home?" Not a sound. We cautiously peered inside and called again. Still no response. The musty air in the well-provisioned kitchen suggested that it hadn't been used for some time. We proceeded to check the other houses and shanties of this "village" and found them also either empty or bolted shut. The inhabitants had disappeared, and except for a few scrawny cats and the untended sheep, the place was deserted. The Tusket Islands were an enigma.

The South Shore of Nova Scotia extends southwest from Halifax around to Yarmouth, where it gradually blends into the Bay of Fundy. From headland to headland it stretches a distance of about 325 km (202 mi.) but, as with the Eastern Shore, inclusion of all the harbours and inlets would inflate this figure considerably. This is a young, submerged coastline, highly irregular, with drowned estuaries and headlands, producing a largely indented coast fringed with islands. These features coupled with localized sediments (from offshore deposits, drumlins, and local subaerial erosion) have contributed to a large number of habitats:

sand and cobble beaches, mud flats, and salt marshes. The predominant feature, however, is the rocky shore.

The South Shore forms part of the province's southern upland. The quartzite and slate bedrock traces its origin to deep-water deposits off the continental shelf of an ancient Africa. Continental drifting shoved this material against North America, where some of it remained after this huge land mass split later on. The granites were formed during this turbulent period as molten magna flooded the cracks, and fissures opened by crustal movement. There is much more slate and granite here than on the Eastern Shore, resulting in somewhat more diverse topography. Extensive bogs, salt marshes, and tidal streams of the Tusket region at the western end contrast with enormous, barren granite slabs at Peggy's Cove, near Halifax.

In between we find the largest bays, the longest sand beaches, and the highest sand dunes along the Atlantic coast of Nova Scotia. Vast areas of the soft slate have been scoured by the glaciers and eroded by the streams to produce more productive soil than on the Eastern Shore, so farming, while still not the major activity, isn't as rare as it is further east. Drumlins are locally abundant and a picturesque rolling landscape decorates much of Lunenburg and Queens Counties.

Several good canoeing rivers (e.g., LaHave, Mersey, Medway) enter the Atlantic here, but their volume is derived from a watershed only marginally larger than that of the Eastern Shore and by early summer they resemble little more than rock gardens. Their influence on the coastal paddler is insignificant.

The offshore islands are, in general, larger and further spaced than those on the Eastern Shore. Major exceptions are Mahone Bay and Lobster Bay, each with over 350 islands. Bring your own drinking water. The small ponds are usually coloured a deep brown, due to high concentrations of organic and inorganic material.

The vegetative cover is determined by the cool, moist, and acidic soil conditions that favour conifers, especially white spruce, which has a high salt tolerance. On headlands and exposed ridges, any trees are severely stunted and distorted; the zone is called "krummholz." Barrens with low heath vegetation are common, and sphagnum bogs frequently fill the depressions. The hardwoods are restricted to higher, better-drained soils, protected from the salt-laden winds, hence, there are few on the islands. The inland forest is noticeably more "lush" than along the Eastern Shore.

Diverse feeding and breeding habitat exists for native and migratory birds. In addition to the sea birds found on the Eastern Shore, there are small populations of Atlantic Puffins and Razorbills. Grey and Harbour Seals are frequently seen but porpoises and whales are not. The latter are usually on their way to feeding grounds at the entrance to the Bay of Fundy. Deer live on the larger islands, and sheep are still pastured, a practice that was abandoned long ago on the Eastern Shore. The plague of coyotes on the mainland now makes these island pastures even more appealing. The name "Ram Island," of which there are many, originated from the practice of placing ewes and rams on separate islands until the appropriate mating time to ensure that the lambs were born in the spring.

Clam beds are often to be found in the sheltered coves.

The climate of the South Shore features moderate daily and seasonal temperatures, high precipitation and humidity, strong winds, and salt spray. Conditions are marginally less harsh than along the Eastern Shore. In winter, few of the harbours freeze, and spring arrives sooner, but fog is common early in the season (less so in Mahone Bay). The Tusket area is particularly "blessed" in that respect, with an average of 120 fog days a year. Summer water temperatures vary from 13°C to 18°C (58°F to 65°F), higher in sheltered inlets and lower in the extreme southwest (Tusket), where the influence of the cool Fundy water is still considerable.

The tidal variation ranges from 1 m (4 ft.) in Halifax Harbour to over 4 m (12 ft.) among the Tusket Islands (again due to the influence of the Bay of Fundy). The currents are particularly significant only in the western region, where considerable caution must be exercised (refer to the Tusket Islands Route 9). Prevailing winds in the summer are from the southwest and should be considered when planning your trip. Count on a fresh sea breeze (20 knots or more) on a sunny day. The stable weather patterns in the summer mean few storms, and those that do occur usually pass through quickly. Electrical storms are even more rare. However, under unsettled conditions, keep an eye out for squalls. The weather report may indicate sunny and warm in Halifax, while a local blow might be hiding around the next headland.

The history of this shore predates the arrival of the Europeans by over two thousand years. The Mi'kmaq spent their summer months along the coast (including the offshore islands) next to a bountiful sea, an unencumbered highway for their birch bark canoes—kayaks were unknown at this latitude. In the winter they moved inland to the shelter of the forests.

When the early European fishermen discovered these rich waters, they sought out many of these sheltered coves and harbours to salt and dry their catch. Samuel de Champlain made his landfall here in 1604 (Cape LaHave), en route to found the first permanent European settlement in Canada at Port Royal. His detailed maps carry place names that remain with us to this day (e.g., LaHave, Port Mouton, Rossignol).

The French subsequently settled along several areas of the South Shore, fighting among themselves and with the English until the mid 1700s. During the infamous Expulsion, they were evicted along with most of the Acadians in the region. The British government brought over settlers in 1783 (mainly German farmers) to fill the resulting void, and they founded the town of Lunenburg. Following the War of Independence, an influx of "Loyalists" arrived, escaping from the newly created United States. They temporarily made Shelburne the largest community in British North America. For a short period, the new town vied with Halifax for dominance in the region. The fortunes of the South Shore have historically paralleled the highs and lows of the fishing industry. It has always been the major source of employment, and when fish were plentiful and the prices high, the population prospered. But when either fell, so did the area's fortunes. Georges Bank, one of the most prolific fishing areas in the world, is close by, and Lunenburg is home of the largest fish processing plant in the country. Recently, the region has fallen on hard times and the decline in catches has forced closure of the processing plants in Lockeport and Port Mouton. Economic diversification in the forestry, manufacturing, and tourism industries has mitigated the problems to some degree, but they can't completely supplant the fishery.

The large offshore islands were all inhabited at one time, but as elsewhere along Nova Scotia's coastline, this is seldom the case these days. Isolated coves and sand beaches may seem romantic to those of us who spend most of our lives in a bustling city, but the early settlers often saw it differently. Cold, foggy, salt-laden air and long, dreary winters gradually pushed them into the comfortable mainland communities, their decision aided by the borderline economics of island life.

One notable exception is Big Tancook Island. This prosperous fishing village has resisted the trend and still has its own general store, elementary school, church, and (until recently) unregulated roads. A regular passenger ferry service links it with the mainland. Many of the other islands continue to be used seasonally, mainly by the lobster fishermen, and the Tusket group is particularly busy over the winter and into late spring. But by August, when I arrived while on my canoe voyage around the province, only the sheep, cats, and empty houses were there to greet me. Elsewhere, locals and tourists maintain a scattering of cottages, especially in Mahone Bay and on the LaHave Islands. The inshore boat traffic, although more apparent than on the Eastern Shore, is significant only in Mahone Bay and near the harbours of the larger fishing communities. Otherwise wilderness prevails. Even the lighthouses have been abandoned and boarded up, the keepers replaced by automation.

The South Shore has its share of tales and mysteries. Perhaps the most famous is the fabled money pit on Oak Island, in Mahone Bay. For almost two centuries, treasure hunters have sought what many believe to be pirate booty or others believe to be the plunder of the Spanish fleet. Some even think the tunnels are the work of pre-Columbian visitors. Millions of dollars have been spent and several lives lost, but to date no money has been recovered, except by authors who have taken advantage of all the hype. Others, myself included, suggest that the whole thing is nonsense, and the tunnels are only the result of natural erosion in the limestone. McNutts Island holds another mystery in the unusual inscriptions carved into the bedrock on its southern tip. There is some evidence to suggest that they originated with Phoenician traders, who visited North America centuries before Columbus.

The South Shore is often referred to as the Lighthouse Route.

Many a ship has foundered along this coast. The largest marine disaster on the North Atlantic seaboard occurred when the *Atlantic* went down off Prospect, near Halifax. (The *Titanic*, although associated with greater loss of life, sank offshore.) These days, drug smugglers take advantage of the sparsely populated coast to bring their product into North America. Canada's largest ever drug bust took place recently, near Liverpool.

The province's South Shore is unspoilt, easily accessible, and you can put in almost anywhere. Camping on the islands isn't a problem. Services—gas stations, grocery stores, and accommodation—are available in the numerous towns and villages, and tourists are welcome. If the weather is poor, you can find sheltered groups of islands for your trip or head inland to Kejimkujik National Park. If the weather is good, your options along the coast are limitless. There is currently a project underway to develop a coastal water trail from Lunenburg to Halifax which may, eventually, encompass the entire coastline.

HALIFAX HARBOUR

DEPARTURE POINT:
Black Rock Beach (Point Pleasant Park) or **Eastern Passage** (Fishermans Cove, Dartmouth).

These are good launch sites, one on each side of the harbour. There are plenty of others, including the Dingle, on the Northwest Arm.

ARRIVAL POINT:
Same as the departure points.

TRIP LENGTH:
Day-long or a weekend, with camping on one of the islands, 15 km to 25 km (9 mi. to 15 mi.).

CHARTS AND MAPS:
Topographical maps: 11/D/11,12
Marine charts: Point Pleasant-Bedford Basin (#4202: 10,000); Black Point-Point Pleasant (#4203: 10,000).

ROUTE DESCRIPTION:
This is the only route description near a densely populated region. In fact, Halifax/Dartmouth is the largest metropolitan area in Atlantic Canada. However, in spite of this, and partially because of it, Halifax Harbour is of particular interest to the paddler. The city of Halifax was founded in 1749 as a military counterpoint to the French fortress at Louisbourg. With the fall of the latter, it rapidly grew in size and importance. In addition to becoming the capital of Nova Scotia, it has remained a major navy base and the commercial centre of the province. Across the harbour, Dartmouth—once considered the bedroom of the capital—has grown in recent years and acquired a dynamic all its own. Passenger ferries and bridges link the two cities.

A tour of the harbour is a journey through more than two hundred years of Nova Scotia's past. Historic buildings contrast with city skyscrapers; modern navel facilities contrast with nineteenth-century fortifications; yacht marinas contrast with commercial container piers; and quaint waterfront boutiques contrast with large oil refineries. However, this diversity and prosperity

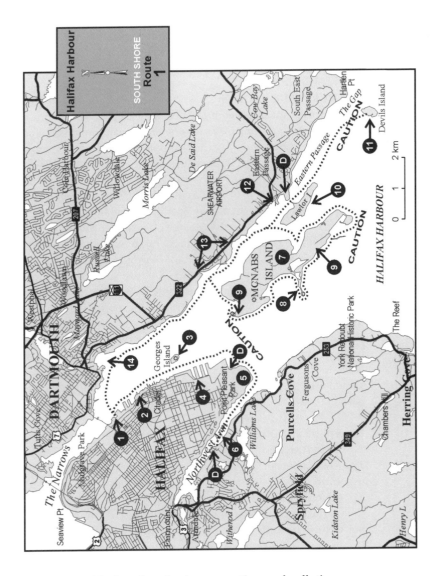

Halifax Harbour

have come with the price of noise, congestion, and pollution.

McNabs Island, Lawlor Island, and Devils Island provide seldom used havens from the bustle of these port cities. The largest Osprey colony along this coast is within the sight and sound of Halifax, on McNabs Island. Lawlor Island, sandwiched between McNabs and the mainland, has a large Blue Heron colony hidden among the ragged spruce and impenetrable brambles, and Devils

Island is supposedly haunted. I can vividly remember one memorable campsite on an island beach, wooded seclusion to my back and city lights on the horizon. Civilization is so near, and yet so far.

SAFETY CONSIDERATIONS:

City harbours mean boats, big boats, and exceptional care must be exercised in paddling these waters. Ideally, you should remain close to the shore, avoiding the shipping channels, and always paddle defensively. The skills of judgement appropriate on open water and along isolated parts of the province are often not enough in the mayhem of Halifax Harbour. Usually people-powered crafts have the right of way over motorized boats but not in Halifax Harbour. Assume that no one else can see you (often the case if you are poking around the piers). Even if they do, they may not be able to stop or veer in time to avoid a collision.

Don't set out in poor weather or in fog. Obtain a marine chart of the harbour, and make sure you know what the symbols mean. Avoid the shipping channels and use particular caution near the ferry routes. The sea conditions are less of a problem than in more exposed waters, although a strong blow down the harbour can create quite a mess. Around Devils Island the water is shallow and sprinkled with shoals. Both the wind and tide level should be noted or you could spend an unplanned night on the island.

POINTS OF INTEREST:

1. Department of National Defence

This is the home of Canada's east coast fleet. Some warships are usually in port.

2. Historic Properties

This is the focus of downtown waterfront activity. A large number of historic buildings have been renovated, becoming boutiques and restaurants. A provincial tourism bureau and the regional offices for the Canadian Parks Service are located here. The Maritime Museum of the Atlantic and the harbour ferry are nearby. The Bluenose II (our provincial symbol) berths here most of the summer.

3. Georges Island

A drumlin long denuded of its trees, it was fortified early on, first in anticipation of a visit by the French and later by the Germans. It is supposedly undermined with tunnels, one of which, as myth has it, connects with the Citadel. Acadians were held prisoner here during the Expulsion.

4. The ocean terminals

Most immigrants to Canada during the early part of this century had their first glimpse of the country at these piers. Passenger liners berth here today.

5. Point Pleasant Park

This is the major parkland in Halifax. Vehicular traffic isn't allowed and a network of trails is used by bikers, joggers, and family dogs. Several species of introduced trees (e.g., Douglas fir, European beech) mix with an assortment of indigenous varieties—and with the ruins of military fortifications. A good departure point.

6. The Northwest Arm

The sheltered finger of ocean that makes Halifax a peninsula borders the affluent South End (and the effluent from the sewer system) and harbours many of the area's yacht clubs.

7. McNabs Island

This was once considered by the French as a location for a North American fortress, but the 1713 Treaty of Utrecht left them with Isle Royale (Cape Breton), so they built at Louisbourg. The British ignored the island until the 1800s, well after Georges Island had been fortified. Peter McNab bought it in 1783, and his family lived there for four generations. Many of the local elite put up cottages. Fruit trees were planted, and land was cleared for a sheep pasture. It was a pleasant retreat from the rowdy military town of Halifax. As late as 1956 there were over fifty permanent residents. That number has dwindled to less than a handful, and today much of the island is owned by Parks Canada. Plans to construct a bridge link have been abandoned, and the island maintains much of its original pastoral allure. A seasonal ferry carries hikers and picnickers over and a tea room operates near the wharf. A recent proposal to site a sewage treatment facility here has created a controversy.

8. Maugher Beach

This was dubbed Hangman's Beach by locals when the Royal Navy erected a gibbet at the end of the sand spit to punish mutineers and deter any other sailors who might have been harbouring similar plans.

9. Ruins of two forts

Fort McNab and Ives Point Battery were constructed in the late nineteenth century and in use until the end of the last world war.

10. Lawlor Island

Now overgrown with spruce and brambles, it was once totally cleared as a pasture for sheep and was the sight of a major quarantine station in the 1800s. Today's inhabitants include Blue Herons and Ospreys.

11. Devils Island

The windswept sentinel at the harbour entrance. A fire destroyed the original forest, and the harsh conditions and sparse soil prevented its return. The light tower is now automated, and the keepers are gone. Only the legendary ghosts stalks the island.

12. Fisherman's Cove

This restored 200-year-old fishing village is a colourful collection of new and old sheds, craft shops, fishing charters and restaurants. The adjacent beach is a good launching spot.

13. Oil refineries.

14. Canadian Coast Guard station.

Lower Prospect

DEPARTURE POINT:
Lower Prospect Government Wharf
Exit at Whites Lake on Route 333. Continue past Terence Bay to the wharf at the end of the road, approximately 30 km (19 mi.) from Halifax.

ARRIVAL POINT:
Same as the departure point. Alternatively at Prospect, 15 km (9 mi.) east of Lower Prospect.

TRIP LENGTH:
Day-long or weekend, 13 km (8 mi.).

CHARTS AND MAPS:
Topographical Map: 11/D/5
Marine Chart: Osborne Head to Betty Island (#4385: 36,500)

ROUTE DESCRIPTION:
The coastline between Terence Bay and Prospect Bay is near the metropolitan area, but it still offers a "wilderness" saltwater paddle. Other than a few summer homes and hunting cabins, the islands are uninhabited and the shoreline, except for that bordering the village, is undeveloped. The topography contrasts sharply with the coast east of Halifax/Dartmouth. Instead of eroding headlands of loose glacial debris, long shallow inlets, and extensive salt marshes (refer to Porters Lake to Chezzetcook Route 1 on the Eastern Shore), this shore is characterized by stark granite outcrops, of which the most famous example is found at Peggy's Cove. It is an austere but compelling landscape. Along the Eastern Shore only Canso displays similar bedrock. Soil is sparse and glacial erratics compete with shrubs and stunted trees for a place on the pitted surface. Beaches and good campsites are not plentiful.

Gulls and terns nest on the islands, and seals, although not as common as along the Eastern Shore or in many other locations on the South Shore, will usually make an appearance. Humans, on the other hand, with their sail- and motorboats, frequent the place on sunny weekends during the summer. Expect their company on the few sandy coves.

Safety Considerations:

The numerous islands close to shore shelter the paddler. However, shoals dot the area, and the exposed outer region can be treacherous in poor weather. The waters are always cold, the air temperature is usually at least 6°C (10°F) lower than in the city, and fog is common, even in summer.

Points of Interest:

1. Back Bay

This inlet offers a sheltered introduction to a rugged, inhospitable coastline. The barren, salt-and-pepper, granite hills support little vegetation—and almost no suitable campsites. However, the cove is peaceful and the crowds of Peggy's Cove are nowhere to be seen.

More popular with sailers than the Eastern Shore, you will sometimes share an isolated cove with these other visitors.

2. Narrow passage

Between Roost Island and the mainland, it can scarcely be navigated at low tide, even with a canoe or sea kayak. As in similar sheltered locations with a continual current bringing nutrients, blue mussels flourish on the bottom.

3. Rogues Roost

A familiar name to the Halifax yachting crowd. It is one of the few places with coastal islands near the city and sufficient anchorage

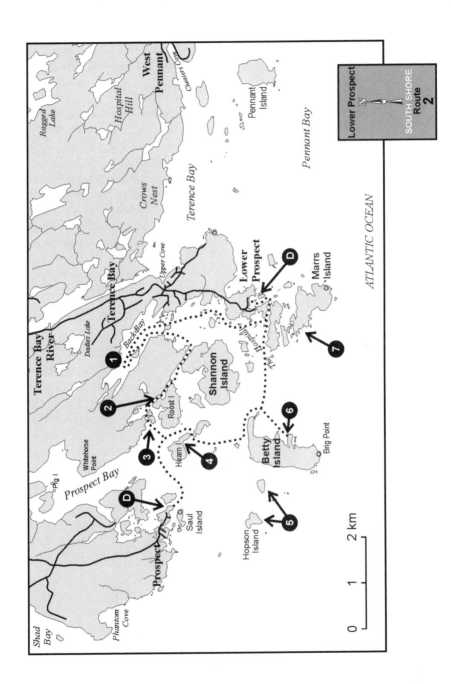

to entice the normally wary sailor. (Sailboats seldom venture in among the Eastern Shore islands.) Expect to find a sailboat (or several) in the summer.

4. Hearn Island

An idyllic view overlooks one of the few sandy beaches on this route.

5. Hopson and Duck Islets

High, treeless islets provide a commanding view of the surrounding coastline. During one of my first coastal paddling trips, my canoe was "retrieved" by a passing fisherman while I was sipping tea and courting my companion in the seclusion of the other side of Hopson. A large fire and some frantic waving eventually attracted a second fisherman and passage back to the mainland.

6. Sandy Cove

From this appropriately named spot on Betty Island a trail leads to the automated light station on the southern tip of the island.

7. Marrs Island

The SS *Atlantic* struck a reef off this island in the early morning hours of April 1, 1873, while making for Halifax to take on coal. From a crew and passengers of nearly one thousand, over six hundred perished. This was the greatest loss of life from any shipwreck on this side of the Atlantic. (The *Titanic* was lost at sea.) Many of the victims are buried in the local cemetery. The waters surrounding Marrs Island are popular for divers. Occasionally, artifacts from the wreck are recovered.

THE TANCOOKS

DEPARTURE POINT:
Chester Government Wharf
Exit 7 on Route 103 and continue on to Chester, approximately 56 km (35 mi.) from Halifax. A forty-minute ferry ride will take you and your kayak or canoe, but not your car, from the Government Wharf to Big Tancook Island and back. Parking is available near the wharf.

Blandford or New Harbour
Exit Route 103 as above, but then follow Route 3 to East River. Continue along Route 329 to Blandford or New Harbour. The distance is about the same as to Chester.

ARRIVAL POINT:
Same as the departure points.

TRIP LENGTH:
Day-long or weekend, Route 3A is about 20 km (12 mi.); Route 3B is about 32 km (20 mi.).

CHARTS AND MAPS:
Topographical map: 21/A/8
Marine charts: Mahone Bay (#4381: 38,000)

ROUTE DESCRIPTION:
These islands are the largest and outermost of Mahone Bay's 365, plus, islands. They also are the only ones that are inhabited year-round. Other than Brier and Long Islands (in the Bay of Fundy) and Pictou Island in the Northumberland Strait, these are the only offshore islands in the province, not linked via a highway, which still maintain a permanent, though dwindling, population. Much of the character of early Nova Scotia is found on these outposts, preserved to an extent by their separation from the mainland. A paddling tour in this region offers both an intimate view of maritime coastal community life and an insight into our coastal biology and geology. The exposed shores illustrate the meeting of two geological periods. Seabirds, including the Atlantic Puffin, nest in the area.

SAFETY CONSIDERATIONS:

Since they are on the outer fringe of Mahone Bay, the Tancook Islands are open to the caprices of the ocean. It may be sunny and warm in Chester but shrouded in a chilling sea fog out here. Keep in mind when rounding the more exposed or south side of the islands that the slate and quartzite cliffs slide into the water at a steep angle, preventing any landing, except during the calmest of days. Plan accordingly.

The paddle from Blandford is relatively short and sheltered from the prevailing southwesterlies, but particular caution is recommended on Route 3B. Pearl (Green) Island is significantly more exposed and should be visited only during good weather by experienced paddlers. It is very low and will be obscured by the slightest bit of fog or haze (common early in the season). Good compass skills are a must.

POINTS OF INTEREST:

The Blue Flag, an iris, is a common early summer flower in damp coastal areas.

1. Little Tancook

This island has a small permanent population of about fifty. It is linked to the mainland by a passenger/freight ferry.

2. Boundary of Halifax/Goldenville formations

The bedrock underlying most of southern Nova Scotia is meta-

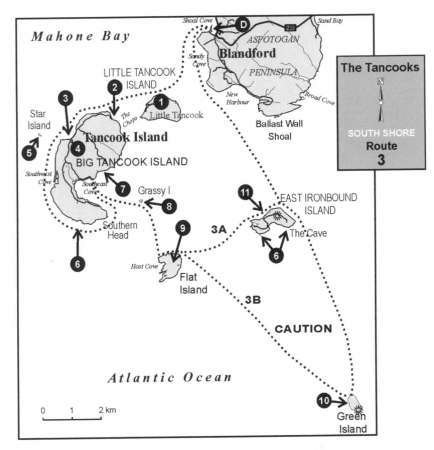

morphic rock, originating from deep-water sediments on the continental shelf of an early Africa (about 500 million years ago). The earlier deposits were mostly coarse material, such as sand, the later finer deposits were materials, such as silts and clays. The total depth exceeded several kilometres. Although the boundary between the two rock zones is generally intermediate, a sharp delineation is exposed on Big Tancook Island.

3. Cobble Beach

To the east of the Government Wharf is a cobble beach with numerous brachiopod fossils, originating from the limestone bedrock of some of the other islands.

4. Big Tancook

This island was settled in the late eighteenth century by German and Dutch immigrants. The soil was fertile, and for many years farming was the main occupation, unlike on most other offshore islands. Only much later did fishing predominate and with it, boat construction. The Tancook whalers were renown for their speed and seaworthiness. The population of the island peaked at over two thousand in the early part of this century, but it has since declined to under three hundred. An elementary school still operates but the high school kids "commute" to Chester by ferry. Fishing is the mainstay but cabbages and sauerkraut provide additional income for some of the residents. The roads are unpaved and potholed, and the cars travel unhindered by mainland maintenance restrictions—

Trawling for pollock.

mufflers seem in short supply. Much of the island is cleared and the remaining spruce/fir wood is crisscrossed with trails. The hiking possibilities are numerous.

5. Star Island
This is a small, grass-covered but eroding drumlin characteristic of many of the inner islands.

6. South Coast of Big Tancook and East Ironbound islands
These have impressive layered slate and quartzite, dipping sharply into the ocean. Greys, blacks, and rust browns colour the sheets of rock. Landing sites are sparse.

7. Remains of a Tancook gold mine
On the north shore of Southeast Cove, hidden among the cobbles on the beach, are some deteriorating wooden beams, all that remain of the Tancook gold mine. The storms and a rising sea level have obliterated the opening of the tunnels, and any remaining gold, is entombed below the island.

8. Grassy Island
Only a remnant of its former self, the grass on this islet is sparse. Loose gravel coats most of the horizontal bedrock. It is, however, home for a colony of terns.

9. Flat Island
Early settlers cleared the hardwood forest in the 1800s. The stone foundations are hidden among the coniferous cover at Sheep Pound Cove, on the north shore. The island is now uninhabited.

10. Pearl Island
One of Nova Scotia's most remote offshore islands, 12 km (7 mi.) from New Harbour, itself on the tip of a peninsula. It was here that I was initiated to our coastal archipelago. In the early 1970s I helped a friend with a study of the Leach's Storm-Petrel, a sparrow-size bird, which nests in burrows and feeds on plankton far out at sea. The remoteness of Pearl Island (also called Green Island on some charts) attracts sea birds. The petrels are now gone, probably eradicated by the gulls-terns, Black Guillemots, and Razorbills that nest along the island's rocky perimeter or among the grasses. There are no trees. Of particular note are the dozen or so parrotlike Atlantic Puffins that have resisted gull predation.

The island had a manned light until the late 1950s and the lighthouse keeper's home stood until recently, when it was destroyed by the Department of Transport, as has been the case with many abandoned lighthouses. Visit Pearl Island only during calm weather, and only if you are an experienced coastal paddler with good map and compass skills. The island lies low and is easily obscured by haze or fog. There are no nearby reference points. Camping is prohibited until after nesting season.

11. East Ironbound Island

This island figures in Rockbound, Frank Parker Day's classic novel about life on Nova Scotia's offshore islands during the early part of this century. Its candid description of the unsavoury as well as the good in people, apparently using some thinly disguised contemporary locals as models, resulted in a flurry of protest following its publication. The book has recently been reprinted and is a worthwhile read while visiting the area. Today fewer than a dozen people remain on East Ironbound; the ferry visits irregularly to bring supplies. A sea cave cuts the south coast cliffs and a few puffins nest above them.

Mahone Bay 🛶

DEPARTURE POINT:
Mahone Bay Harbour
Exit 10 on Route 103 and continue west on Route 3 to Mahone Bay, approximately 90 km from Halifax. You can launch at the public slipway on the south side of the harbour. Ample parking (not overnight). An alternative launch spot beyond the harbour is at Westhaver Beach, a further 3 km along the coastal road.

ARRIVAL POINT:
Route 4A: Same as departure points
Route 4B: Chester Harbour Government Wharf

TRIP LENGTH:
Route 4A: 16-20 km (10-12.5 mi.), depending on departure point
Route 4B: 22-25 km (14-16 mi.), depending on departure point

CHARTS AND MAPS:
Topographical maps: 21/A/8,9
Marine chart: Mahone Bay (#4381; 38,900)

ROUTE DESCRIPTION:
If it is untrodden wilderness that you are seeking, this may not be the destination for you (try the Eastern Shore). However, inner Mahone Bay is nevertheless a unique paddling destination with plenty to offer. Its intriguing melange of deserted island and crowded mainland, traditional homesteads and ostentatious summer mansions, lobster boats and sleek yachts, will keep your interest. The inner islands vary in size, from a few acres to several hundred and are mostly drumlins, relics from the last ice age, slowly succumbing to the rising seas. Abundant sediment released by the eroding cliffs provides material for the beautiful beaches that grace the coves and spits throughout the group. Most of the islands were cleared and farmed in the 1800s but, today, there are no permanent residents. However, unlike the Eastern Shore where many of the islands have reverted to public ownership (or were never granted in the first place), the Mahone Bay islands remain private and summer homes (some very substantial) are often the prominent landmark on them. Although you may officially stop and

lounge about up to mid high-tide, the camping enthusiast should be forewarned. The only official campground is the (less than ideal) provincial park at Graves Island.

One of the more interesting aspects of this route is just the decidedly non-wilderness setting that you get paddling in Mahone Harbour along Indian Point, and in Chester Harbour. The bright colours, ornate shapes, and diverse sizes of the waterfront properties are reason in themselves for poking along these shorelines. You may be next to one of the most popular summer destinations in the province but you will feel a certain remoteness from the private perspective of your craft. The options also exist for Inn to Inn trips, not to mention the after-paddling opportunities provided by several good (and not so good) restaurants, craft shops, and the view of Hansel-and-Gretel residences reminiscent of Freeport, Maine.

SAFETY CONSIDERATIONS:
Mahone Bay cuts deep into the Nova Scotia coast and the marine climate is moderated by the adjoining mainland. In the summer there is less fog, and the water is warmer, than along much of the South Shore. However, as elsewhere, the sea breezes can be quite brisk in the afternoon (over 20 kph) and so be prudent if planning to visit the outer islands (e.g., Mason, Rafuse). Since the prevailing breezes in summer flow from the southwest, it is recommended to begin in Mahone Bay and head towards Chester.

One of the main concerns for the paddler in this major tourist locale is the heavy pleasure-boat traffic. Note the boating channels, and remember that these motorized craft are not used to looking out for small kayaks.

POINTS OF INTEREST:
1. **Hermans Islands Passage**
At low water this channel of mud and eel grass is impassable. Once through, the cove is often crowded with moored sailboats.
2. **Coveys Island**
A large stand of white pine tops the hill at the south end. The former fields are overgrown with alder and spruce. History records an Indian massacre on this island.
3. **Backmans Cove**
This picturesque horseshoe shaped cove, bordered by a sandy beach, is a secluded respite from an otherwise populated archipelago.

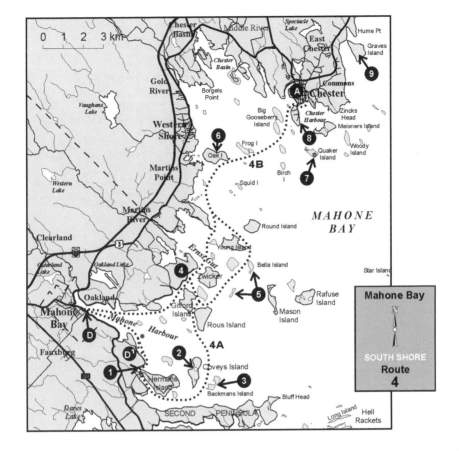

4. Indian Point
Colourful array of houses, wharves and boat houses.

5. Spectacle Island & Bella Island
Two uninhabited drumlin islands with charming sand beaches.

6. Oak Island
This unimposing island still has a few oak trees, but these days is mainly covered with spruce and alder. The island of money-pit fame has had it share of hype over the years—hype that has unfortunately lead to several deaths. To date, the only money associated with this place has been the exorbitant amount spent on seeking the nonexistent (in my mind) treasure. However, the treasure myth has been useful in recruiting tourists to our fair shores (although the island itself is private and off bounds).

7. Quaker Island

Surmounted by a navigational beacon, and not much else, this bald drumlin stands in stark contrast with the other forested islands in the area. It gains its name from members of that religious order who first tried to settle here over 200 years ago.

8. The Peninsula

This former farmland is now rimmed with some incredible summer estates.

9. Graves Island Provincial Park

This is an excellent camping park but less than ideal as a base from which to paddle since the tent sites are a fair distance from the water. However, there has been some talk recently of having boat trailers available for moving the canoes and kayaks.

Blue Rocks ⟿

Departure Point:
Blue Rocks Harbour
Exit 11 on Route 103. Continue on Route 324, bypassing Lunenburg and through Blue Rocks, approximately 100 km (62 mi.) from Halifax. Ample parking at the end of the road. An alternative departure is at Stonehurst East but parking is limited and make sure not to block the path to the water or the turnabout.

Arrival Point:
Same as the departure point.

Trip Length:
Day-long or weekend. Route 5A, ideal for novices, is a compact area with a paddling loop options from 6-16 km (4-10 mi.). Route 5B is a more exposed and longer trip for the experienced paddler, 18 km (11 mi.).

Charts and Maps:
Topographical map: 21/A/8
Marine chart: Lunenburg Bay (#4328; 18,000)

Route Description:
Lunenburg Bay has been a fishing community for over two centuries. The first settlers, mainly German, arrived in 1783, shortly after Halifax was founded. The offshore islands were settled but, as is the case elsewhere, they are used now only as a summer retreat, if at all. Small boat traffic is common due to the proximity of Lunenburg, a large fishing port, and the tourist appeal of Chester. Several sea bird nesting sites and an unmanned lighthouse will be found on the outer islands.

The name "Blue Rocks" is derived from the greenish-blue slate that predominates in the area. The extensive laminate of parallel striations is the result of aeons of geological evolution, beginning with the deposition of sand and mud on the ocean floor and followed by heat, pressure, and uplifting. The direction of the crustal folding is clearly apparent by the lay of the inner islands. At low water the tiny islets are draped with brown algae (rockweed and knotted wrack) that turn a brilliant golden-yellow by mid summer. This is one of our most spectacular paddling routes.

SAFETY CONSIDERATIONS:

Among the inner islands of Blue Rocks is one of the most protected coastal paddling regions along the entire Atlantic coast (Route 5A). The maze of islets and channels, some scarcely wider than a canoe or kayak, offer considerable protection from any surprises that the weather might throw at you. Few inland lakes provide as much protection. It is an ideal place to take the novice paddler, who will surely leave this route with a desire to explore more of the coastline. Note, however, that these waters are shallow and not all the passages can be navigated at low tide.

The textured bluish-gray slate has given the village of Blue Rocks its name.

Route 5B should be approached with considerably more caution. This area is exposed and shoals are common. It should be reserved for experienced paddlers and in calm weather.

POINTS OF INTEREST:

1. Millers Island

A road, overgrown with alders, leads to decaying wooden bridges that once connected Little East Point Island. This had been a fishing community, but a severe storm in the early 1900s

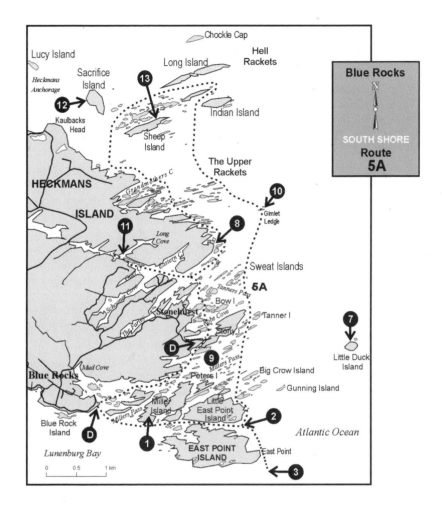

took a heavy toll on the fleet and hastened its demise. Camping is not permitted.

2. East Point Island Passage

There is often yacht traffic in the narrow gut between here and the larger East Point Island. Keep your eyes open.

3. East Point Ledge

Look for seals hauled out at low tide.

4. Cross Island

A narrow channel cuts through this slate headland and into a protected harbour on Cross Island. Several cottages now occupy this former fishing settlement. In late summer the rockweed turns a brilliant yellow orange, a sign of nutrient depletion in a calm ocean.

5. Light tower

A road leads to the automated, fibreglass light tower at the tip of Cross Island. It was flown in by helicopter in sections to replace the original structure.

6. Big Duck Island

The intense smell of droppings attest to this island's popularity with birds. It is a nesting site for gulls, petrels, and Eider Ducks, and puffins have been reported. It has an lovely tiny cove (Western Harbour on the topographical maps) at the southwestern end, well worth a visit on a sunny day.

7. Little Duck Island

Here there is a large cormorant colony in the mostly dead spruce wood. The thick ring of shoulder-high wild rose guarding the perimeter makes it difficult for those wishing a close-up view of the birds. If you're into stone skipping this is the spot!

8. Mountain Cove

The large slate outcrops offers a spectacular sheltered view of the bay. The perfect lunch spot on a sunny summer day!

9. Islets

The best time to paddle this area is from mid- to high tide. Many of the narrow passages are "dry" at low water. Blue mussels are

The islands of Blue Rocks form an intricate water maze.

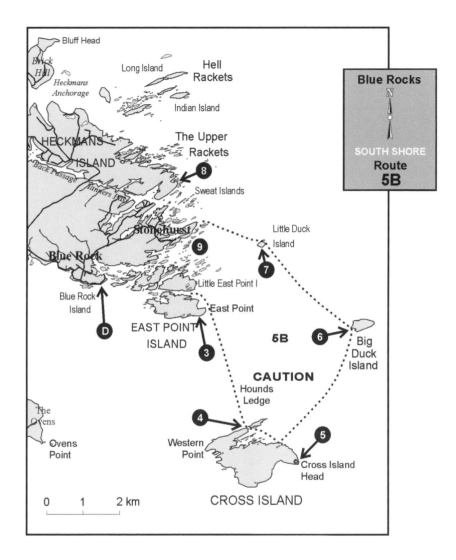

plentiful. Flanked by long, narrow channels and slates aligned in a southwest/northeast direction, these islands offer a good example of crustal folding.

10. Gimlet Ledge & Shag Ledge

These shoals (and others in this area) are exposed at low water and the seals use them to haul out and sun themselves.

11. Tanners Pass

This section of the passageway between Heckmans Island and the mainland highlights the rugged nature of this coast and the textured, layered, slate bedrock. At low tide the section beyond the bridge is an impassable mixture of eel grass and mud, and not particularly interesting.

12. Sacrifice Island

Site of a reputed massacre in early colonial days.

13. Sheep Island

This is one of the few public islands in the area, and one with several good campsites.

THE LAHAVE ISLANDS ⟵⟶ 6

DEPARTURE POINT:
Bush Island Government Wharf
Exit 12 on Route 103. Follow Route 331 (a scenic drive along the
LaHave River) to Crescent Beach. Turn left and continue to the
wharf on Bush Island, approximately 120 km (74 mi.) from
Halifax. Alternatively, depart from the small beach at the end of
the road (D') on the east end of Bush Island.

ARRIVAL POINT:
Same as the departure point.

TRIP LENGTH:
Day-long or weekend 10 km to 15 km (6 mi. to 9 mi.).

CHARTS AND MAPS:
Topographical map: 21/A/1
Marine chart: Pearl Island-Cape LaHave (#4384: 39,000)

ROUTE DESCRIPTION:
This compact group of offshore islands is partly linked by a road
to the mainland. Their importance in the fishing industry predates
the founding of Halifax. Samuel de Champlain mapped and
named them, and French fishermen visited during the summers.
The English moved in after the Acadian Expulsion, but they too
left by the early part of this century. Today, only seasonal inhabitants reside on the outer islands.

The LaHave Islands are a collage of white sand beaches, granite rock, eroding drumlins, sheltered salt marsh, oldfield, layered
slate, and exposed shoals. Variety is the norm, and although one of
the province's most popular beaches (Rissers) is nearby, few venture where the road does not. You will seldom have to share these
deserted beaches and salt marshes with more than migratory
shorebirds and white-tailed deer (although it has become popular
in recent years.)

SAFETY CONSIDERATIONS:
Within the large bay separating Cape LaHave and the inner
islands, you are protected from the ocean swells. However, the

fetch is considerable—3 km (2 mi.)—resulting in quite a chop during a strong wind. The water is shallow, particularly in Cape Bay, so note the tides or you could end up stranded in ooze that allows little wandering. Be especially wary when rounding the exposed southern side of Cape LaHave Island. Seal Point, and Cape LaHave jut into treacherous waters; should the wind pick up, there are few safe landing sites. Often, the Bay Beach is guarded by a wide surf zone. Also be cautious in the passage southeast of Mosher Island, especially when the current runs against the ocean.

POINTS OF INTEREST:

1. Rissers Beach Provincial Campground
This campground is situated in the woods just behind the beach. It is a popular location and often full in the high season (reservations: 688-2034/2010).

2. Crescent Beach
One of the most spectacular sand beaches along Nova Scotia's Atlantic coast, it is part of a tombolo and is a favourite with bathers. Motorbikes, dune buggies, and rowdy crowds may also frequent the beach area.

3. Cape Bay
This bay would cut Cape LaHave Island in half if not for the barrier beach at its apex. It is very shallow with dense beds of eel grass and is impassable at low water, even for kayaks. Blue mussels are plentiful.

4. Barrier Beach
This idyllic little spot has a barrier beach, expansive dunes, slate outcrops, and a hidden inlet that slices deep into the island and empties at low tide. A good camping spot and an easy portage over the dunes.

5. The Bay Beach
Only half the size of Crescent Beach, it still has over a kilometre of gently sloping, white sand, backed by impressive dunes. Most importantly, the summer throngs that pack Rissers and Crescent Beaches are absent. A high tide will carry you in close to the beach from the north, and if the weather permits, you can portage and continue around the island.

6. Cape LaHave
At over 30 m (l00 ft.) this is the highest point on the island and a good example of an actively eroding drumlin. The soft cliffs lose up to 2 m (8 ft.) a year to the ocean. Similar mounds of glacial

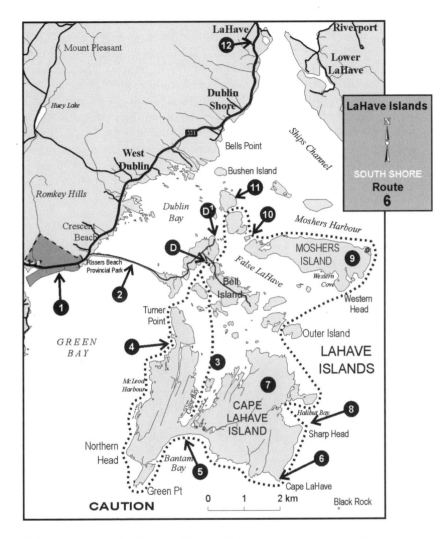

debris are spread the length of the South Shore and provide much of the sand for the beaches. Samuel de Champlain landed near here on his journey to found the first permanent European settlement in Canada, Port Royal, 1605. He named the spot after Cap de la Hève, the lighthouse at the entrance to Havre (his port of origin). He also began his series of excellent harbour charts with this coast.

7. Cape LaHave Island

This is the largest in the archipelago, although unlike some of the others, it never had a significant settlement. This was possibly due to the shallow waters on its protected side and the exposed cliffs on the other. Most of the island is common municipal land, where hay was harvested, and until recently, cattle grazed. Regenerating oldfields provide forage for a permanent deer population.

8. Halibut Bay and Halibut Head

Sea kayaking is an activity for kids of all ages and boats of all kinds.

These offer some of the best campsites on this route, particularly by the beach on the northern side of Halibut Head. The Shelburne dyke outcrops here. It was formed during the continental rifting of the late Triassic age, when molten rock flowed into open fissures. It stretches over 100 km (62 mi.) across the western part of the province.

9. Mosher Island

There were once a number of homesteads here as several fields testify. The southeastern end has some interesting coves and inlets. The northeastern end has a small sheltered beach leading to a great view by the automated lighthouse. There are no longer permanent residents on the island.

10. The Squam

Located between Hirtle and Mosher Islands, this is a good clam digging spot when exposed at low tide.

11. Covey Island

As well as Hirtle and Mosher Islands, it is linked to the mainland by an underwater power cable. The Covey Island boat yard operated on the island, until it recently moved its operation to Petite Riviere.

12. LaHave

Stock up with some excellent bread and pastries at the historic LaHave Bakery.

PORT MOUTON

DEPARTURE POINT:

St. Catherines River

Exit at Port Joli on Route 103. Continue another 6 km (4 mi.) to the wharf remains at the end of the gravel road, approximately 175 km (109 mi.) from Halifax.

ARRIVAL POINT:

Same as departure point or South West Port Mouton: Exit 21 on Route 103. Continue another 6 km (4 mi.) on pavement to gravel road, about 1 km (0.6 mi.) from dead end, on the left leading to the Government Wharf. Two cars are definitely needed for this trip as there is no public transport (nor much traffic, should you be considering hitchhiking) between Port Mouton and St. Catherines River, 20 km (12 mi.) apart.

TRIP LENGTH:

Day-long or weekend. Route 7A, is a compact area with a paddling loop from 12 km to 14 km (7 mi. to 9 mi.). Route 7B is a more exposed and longer trip for the experienced paddler, 20 km to 25 km (12 mi. to 15 mi.).

CHARTS AND MAPS:

Topographical map: 20/P/15
Marine chart: Liverpool Harbour-Lockport Harbour (#4240: 60,000)

ROUTE DESCRIPTION:

Port Mouton (pronounced "ma-toon," as in "cartoon") owes its name not to the sheep that were pastured on the islands but to the first Champlain expedition in 1604, when a sheep fell off a ship into the harbour and drowned. DeMonts, the leader of that famous voyage, established a base in Port Mouton for several weeks, while they waited for their second ship to arrive. During that time, Champlain further explored the southwest coast in a small, collapsible boat they had brought along for the purpose. Port Mouton was settled much later by British immigrants. Fishing offered a prosperous livelihood, until the fishing crisis in Atlantic Canada recently forced the town's major employer, its only processing plant, to close.

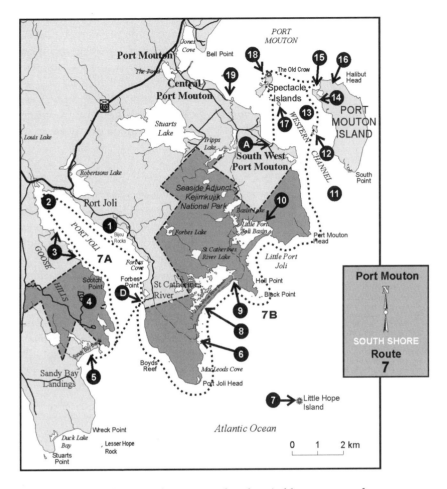

The surrounding area has a rugged and varied beauty, one of the reasons that the Canadian Parks Service acquired much of it for a marine adjunct to Kejimkujik National Park, about 100 km (62 mi.) away. The large, blunt peninsula between Port Mouton and Port Joli is covered mainly with the usual coastal spruce and fir, but the two major headlands are open, probably cleared by settlers years ago. Two substantial barrier beaches front a ragged lake and a saltwater basin, respectively. A hiking trail leads along the shore, but development is limited and tourists few. Granite is the dominant rock; its erosion produces a whiter sand than along the Eastern Shore. The endangered Piping Plover nests on the upper edge of the beaches.

The islands of Port Mouton Harbour are a counterpoint to the exposed mainland coast. They are an eclectic combination of huge sand dunes and scattered shoals, cormorant and gull colonies, abandoned fields, and a lighthouse—and of a drowned forest. The sheltered Port Joli Basin is shallow and warm in the upper reaches with salt marsh and mud flats, cut by channels, exposed at low tide. Numerous shorebirds frequent the area during migratory season.

SAFETY CONSIDERATIONS:

This trip around the large peninsula is one to make in good weather only. The exposure to open sea coupled with the many shoals can quickly lead to treacherous conditions should a wind pick up. Consider this when contemplating a journey that will be at least 16 km (10 mi.) before the first take out. Recently, Parks Canada removed the only official wilderness campsite in the park, restricting this shoreline to only very experienced paddlers, since you are expected to complete the entire route within one day. I disagree strongly with this policy as it is unnecessary and potentially dangerous. If, when following this route, conditions deteriorate, do not hesitate to stop and find shelter within the park boundary. Your safety comes before park regulations. Should inclement weather arrive in this area just as you do, it might still be possible to explore the Port Joli Basin or the smaller islets and visit Port Mouton Island (although there are plans to develop it as a tourist resort). The mainland will offer some protection from the prevailing southwesterlies.

POINTS OF INTEREST:

1. Bijou Rocks
Arctic and Common terns nest on these tiny outcrops.

2. Upper Basin
At high water you can paddle throughout this area. However, when the tide falls the salt marsh takes over and your route will be restricted to a few channels, often with dead ends.

3. West shore
This irregular coast harbours several beaches. The observant will find shellfish middens, mounds of shells left by the early native inhabitants who spent the summer in these productive coastal inlets.

4. Thomas Randall Provincial Park
The wooded campground is, unfortunately, not set close enough to the water to allow for an easy launch.

5. Sandy Bay Beach

This beautiful beach is partially sheltered from the normally prevailing southwesterlies.

6. Cove

An idyllic tiny cove is nestled behind the Harbour Rocks and is a relatively protected landing spot during a southwest wind. The park trail passes this way where there was once a National Park wilderness campsite, but it has been removed following park policy to prohibit camping in the adjunct. There is a foundation of an early homestead and a striking outcrop of metamorphosed granite. Harbour and Grey Seals are common among the shoals.

7. Little Hope Island

Barely a rock above high tide, it lies about 4 km (2 mi.) offshore. It is dominated by a tall, cylindrical, unmanned light tower. The name probably refers to the chances of survival prior to the establishment of the first light house (1866).

8. St. Catherines River Beach

One of the largest crescent beaches of its kind along the entire Atlantic coast of Nova Scotia is spared foot and vehicular traffic because of its isolation.

9. Eastern end St. Catherines River Beach

Ocean currents and wave action have formed a bar that, except for a narrow entrance, almost connects the headlands. (Since both the topographical map and the marine chart indicate a complete barrier, this entrance was probably closed several years ago. It is not uncommon for severe storms to block, open, or relocate such passages.) This and the adjoining beach are among the few places where the Piping Plover can nest in peace. Take care during the nesting season—mid-May to July-for they blend in extremely well with the sand and dune grass.

10. Little Port Joli Basin

Protected from the open sea by a barrier beach, this spit also runs northeast, leaving a narrow channel. At low water the basin is an expansive combination of mud flat and salt marsh, with the ebbing tide creating a strong current at the entrance. At high tide, it can be explored by kayak.

11. Western Channel

During the summer you may spot groups of Pilot whales.

12. Jackies Islands and Thrum Cap

This small island and islet are home to cormorant, Black-backed Gull, and heron colonies.

13. Wreck

A dragger was sunk here intentionally as part of a dive park. At low water you can clearly view the wreck from the kayak.

14. Back Beach

Located on Port Mouton Island, the name "Back Beach" refers to enormous sand dunes that extend well inland into the woods. While most dunes rarely exceed 6-7 m (approximately 20 ft.) some of these attain 15 m (50 ft.)—among the largest on Nova Scotia's Atlantic coast. Favourable winds and currents, along with a good supply of white granitic sand have combined to produce this unique coastal feature.

15. Island Cove

This cove illustrates the rising tide level and the destructive power of the ocean in a dramatic fashion. Large tree stumps, anchored in the rocky beach, are exposed at low tide. Very probably a strong storm from the northwest wreaked havoc with this shoreline sometime during the past century, excavating the soil and destroying the trees. Only a narrow barrier protects the freshwater pond from an incursion by the ocean.

16. Island clearing

Among the fields, you will find a well, building foundations, an apple tree, and, if you visit at the right time, a garden of day lilies. Hidden at the back of the hill, bordering the woods, is a large abandoned (and definitely out of place) Quonset hut. It was built over a decade ago by the American owner for a barn in his attempt to raise sheep on the island.

17. Massacre Island

This name comes from a reputed native attack in the 1600s on a group of French sailors.

18. Spectacle Islands

Steelhead trout are raised in floating pens.

19. Carters Beach

This beach borders extremely high sand dunes, similar to those on Port Mouton Island, which exhibit excellent examples of dune succession.

McNutts Island 🛶 **8**

DEPARTURE POINT:
Carlton Village Government Wharf
Exit 29 on Route 103. Continue past Gunning Cove 10 km (6 mi.) and turn left down the first gravel road after the church. Plenty of parking at the waterfront, approximately 210 km (130 mi.) from Halifax.

ARRIVAL POINT:
Same as the departure point.

TRIP LENGTH:
Weekend, 17 km to 20 km (11 mi. to 12 mi.).

CHARTS AND MAPS:
Topographical map: 20/P/11
Marine chart: Shelburne Harbour (#4382: 24,300)

ROUTE DESCRIPTION:
McNutts Island, one of Nova Scotia's largest offshore outposts, is known by few and visited by even fewer. Its more than 800 ha (2,000 acres) are a diverse combination of dense wood, fields, steep bedrock cliffs, cobble shores, and sand beaches. A narrow trail about 4 km (2 mi.) long leads from the wharf to the lighthouse, but is fighting a losing battle with alders and white spruce. Another road, in scarcely better shape, skirts the western shore where most of the early settlers lived. Sheep are still pastured in the open perimeter, and it is a good hiking area. The bedrock is mainly greyish quartzite, with spectacular vertical blocks near the lighthouse, but beaches are often white from the sand of the mainland granite.

This is an ideal place, especially for the novice paddler and those with kids to spend some time exploring an Atlantic coastal island. The distance from the mainland is only about 1 km (0.6 mi.) and protected from the prevailing winds. There is plenty of room to roam and explore for a weekend or longer, and there is much that is notable: a large, abandoned light station, early homesteads, a deserted military battery, and some cryptic rock inscriptions.

SAFETY CONSIDERATIONS:

Although the distance to McNutts Island from Carlton Village is short and normally quite sheltered from the prevailing southwesterlies, any shift to a south/north axis can be cause for concern. A strong breeze along the extended fetch will create a choppy beam sea. Be wary, too, of rounding the south end of the island; here, you are exposed to the open ocean with only steep boulder beaches or protruding bedrock to greet an emergency landing. In poor weather, hike to the light station via the interior trail or shoreline.

POINTS OF INTEREST:

1. Shelburne

In May 1783, a fleet of over twenty vessels guarded by two warships sailed along the shores of McNutts Island up the Eastern Way. Their destination was the head of Shelburne Harbour, and their cargo was thousands of British refugees. These destitute exiles had supported the losing side during the War of Independence and were forced to flee. Shelburne (or Port Razoir, as it was called then) was chosen mainly for its shelter and defensibility. There was little else to recommend the area. The ground was either rocky or boggy, so farming was next to impossible. However, these "Loyalists," as we call them, continued to arrive, and by 1786 over sixteen thousand had made Shelburne the largest community in Canada and one of the largest in North America. That status changed within a decade as harsh reality set in and most of the inhabitants left for more hospitable areas. Today, Shelburne is a quiet fishing town with a population under two thousand.

2. McNutts Island

The story of this island predates that of Shelburne by a few years. Following the Seven Years War (1756-1763), the British government awarded many land grants in Nova Scotia. Alexander McNutt acquired this island (as well as several other tracts in the province). Although his dream of founding a "New Jerusalem" did not materialize, he did settle for a time on the island. However, his sympathies were with the Americans, and during the revolution he moved south. Several families subsequently settled the island, and until a few decades ago, there was still a small community, complete with school. Now all are gone, the roads are in disrepair and succumbing to alders, and visitors are few. The only permanent inhabitants are the sheep.

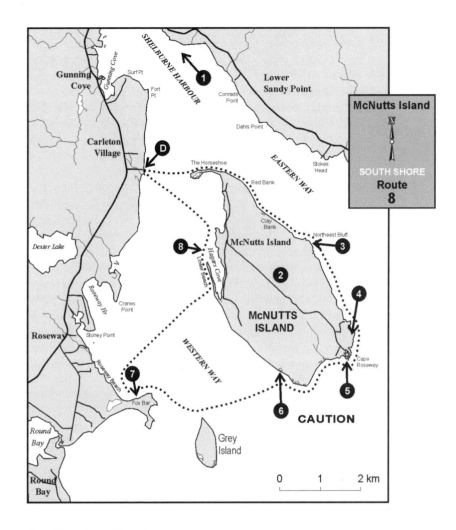

3. Remains of trawler

Just south of Northeast Bluff, the most prominent cliff on this shore, are the rusting remains of a large trawler.

4. Remains of coastal battery

Among the dense woods, off the main trail, are the remains of a major coastal battery. Constructed during the Second World War, it was meant to deter the Germans from entering Shelburne Harbour, one of the largest in Nova Scotia. Whether it deterred them is doubtful, and in any case, no shots were fired in anger, although one of the former keepers mentioned that the initial practice round nearly took out the light tower. The concrete gun emplacements, connecting tunnels and chambers, are cracking, slowly succumbing to the elements and vegetation. Two enormous 25 cm (10 in.) canons remain—apparently the largest in the country. An attempt had been made to salvage one by cutting it in pieces, but it proved too expensive. The buildings have long since been removed, but the rectangular concrete posts upon which they stood are scattered among the new forest growth.

5. Abandoned light house

Middle Eastern script or graffiti from a former light keeper? Intriguing engravings are sometimes found on the off-shore islands.

The first Cape Roseway lighthouse was constructed in 1788, following one at Louisbourg (1737) and one at Sambro (1752). It survived until the sixties, when it was destroyed by fire and replaced by the present modern structure. This too has been abandoned and the various buildings boarded up. They have taken on a particularly ghostly air of remoteness—especially after a 4 km (2 mi.) hike from the other side of the island. The bedrock near the tower is covered with graffiti, some of which dates back to the early 1800s and includes names, dates, and sketches of lighthouses. Of particular note is an inscription of unknown origin, midway between the tower and the keeper's house. The symbols are believed by some to be Carthaginian; others believe they are just

the prank of a bored lighthouse keeper with some knowledge of ancient script. It has been translated as: "Inscribed and left behind as a memorial to (or by) Chief Kese."

6. A boulder

An enormous boulder stands out against the high-energy, cobble beaches of the southwest shore. It is noted even on the marine chart.

7. Fox Bar

This is an imposing sand and cobble promontory which, during low water, connects with marsh-covered Grey Island, a popular nesting site for sea birds.

8. Hagars Cove

This sheltered harbour is the site of an early settlement. A couple of buildings are still standing.

9   CAPE NEGRO ISLAND

DEPARTURE POINT:
Cape Negro Government Wharf
Exit 28 (Port Clyde) on Route 103. Continue south through Port Clyde to the Blanche turn-off, about 9 km (6 mi.) and follow gravel road to wharf on the left, 2 km (1 mi.). Parking by the wharf. Approximately 225 km (140 mi.) from Halifax.

ARRIVAL POINT:
Same as the departure point.

TRIP LENGTH:
Weekend, 25 km to 30 km (15 mi. to 19 mi.).

CHARTS AND MAPS:
Topographical maps: 20/P/11,6
Marine chart: Lockeport to Cape Sable (#4241: 60,000)

ROUTE DESCRIPTION:
Near the southwestern extremity of the province, the Cape Negro/Port La Tour region is an irregular composite of long, shallow harbours, cobble beaches, islands, shoals, and sand bars. The low relief carries a stunted fir/spruce forest and large expanses of bog, characteristic of much of this area of Nova Scotia. Glacial erratics dot the terrain. Some of the islands were cleared by early settlers, and heavy foraging by free ranging sheep has kept their perimeters well cropped.

Natives spent their summers along the coast, and by the 1500s European fishermen were frequent visitors, stopping to salt and dry their catch before returning to Europe. However, it was Champlain who offered the first accurate description of this coast, and he bestowed the name "Cape Negro," apparently in reference to black rocks, although it is not clear exactly what he meant. This section of Nova Scotia coast was settled by Acadians who were replaced by New Englanders after the Expulsion of 1755.

Cape Negro Island once supported several families but has been uninhabited, except for the sheep, since the Second World War. One well-built but rapidly disintegrating home is all that remains of this earlier settlement. Several hunting/summer cabins

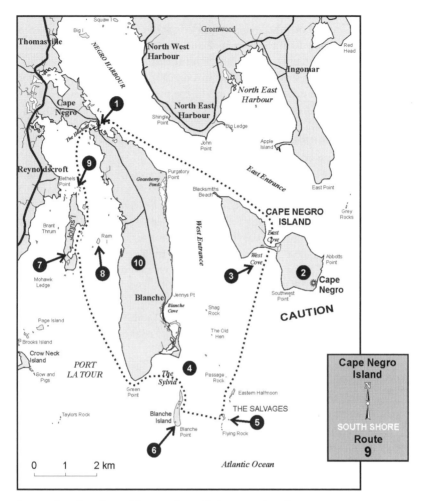

Atlantic Ocean

0   1   2 km

have taken its place. The southern light tower has been automated. The island can be reached relatively easily from several points on the mainland. Its large size and hiking possibilities make it worth a trip, even if the weather prevents you from rounding Green Point, the tip of Blanche peninsula, to complete the circuit.

SAFETY CONSIDERATIONS:

As with our other coastal areas, special caution is advised when rounding the exposed headlands and islands. Cape Negro and Green Point bear the full brunt of the southwesterlies. The waters around the Salvages are very shallow and conditions vary, depending upon both the weather and tide state. Tides in this region are influenced by the Bay of Fundy and can exceed 2 m (8 ft.). Currents may also be strong. The shoals and bars, exposed at low water often serve as barriers to a nasty sea and shelter low draught boats like a kayak. Although there are many beaches, most are boulder. They are steep, exposed, and subject to a dumping surf.

POINTS OF INTEREST:

1. The Haulover
Natives used it to portage their canoes from Cape Negro Harbour to Port La Tour long before the Europeans arrived. The Acadians probably did the same. Larger vessels had to round Blanche Point. Eventually, increasing fishing activity led to a demand for a safer route between the two harbours. This narrow canal, only about 450 m (1,400 ft.) long was completed in 1828. It is still used today, although in disrepair; canoes and kayaks will have no problem, except during the lowest tides.

2. Cape Negro Island
Except for the steep, double-crescent cobblestone beach, this island would be two separate ones. The island was inhabited until recently, and sheep are still pastured. The northern half is mostly wooded, while the southern half has large sections of well-cropped grass. The sheep leave little other vegetation, except thistles and nettles, but they leave their droppings, which are scattered everywhere. Large tracts of huckleberry cover much of the interior of the southern island, creating a dense red carpet in the fall. A more appropriate name for the place might have been "Cape Rouge." The trails marked on the topographical map are overgrown, but a hike around the open perimeter allows a spectacular view. The classic light tower has been automated.

3. East Cove and West Cove
A tombolo separates the coves and links the two halves of Cape Negro Island. Here are the remains of the main wharf, a house in ruins (now used by the island sheep), and many signs of the previous homesteads—carved granite stones, rock piles and walls, and wells. A sheep pen at one end of the beach suggests how the animals are rounded up during spring shearing. The beach stones are mostly metamorphic rock and have an interesting pattern of dark crystals (probably andalusite).

4. Sheep Ledge and Blanche Island Bar
These are only two of the numerous bars, shoals, and islets that

make up this shallow area just south of the Blanche peninsula. It has always been a dangerous place for fishing boats, one of the reasons for constructing the canal through the Haulover. At low tide the exposed bar connects Blanche Island with the mainland, and Sheep Ledge stretches over a kilometre into the harbour. The tide state can alter your route considerably.

5. The Salvages

These are the islets off the eastern fringe of Blanche peninsula. An automated lighthouse is bolted and cemented onto the southern-most island (Western Halfmoon). Scarcely more than a rock at high tide, storm waves can sweep over both island and house. During settled weather, you might be able to find a spot to camp (perhaps in the remains of the basement). Be sure to bring your camp stove; there is precious little driftwood.

6. Blanche Island

This island may have once been a summer fishing station—remains of a wharf can be found at low tide near the middle of the eastern shore. Today it is a nesting spot for sea birds. Sheep are sometimes pastured here during the summer months, and a crude pen sits in one of the hollows.

7. Johns Island

A narrow entrance leads into a sheltered pond/salt marsh on Johns Island. The current is strong during midtide, and large granite boulders, with protruding cubic crystals, determine the entrance.

8. Ram Island

The name was often used to designate an island where male sheep would be segregated until mating time to ensure that the lambs would arrive in late spring, with a better chance of survival. However, this particular Ram Island is scarcely more than a out-crop of bedrock, crowned with scraggy spruce. It probably got its name from more than one encounter with a returning fishing boat.

9. Boulders

An unusual collection of angular boulders, some almost a pyramid shape, lie in the shallow water off the northern tip of Johns Island.

10. The Blanche Peninsula

This is technically an island, with The Haulover separating it from the rest of the mainland. Until the 1950s it was one large sheep pasture. The animals ran free while the residents fenced in their homes and gardens, rather than the reverse. In early June each year, the sheep were driven into a large community shearing pen located on the point. In recent years the population has dwindled considerably.

LOBSTER BAY

DEPARTURE POINT:
Morris Island Government Wharf
Exit 33 on Route 103 and continue on Route 308 to wharf, approximately 310 km (194 mi.) from Halifax. This wharf is one of many that have been transferred to local harbour authorities and you may be required to pay a boat launching fee ($10 in this case).

ALTERNATE DEPARTURE POINT:
Argyle Sound
Exit 31 on Route 103 and continue on Route 335 to West Pubnico. Follow Argyle Sound Road 2.5 km to turnoff for public launch. Argyle Sound is approximately 280 km (175 mi.) from Halifax. At very low tide you will have to traverse a few metres of mud to reach the water.

ARRIVAL POINT:
Same as the departure points.

TRIP LENGTH:
Day-long to weekend, 20 km to 27 km (13 mi. to 17 mi.)

CHARTS AND MAPS:
Topographical maps: 20/P/12 (also 20/P/13 if you wish to explore further into the bay)
Marine chart: Wedgeport and Vicinity (#4244, 30,000)

ROUTE DESCRIPTION:
Lobster Bay has been well named. This is a rich lobster fishing area and, in season (from November to May), it is bustling with activity as hundreds of "Cape Islanders" and thousands of buoys dot the waters. During the spring and summer months, the usual season for paddling in these parts, the fishery is still active. Draggers and herring seiners head to and from the deeper waters, while rockweed harvesters and aquaculture lease holders operate closer to shore. The groundfishery collapse, which has decimated many fishing communities in Atlantic Canada, has had much less impact on the more diverse fishing industry of this area.

This route illustrates most of the island and coastal diversity characteristic of the region: broad salt marsh and mud flats,

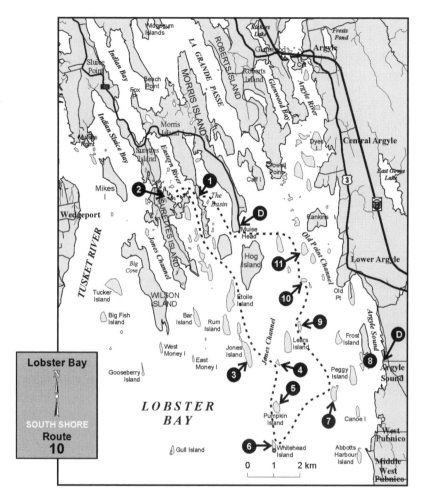

forested and cleared islands, tidal rivers, and elongated drumlins
being dissolved by the sea. The topography is relatively flat
although panoramic views are possible atop some of the barren
islands. Where there is tree cover (usually a tight mix of spruce, fir,
and birch), this often extends to the high tide mark. Similar to the
Tusket Islands, an array of names describe shapes (e.g., pumpkin),
plant cover (e.g., Gooseberry, Bramble, Birch), domestic animals
(e.g., Inner/Outer Sheep, Ram, Hog) as well as early ownership
(e.g., Jones, Muises, Frost). Unlike the Tuskets, however, the
islands no longer serve as active fishing bases (although sheep are
still pastured here). There are no houses (except for a large modern

two story abode perched alone atop an otherwise barren Lear Island). The islands (except for Whitehead with its light tower) are private, although the owners appear more welcoming to visitors (locals camp frequently) than Mahone Bay. However, if camping be discreet, clean, and avoid areas where sheep are pastured. For the birder, Lobster Bay has an exceptional range of species. Indigents such as osprey, great blue herons, eiders, terns, and gulls share the marshes and mud flats with the numerous migrants that seek out food and rest on their long journeys.

This is one of the Acadian areas of Nova Scotia where the French speaking community has lived and worked continuously since 1653 (except for a short period, when the local population was expelled in the mid 1700s). The distinctive Acadian dialect is still the main language on the adjacent mainland.

SAFETY CONSIDERATIONS:

Early settlers raised sheep on the South Shore islands and some are still pastured year round, where there are neither fences nor foxes.

A glance at the map will quickly indicate that this route deep within Lobster Bay is significantly more sheltered than the Tusket Islands. However, the outer islands are exposed and, in some of the narrow inner channels, currents can still present a problem. Fishing boat traffic is more frequent than in most other paddling areas and you should be careful, especially in those passages leading into the major wharves. Fog is a common companion and can surprise if you are not vigilant.

POINTS OF INTEREST:

1. Bridge remains

The stone foundations of an early bridge that carried a pathway out along this headland, ultimately to Muises Head Island (where there are also stone remains). The trail is now unused and overgrown. At most tide levels you can paddle through this passage. At very low tide you will have a short carry.

2. Saltmarsh

When driving along the shoreline to Morris Point, as elsewhere in this region, one is struck by the extent of the salt marshes, which border vast areas of this indented coast. They range from a verdant green in the spring, to a rich golden-brown in the fall and are invaded by meandering channels, which are often reduced to glistening mud passages at ebb tide. At high water you can poke about this particular marsh right up to the roadway. When the tide is falling be careful not to be trapped in a dead end channel on a mud bank.

3. Jones Island

Treeless, except for a few sentinel spruce, the grasses share the rough terrain with Canada Thistle, one of the few plants which are not browsed by the sheep which are pastured here.

4. Thrum Island

This tiny islet is the site of a tern colony. There are several small rounded islands named Thrum or Thrumcap in Nova Scotia (another is in Mahone Bay). The name means a tassel, and refers to the warp threads remaining on a loom beam after the web has been cut off. It probably arose as the result of the caps worn by many Maritime sailors during the past century, which were embroidered with thrums.

5. Pumpkin Island

Eiders nest along with a large Herring Gull colony.

6. Whitehead Island

The light keeper's home has been removed to the mainland. Only the automated light tower remains, along with an impressive panorama of the bay.

7. Ram Island

Possibly named when rams were segregated from ewes in order to help determine the timing of the birth of the lambs (preferably in the spring). There is a fish farm (steelhead trout) on the eastern side.

8. Argyle Sound

This suggested departure spot is mainly mud and eel grass at low water on its south end. Mussels are common.

9. Little Gooseberry Island

This small drumlin island has only a few trees, home to a cormorant colony.

10. Channel Island

Site of a Blue Heron colony.

11. Board Island

During the rum-running days of the 1930s, this was reputed to be one of the places where the rum casks were hidden. In order to deter kids from poking around, a rumour was spread (widely believed until recently) that the island was full of snakes.

DEPARTURE POINT:
Little River Harbour Government Wharf
Exit 33 on Route 103. Continue west on Route 3 to Arcadia, turn left on Route 334 and follow signs to Little River Harbour, approximately 315 km (196 mi.) from Halifax. Resist the temptation to depart from the tip of the peninsula. You may be closer to the islands, but your car will be left unprotected.

ALTERNATIVE DEPARTURE POINT:
Lower Wedgeport government wharf.

ARRIVAL POINT:
Same as the departure point.

TRIP LENGTH:
Day-long or longer. Route 11A: 21 km (13 mi.); Route 11B: 8 km (5 mi.).

CHARTS AND MAPS:
Topographical map: 20/0/9
Marine chart: Wedgeport and Vicinity (#4244: 30,000)

ROUTE DESCRIPTION:
A paddle among the Tusket Islands is a trip into our past. Twelve thousand years ago the world was a much different place, and Nova Scotia was covered by a massive ice sheet over 1 km (0.6 mi.) thick. As it pushed and scoured its way out towards the continental shelf, it deposited loose glacial debris in large mounds over the province. Some of these mounds were left offshore to become the Tusket Islands, where they are slowly succumbing to the onslaught of a continually rising sea level. The finer material has produced the sand beaches, while the boulders have been tossed up by the sea to form the characteristic white cobble shores. Saltwater marshes border much of the largest island and in the interior, the islands vary from thick wood, to open field, to heath barren and bog. Seals are common in the nutrient-rich waters, and several species of sea birds nest on the outer, uninhabited islands.

On the Tuskets, you will find the islands being used much as they were over a hundred years ago, when most of Nova Scotia's hidden coves and island outposts were bases for the fishing industry. People and sheep coexist until late spring, with smoke rising from the chimneys, boats tied up to the wharves, and lobster boxes floating in the currents. At the end of the season, in May, only the sheep remain, along with the deserted houses, cabins, and wharves—a ghost settlement. The lighthouses, of which there are many in these treacherous waters, all lost their keepers by the mid-1980s, but the buildings remain, for now. During the summer many of the shanties are used as a holiday getaway by the locals. Prior to the Europeans, the natives assembled here during the summers to live off the rich marine life. Oyster middens (oysters have long since disappeared in these waters) have recently been found in the area.

Irish moss (Chondrus crispus) is a red seaweed that produces an extract used as an emulsifier in ice cream, chocolate milk and many cosmetics.

SAFETY CONSIDERATIONS:

Much of what will be said about the Bay of Fundy also applies to the Tusket Islands. The influence of the bay extends well past Yarmouth, spilling onto the south coast of Nova Scotia. The tidal range here can exceed 4 m (12 ft.). The water temperature remains very cold throughout the summer season, but most important are the currents, which, due to the shallow bottom and

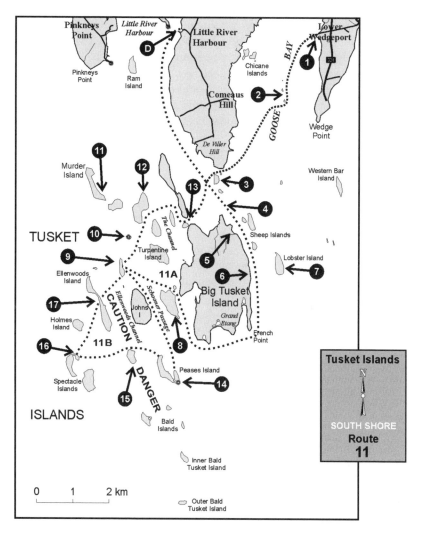

numerous shoals, are strong and often treacherous. Hence, extreme caution is advised when paddling in this area. Hug the island shorelines, and cross channels only when the current is slack. Anywhere but the innermost islands should be left to experts. Of utmost importance is the ability to judge the water conditions, especially the speed and direction of the current. Two particular examples are "Hells Gate/The Sluice" and Schooner Passage where in addition to the currents you might have to compete with fishing/sailing vessels that use these passages to avoid having to round the more difficult waters of the outer Tuskets.

The Tusket region is also noted for its fog. This can hang around for the better part of a summer and serves to augment hazards with currents and fishing boat traffic. Avoid Route 9B unless you are a very proficient coastal paddler, and then only if the weather is favourable (i.e., no wind). If you misjudge, you may end up trapped on a barren island, with cold mist and sea birds for company—or worse.

POINTS OF INTEREST:

1. Lower Wedgeport

The Wedgeport Tuna Fishing Museum at this alternative departure point highlights the colourful history of the local tuna fishery.

2. Goose Island Ledges

Seals are often hauled out on these rocks at low water. The bay is shallow and at low tide much becomes exposed mud and the local boats will be sharing the main channel with you. Be particularly careful at these times.

3. Turnip Island

Like other islands in this grouping, it was named for the crop once grown on it. Even before the arrival of the Europeans, Native people visited, as attested by the large amounts of shells and bones found here and on neighbouring Big Tusket Island.

4. The Sluice

This is the channel between Big Tusket and the mainland, permitting fishing boats to avoid the more dangerous outer waters when crossing from one bay to the other. Hells Gate is the section that was widened in the mid 1800s and again in this century, to allow larger boats to pass through. As the name implies, the peak current can be rather strong here. During the flood tide the water flows from east to west. I was witness to one incident in which paddlers in a double kayak attempted to cross the stream, misjudged the flow, and ended up broadside to one of the large platforms marking the channel. They capsized and had to be rescued.

5. Big Tusket Island

The largest island in the group has a sample of everything: forest, field, pond, and salt marsh. This particular spot (indicated by the arrow on the map) skirts both a freshwater cattail marsh and a saltwater marsh. It is relatively level, with room for a number of tents. At low tide the shallow and muddy slope extends well offshore. Big Tusket was a reputed native burial ground.

6. Abandoned fishing shanties

These are common. Some are used for shelter by the sheep that run loose on the island.

7. Lobster Island

Once a fishing station, the perimeter is characterized by striking layered bands in the metamorphic rocks.

8. Harris Island

This tight and colourful cluster of cabins, shanties, boasts, wharves, and lobster cages is home to a continual bustle during the fishing season.

9. Owls Head Island

An excellent site for a base camp, although the landing is a little rough (boulders, no sand beach). It is both centrally located and unused by fishermen. It also features the deteriorating remains of the Acadian Tuna Club, an elaborate stone lodge, built in the late 1930s by Americans in search of prize-winning bluefin. The location was too isolated, and by 1955 the Americans had left, as had the tuna. Within a decade of the peak catch—1,780 fish in one year—the catches dropped to less than 10. Woods now surround the beach-stone pillars, where the cabins were placed.

The Tusket Islands are still used as a base during lobster season and the wharves are built to take into account the 12 foot tidal range.

10. Candlebox Island

The light was automated in the mid-1980s. A visible path around the perimeter of the tiny island was worn in by the jogging of the lighthouse keeper.

11. Murder Island

The origin of this name is obscure. One source has it as an

Iroquois warrior party overrunning a Mi'kmaq encampment. Another tells a grisly tale of hundreds of corpses lining the shoreline in the late 1700s, and of divers finding skulls and bones more recently in the shallow pond. It has also been linked with the Oak Island mystery (Mahone Bay) as the site where the construction workers from the fabled money pit were taken and killed in order to preserve Oak Island's secret.

12. Deep Cove Island

During lobster season many fishermen move to several of these outposts, including Deep Cove Island, to be nearer the fishing grounds. The shallow, rocky bottom makes excellent lobster habitat. This is that mysterious island where we stopped during our circumnavigation, where we found "shanties" and all the comfort of home. Submarine cables provide electricity for the stoves, fridges, and televisions. In the summer off-season, most return to the mainland.

13. Between Inner Spectacle Island and Big Tusket

This watercourse meanders through the mud flats as if through a maze. At very low tides, the passage is impassable, even for canoes and kayaks.

14. Peases Island

This one offers a panorama of the outer islands. The lighthouse is unmanned.

15. Marks Island

There is a protected cobblestone beach on the northern side. The grass along the shore has been cropped by the sheep and resembles that of a lawn. Beware of the nettle and thistles which have been spared by the animals. The sheep are left year-round to forage on the grass and seaweed. In spring they are sheared.

16. Spectacle Island

There is a colony of Arctic terns here, one of the few sea bird colonies on the inner islands.

17. Ellenwoods Island

This is a seasonal fishing community, and with the entire island cleared, it resembles a remote Newfoundland outport. It is uncharacteristic of late early twenty-first century Nova Scotia.

COASTAL PADDLING ROUTES
OF THE BAY OF FUNDY

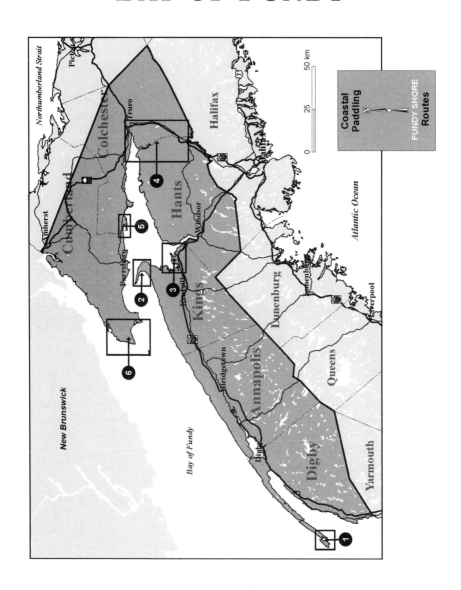

INTRODUCTION

We struggled along the serpentine channel of the Missaguash River towards its entrance as a difficult wind, sweeping in from the hidden bay, pressed the grass against the exposed dyked fields. Staccato salvos jumped over the soft banks to buffet our canoe and our bodies, gradually draining what little energy remained in our exhausted shoulder muscles, sore from the long journey through the marshes. When we finally rounded the last bend into the full fury, we could not go further. Neither did we want to, for before us, and as far as our sight would reach, a chaos of white caps covered the open waters. Here it was, the Bay of Fundy—the big unknown of our voyage around the province.

We found some shelter for our tent behind an irregular jumble of rectangular granite slabs, remnants of the ill-fated ship railway. Cattle and their well-seasoned paddies were our only companions. To the east, the fields and dykes hid the highway from view. To the west was the bay, and a vast plain of marsh, mud, and confused water stretched into the horizon. Mesmerised by the cyclic ebb and flow, we watched as the river mouth disappeared, exposing its wet bed of glistening brown mire. The entire upper region of the Cumberland Basin exchanged its murky solution for mud flats and the throngs of sandpipers who gorged themselves for their flight south. We saw this formidable spectacle reverse itself six hours later. It was an ominous sight, which gave us cause to ponder our situation and our decision to cross the Bay of Fundy.

If you have heard of the Maritimes, you have probably heard of the Bay of Fundy. If you live here, you were probably aware of its reputation early on in life. It is a unique world of salt marsh and mud flats, of labyrinthine creek and channel, and of ingenious dyke systems guarding fertile farmland. However, it also boosts the highest cliffs on mainland Nova Scotia, where gemstones hide in volcanic rock; dinosaur bones are concealed in its layered sandstone; and it hosts some of the largest animals that have ever existed—the Baleen whales. Above all, the Bay of Fundy is the domain of the highest tides on earth.

The Bay of Fundy is a funnel-shaped tongue of ocean separating Nova Scotia from New Brunswick. It stretches over 200 km (120 mi.) from its mouth in the Gulf of Maine to its upper reaches at Amherst and Truro. About three-quarters of the way, Cape

Chignecto splits it into Chignecto Bay and the Minas Basin. Its influence extends well beyond the ill-defined boundaries, blending into the Gulf of Maine and edging around Yarmouth, onto the South Shore.

It has few islands, and except for the Fundy Isles and Brier Island at the entrance, the only ones of note are Isle Haute, and, in the Minas Basin, the Five Islands. Most are basalt reminders of an earlier geologic era, when crustal distortions unleashed lava flows that covered the surface. Basalt cliffs also define the Nova Scotia shoreline from Brier Island to the Minas Basin. Most of the

The Bay of Fundy is not just raging currents and endless mud flats. At times it can be a placid basin, with stunning rock sculptures.

upper regions of the Bay of Fundy, particularly the Cumberland and Minas Basins, are lined by softer strata (sandstone and shale), and erosion has produced extensive, gently sloping sand and mud flats and vast areas of salt marsh.

The Bay of Fundy traces its origins into the Triassic era and the age of the dinosaurs, over 200 million years ago, when all the earth's land mass had been compressed into a single megacontinent, called Pangea. The area that was to become Nova Scotia was then situated near the equator. The terrain was relatively uniform, the climate hot and arid. Eventually the convection currents, responsible for bringing the crustal plates together in the first place, shifted, and Pangea began to break apart. Initially, the surface subsided and the depressions were filled with sediment eroded from the surrounding highland. As the separation progressed, the crust faulted severely, allowing lava to pour out. The final rupture occurred along the continental shelf far to the east, leaving a segment of early Africa attached to North America—part of a future Nova Scotia.

With time, the rift valley widened, continued to subside, and was gradually invaded by the new Atlantic Ocean. Consumed by the sea and scoured by the glaciers, the new bay deepened, and recently, about five thousand years ago, developed the extreme tidal range. The ocean is continuing to rise relative to the land in most areas, and the shoreline is eroding at a rapid rate.

The special nature of the Bay of Fundy follows from its extreme tides. These range from about 6 m (20 ft.) at the entrance to a record of 18 m (58 ft.) at Burntcoat Head, in the Minas Basin. This unusual phenomenon is partially due to the funnel shape of the bay itself—a progressive narrowing and shallowing that accentuates the tides at the apex. However, there are plenty of similarly shaped bays around the globe that do not have Fundy's tides. Resonance also plays a role. This refers to the natural oscillation inherent in every body of water, which means that it tends to slosh back and forth with a certain rhythm. The period of oscillation is dependent upon the size and shape of the basin. If that oscillation approximates that of the tides, which is the case in this bay, it will augment them.

Tides affect the coastal paddler. Extreme tides will, at times, have an extreme effect. The degree will depend upon the shoreline and sea floor features, the weather, and your position in the tidal cycle (i.e., neap, spring, or somewhere in between). Your initial concern at the beginning of a trip will probably be the distance you will have to lug your boat to the water. In areas with a steep slope, such as Cape Chignecto, this distance may be minimal. However, along the low lying upper reaches of the bay, a landing or launch at an inappropriate time could involve carrying or dragging the boat hundreds of metres over a soft ooze that can "crawl" up to your knees.

En route, keep a sharp eye on the water level—and your gear—when stopping for a break. On more than one occasion I've had to scurry after a precious piece heading off to New England. Conversely, inattention may leave you and your fully laden kayaks stranded hundreds of metres above a rapidly receding shoreline. When setting up camp, pay more than cursory attention to your tent site! Be wary of that soft, level, "grassy" area, especially during the full moon.

Once on the water you will have to deal with another direct consequence of tides—the currents. It is here that the coastal paddler must be particularly vigilant in the Bay of Fundy. Under some circumstances, the velocity of the currents can exceed 8 knots, and in a few rivers, such as the Shubenacadie, a bore will sometimes form at the leading edge of an incoming tide. When wind opposes the current, dangerous standing waves can evolve rapidly. This will often follow a change in the tide. Particularly delicate areas are headlands, such as Cape Split and Cape d'Or; narrow passages, such as the one between Brier Island and Long Island; and sudden shallowing over reefs and shoals. These are all situations where the currents speed up in order to get through, around, or over an obstruction. Whirlpools that will grasp your kayak and pull you under are mythical musings, but large eddies do exist and can be confusing. Although you might be going "with the tide," you might still be paddling against the current.

Fortunately, with experience, critical situations can be recognized and avoided. In calm weather and during slack tide, many of the most potentially treacherous areas can be navigated safely. Once, we dallied in the kayaks to pick dulse at the very tip of Cape Split, where at peak flood, you will be swept into an impossible jungle of standing waves. Along linear coastlines, such as the Cape Chignecto fault, frictional drag close to shore will slow the currents, and it often matters little whether you are paddling with or against the flow. On the other hand, in calm weather the bay can lull you into a false sense of security. Ocean swells are absent and there may be no surf—features reminiscent of an inland lake. However, this serenity is often transient and can change as rapidly as the tide. The wind may increase dramatically, transforming a peaceful scene into a caldron of white caps and standing waves in minutes.

Another extremely important feature of the Bay of Fundy is the water temperature. It is cold! The constant turbulence, mixing the colder bottom with the surface layers, maintains a temperature that rarely exceeds 13°C (55°F), even at the height of summer. An unexpected plunge into this milieu, without adequate protection, can have tragic consequences. It is important to remember this fact, since the dramatic contrast between the ambient air and water temperatures can lead the unwary to take foolish risks. Consider wearing a wet or dry suit. An exception to this generalization is in the upper bay, where the shallow water can warm up considerably as it flows over the intertidal flats.

The power of the Bay of Fundy tides has separated rock pinnacles from the solid bedrock.

The climate in the Bay of Fundy is similar to that along the Atlantic coast. The air temperatures are lower than those found inland, and wind is more frequent. However, less surf means less salt spray. Fog is a common companion, and it isn't unusual for it to be sunny and a warm 27°C (80°F) inland, while a chilling mist drapes the coast. The warm, moisture-charged continental air condenses rapidly as it crosses the bay, and summers have passed in which the sun hid until August, especially in outposts like Brier Island.

The turbulence in the Bay of Fundy not only prevents thermal stratification but it also recycles nutrients that would otherwise settle to the bottom. This has made the Fundy one of the most productive natural areas in eastern North America, supporting a prolific food chain that ranges from microscopic phytoplankton to the enormous baleen whales. Fin and Humpback Whales visit regularly in the summer and early fall to feed at the mouth of the bay, and this is the only known breeding ground for the endangered Right whale. The extensive salt marshes are also highly efficient producers of biomass, and even the seemingly sterile mud flats will (upon closer examination) reveal a profusion of invertebrate creatures, including the soft-shell clam. During the migration period, shorebirds congregate in the thousands on these flats to rest and to gorge themselves for their long journey. Brier Island and Grand Manan (in New Brunswick) are among the best bird-watching destinations in the country.

The Fundy shoreline typically displays a transition between a true coastal forest and the more "lush" interior, a reflection of its somewhat more sheltered geography. However, it also touches both extremes of the vegetation spectrum. Arctic alpine relics cling to exposed basalt cliffs, while nearby saltwater marshes, flanked by rich deciduous woods, accompany tidal rivers many kilometres inland. Large areas of these salt marshes have been dyked and converted to agricultural land. Where rock underlies the littoral zone, low water unveils a colourful tapestry of dulse, laver, sea lettuce, and rockweed—a deceptive beauty that can test the most nimble walker.

Humans have long harvested from this natural mecca. Native Americans hunted and gathered in these waters twenty-five hundred years ago, long before Samuel de Champlain explored the Bay of Fundy in 1604, on his way to a disastrous winter in the St. Croix River, New Brunswick. The next year Champlain established the first permanent French settlement in North America at Port Royal, in the Annapolis Basin. Fishermen and more settlers, mostly French, followed, and by the middle of the 1700s the best fertile marshland had been dyked and drained.

The entire basin would probably still be French speaking today if it were not for the Expulsion of 1755, immortalized in Longfellow's poem, "Evangeline." The British, who had gained control of mainland Nova Scotia, feared that the Acadian inhabitants would side with the French regime in future hostilities. Although that would have certainly pleased their country of origin, the Acadians wished only to be left alone to farm their lands. They wanted nothing to do with the endless European squabbles. However, British fear took precedence, and the Acadians were rounded up and shipped out. Many ended up in Louisiana. Their land was confiscated and distributed to new settlers—many from New England—and following the War of Independence, another influx of "Loyalists" arrived. Some Acadians escaped the Expulsion or returned later and established themselves on the southwest shore, near Yarmouth.

In the 1900s, the age of sail transformed the region. Nova Scotia, and particularly the borders of the bay, prospered. By the end of the century every cove, inlet, and river mouth that could be adapted for anchorage became the site of a mill or shipbuilding yard. These glory days were short-lived, and with iron and steam replacing wood and wind, hard times returned. Entire towns were abandoned and many never recovered. Reminders of these early years can be seen in the elaborate homes of obscure villages, which are no longer mentioned on the maps and in the rotting wharf pilings that poke through the shifting mud and sands at deserted river outlets.

However, the fishery in the bay is diverse—herring, scallops, and groundfish—and although not immune to the current problems plaguing the industry, it hasn't been as devastated as the fishery in Newfoundland. Lobster fishing is successful, weirs are still capturing herring, and aquaculture is growing rapidly, particularly with Atlantic salmon.

The reputation of the Bay of Fundy is cloaked in myth, folklore, and fact concerning its tides, currents, and whirlpools. This has coloured people's perceptions, distorting the reality, and many who are suspicious in general about paddling small boats on the ocean would consider a trip on the bay foolhardy. I have paddled for years on the Fundy and have learned to respect this unique body of water. Although potential risks are real, several routes do exist that can be paddled safely during calm weather, by experienced paddlers, and a number of them are exceptional. The following descriptions include details about five of the best.

Brier Island ～🛶～

Departure Point:
Westport Harbour
Exit 26 off Route 101. Continue on Route 303 towards Digby and turn left on Route 217. The journey to Westport includes ten-minute ferry crossings to Long Island and to Brier Island. (Fee is $2/car return.) You can put in at several spots along the sheltered harbour, approximately 315 km (196 mi.) from Halifax.

Arrival Point:
Same as the departure point.

Trip Length:
Day-long, 18 km (11 mi.). However, you should stay on Brier Island at least two days to take advantage of the hiking, birding, and whale-watching.

Charts and Maps:
Topographical maps: 21/B/1,8
Marine chart: St. Marys Bay (#4118: 60,000)

Route Description:
Brier Island is the westernmost part of Nova Scotia, and at 6 km x 3 km (4 mi. x 2 mi.), it is one of our largest offshore islands. The island is composed entirely of basalt bedrock, the end of a ridge with the bold designation "North Mountain" that stretches all the way from Cape Blomidon. To the west, it descends under the bay as a series of ledges and exposed shoals. The shoreline is a mixture of sheer cliffs, ragged coves, and sandy beaches, all washed by powerful currents. The numerous tidepools and distinctive zonation provide an excellent opportunity to study the littoral area of a rocky coast.

Marine mammals frequent the clear, clean waters, and by late summer Fin, Humpback, and occasionally, Right Whales feed near the shore. Sea birds also take advantage of the ample food supply off Brier Island and it is an important staging area for migratory birds. Warblers descend en masse in early spring and huge flocks of phalaropes gather on the surrounding waters in late summer. The interior consists of stunted white spruce and fir woods, as well as freshwater bog, noted for several rare plants and an important orchid flora. It has been proposed as an international ecological site.

Brier Island is only one of a handful of offshore islands that are still inhabited year-round, and its prosperous fishing community takes advantage of the nutrient-rich waters at the entrance to the bay. It will always be remembered to sailors as the birthplace of Joshua Slocum, the first person to sail solo around the world. Excellent bed and breakfast and inn accommodations are available but reserve early for the peak season.

SAFETY CONSIDERATIONS:

While Brier Island offers an exciting paddling opportunity, a trip in these waters must be approached with extreme caution. Tidal currents are strong, especially over shoals and in Grand Passage where they can exceed 6 knots, the waters are cold, even at the height of summer. Add to this the dense and persistent fog, which can shroud the island for days on end, and you have a combination that can be deadly. Before setting out get particulars on local conditions, listen to the weather forecast, and plan to avoid areas with strong currents. Pay particular attention to boat traffic, especially the car ferry, and never paddle in the channel in the fog.

Brier Island has a permanent lifeboat station, so take advantage of the trained personnel available. Let them know when you are leaving and when you expect to return, and expect a degree of skepticism as regards to your ability. This is one of the few areas of the province where, if something does happen, a call for help could bring a quick response—if they know where you are.

POINTS OF INTEREST:

1. Westport

This is the westernmost community in the province and a prosperous fishing village, in spite of the crisis in the east coast fishery. It is the birthplace of Joshua Slocum, the first person to circumnavigate the globe alone—a voyage that began in 1895 and took over three years. It is also a base for whale-watching tours.

2. Grand Passage

It is both a sheltered port and a channel with strong rip tides. Watch out for boat traffic.

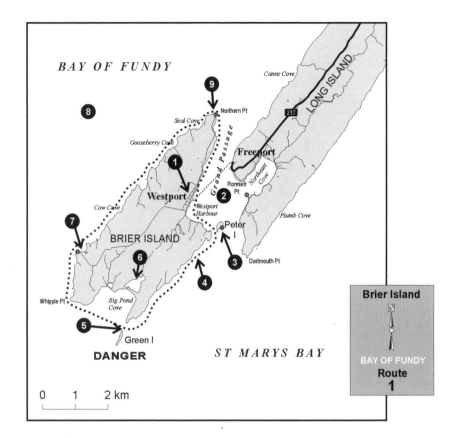

BAY OF FUNDY

Canns Cove

LONG ISLAND

9

Northern Pt

Seal Cove

Gooseberry Cove

Grand Passage

Freeport

217

1

Ronnies
Pt

Northeast
Cove

2

Westport

Cow Cove

Westport
Harbour

Plumb Cove

Peter
I

7

BRIER ISLAND

6

3

Dartmouth Pt

Whipple Pt

Big Pond
Cove

4

5

Green I

DANGER

ST MARYS BAY

0   1   2 km

Brier Island

N

BAY OF FUNDY
**Route
1**

3. Peter Island
This small, treeless islet has Common Tern and Arctic Tern colonies and a lighthouse.

4. Big Cove
Ringed with impressive 30 m (100 ft.) basalt cliffs, this igneous rock was formed around 200 million years ago, when the super-continent of Pangea began to break apart. Molten magma rose up into fissures beneath the earth's crust. As it slowly cooled, it fractured into jointed, usually six-sided columns. Upon subsequent and continuous exposure to frost and water erosion, it produced this organ pipe panorama. South Point, to the east of Big Cove, has a strong current close to shore with a major back eddy.

5. Shoals
These are particularly treacherous at this tip of Brier Island when the currents are accentuated by wind. Wait until conditions are

calm before passing. If necessary, you can take out at Hog Yard Cove, where a dirt road leads back to Westport.

6. Big Pond

A body of shallow fresh water, separated from the ocean by a narrow barrier beach. It is a major resting site for migratory birds.

7. Lighthouse Cove

This is a possible take out point, should the weather deteriorate. A grassy bluff surrounds the automated light tower.

8. Fin and Humpback Whales

Occasionally, they pass close to the shores of the island. If you are lucky and the weather is calm, you may have the unforgettable experience of paddling among them. More likely, though, they will be too far offshore, or the water conditions will be too rough. In that case, take a whale-watching tour out of Westport.

9. Northern Point

As with the other headlands around the island, Northern Point experiences strong currents at midtide. Exercise caution.

CAPE SPLIT

DEPARTURE POINT:
Scots Bay Government Wharf
Exit 11 off Route 101 (New Minas). Follow highway signs to Port Williams, Canning, and Scots Bay (Route 358). The wharf is about 2 km (1 mi.) after the end of the pavement. Cars can be left near the wharf. Approximately 125 km from Halifax.

ARRIVAL POINT:
Blomidon Provincial Park

TRIP LENGTH:
Full day, 28 km (17 mi.). Plan on seven or eight hours, with good weather, to complete this route, including a stop at the split and another along the north shore to look for gemstones. As an alternative to this lengthy tour, consider a return trip to the split, 16 km (10 mi.) or about four hours.

CHARTS AND MAPS:
Topographical map: 21/H/8
Marine chart: None available

ROUTE DESCRIPTION:
Long known as one of the most breathtaking hiking trails in the province, Cape Split is seldom seen from a paddler's perspective. A view from the tip of the peninsula onto swirling currents and standing waves makes it readily apparent why this is so. However, there are times when even this spot can be paddled safely, and in these cases you will be treated to some of Nova Scotia's most magnificent coastal scenery.

The stretch from the wharf to the tip of Cape Split borders a gently sloping shoreline with a jagged fringe of black basalt, topped by a mixed forest. Dark green rockweed, nourished by the rich waters, drape the exposed rocks. Near the tip of the peninsula, the land rises vertically 76 m (250 ft.) to a grassy plateau-the hiker's destination. The split itself is a series of imposing towers, the largest is a flat-topped home for sea birds and the smaller ones are barren pinnacles. They all become islands during high tide.

The northern shoreline is relatively straight, with sheer, columnar

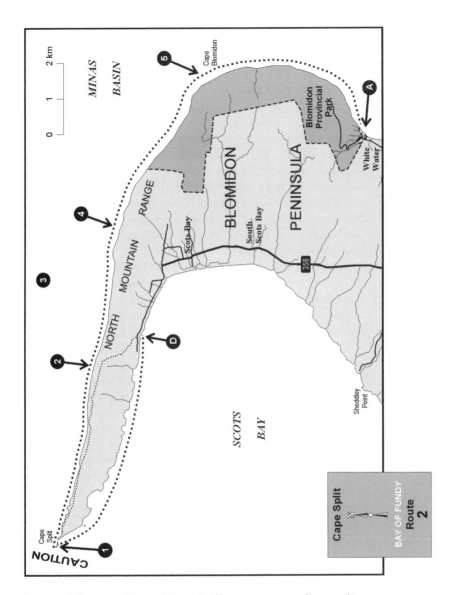

basalt, rising over 122 m (400 ft.). There are no good campsites, and the steep cliffs often descend directly into the bay. Emergency shelter can be found, but if you have to overnight expect a rough mattress on the angular boulders. In the rubble at the base you may find semi-precious stones. At Cape Blomidon, stratified red sandstone flanks the basalt, resembling the buttresses of a huge cathedral. The dark rock eventually disappears entirely under the sandstone.

SAFETY CONSIDERATIONS:

The Bay of Fundy is considered, with justification, one of the most treacherous bodies of water around the province. The extreme tides that rush in and out of the funnel-shaped bay twice a day result in tidal rips, standing waves, back eddies, and whirlpools dwarfing those found elsewhere—and adverse weather will compound these conditions. The Minas Channel is of particular note since the waters of the Minas Basin accelerate through this narrow passage. By choosing a calm day and the appropriate time—slack tide when rounding the tip—the experienced paddler should have little problem.

The most critical section of the entire route, and the one with the greatest potential for danger, is at the tip of Cape Split. Here the powerful currents entering and exiting the Minas Basin at midtide can produce treacherous conditions and must be avoided. The flood waters are captured by Scots Bay and redirected around the tip of Cape Split into the Minas Channel, where they meet the bulk of the incoming current at right angles, resulting in huge standing waves and whirlpools. Rough conditions at the split itself can be dangerous enough, but a mistake that sweeps you into the channel proper could end tragically. During ebb tide, the current through the split is somewhat less severe (it tends to head straight out the bay) but it should still to be avoided.

During slack water—about an hour on either side of low or high tide—the conditions at the tip of Cape Split should allow you to pass. Sometimes it has been so calm that I have lingered to collect dulse from my kayak. For a short time after low tide, you can still avoid the increasing current off the tip of the peninsula by a portage through the pinnacles.

Once on the north shore, the remainder of the route to Blomidon Park presents no major difficulty, regardless of tidal level or direction. However, be prepared for increased currents where any land juts into the channel. Don't assume that a flood tide will help you move towards the Minas Basin, since large back eddies are common. Keep close to the shore where friction slows the currents. The coastline here is relatively straight and it is easy to land, although there are no good campsites.

Note: The tip of Cape Split should be rounded only during slack water, that short period of about one hour near high or low tide, when the current has stopped flowing in one direction and is about to begin moving in the opposite. Whether this is during the high tide slack or the low tide slack will depend upon the time of day that each occurs. You must allow enough daylight to complete the route once past the tip of Cape Split. If you wish to disembark and explore the pinnacles, then choose a day when low tide is during the morning. If, on the other hand, you prefer to paddle through the split choose a morning high tide.

The large tidal range in the Bay of Fundy can leave fishing boats sitting on the bottom.

POINTS OF INTEREST:

1. Cape Split

A part of the great basalt lava flows, which spewed forth in this region when Pangea began to split, are evident here. Several distinctive eruptions are clearly delineated in the escarpment. In addition to Cape Split, North Mountain, several islands and headlands—including the Five Islands—and the entire bottom of the bay are composed of basalt. Some of the pinnacles at Cape Split can be climbed. A few hikers who have ascended them during low tide, when they can be reached from the mainland, have had an unplanned extension by misjudging the speed of tidal rise.

2. High Point

Along the north shore of the peninsula over 150 m (500 ft.) high cliffs of columnar basalt are particularly imposing.

3. Minas Channel

The huge volume of water that enters and leaves the Minas Basin twice a day must pass through the Minas Channel. Although deep, it is only 5 km (3 mi.) across, and the currents can be so strong that ocean freighters have difficulty opposing them. However, along the north shore of Cape Split, frictional drag reduces them to a degree where they may be insignificant next to the land. Back eddies are common.

4. Amethyst Cove

One of several locations along this shore where frequent rockfalls provide good pickings for the rock hunter. Semi-precious stones, such as amethyst, jasper, and jade, are sometimes exposed in chunks of fractured rock but are more often hidden within the basalt, requiring some geological sleuthing. The best time for rock hounding is in the spring or early summer, after the freeze-thaw cycle has brought down new material.

5. Cape Blomidon

This is the legendary home of Glooscap, the Mi'kmaq demigod. It was from here that he ruled all of present day Nova Scotia and New Brunswick. The huge boulders that he hurled at his arch enemy across the channel fell to become the Five Islands. After the Big Eddy (a large back eddy), the basalt escarpment becomes buttressed with the older sandstones that have escaped erosion. This soft, highly stratified rock quickly becomes the dominant terrain, forming sedimentary cliffs up to the take out point, where a wooden stairway leads down to the beach at the entrance to Blomidon Provincial Park.

Minas Basin　～⊂ᚗ

DEPARTURE POINT:
Grand Pré
Exit 10 off Route 101. At Grand Pré continue to Long Island.
Follow the Long Island Road east to the dikes at the very end (the
last km is unpaved and potted). Over the dyke to the right, past a
large clump of bayberry bushes, is a nose of compact clay and salt
marsh grass pointing to Boot Island. You can carry over (or beside)
this point and down over packed sand and gravel. Even at low
water you can launch without getting unduly muddy.
Alternatively, you can put in at the bridge at Melanson, on the
Gaspereau River or, if there is sufficient flow, beside the bridge at
the village of Gaspereau. However, when launching here make
sure that by the time you reach the tidal section (at Melanson), the
water is ebbing. You won't be able to paddle against the incoming
flood.

ARRIVAL POINT:
Same as departure point (or A[1]: Blue Beach, which involves a 200
m carry to the parking lot).
　　Note: If you choose to end up the Gaspereau River (as far as
Melanson) you will need the incoming tide to help you up the river.
You will not be able to paddle against the ebbing current.

TRIP LENGTH:
Day-long, 12 km to 18 km (8 mi. to 11 mi.)

CHARTS AND MAPS:
Topographical map: 21/H/1
Marine chart: Avon River and Approaches (#4140: 37,500)

ROUTE DESCRIPTION:
The Minas Basin developed several thousand years ago when the
rising sea level entered the Minas Channel, gradually flooded
river deltas, and began to erode the surrounding soft triassic strata. Vast deposits of sand and silt are added to the Basin each year.
These are continually shifting about due to the extreme tides and
river outflows, defining the changing contours of the bottom and

shoreline, and forming the basis for the vast salt marshes and mud flats.

This is a highly productive biological area and the Native populations prized the large shellfish beds and fish habitat. The Europeans were also drawn here since clearing the inland forests was difficult and these lowlands offered ready-made farmland. The early settlers were French (called Acadians) and while they initially harvested the salt marsh grass, over time they dyked and drained much of the area to allow traditional crops to be grown. The Acadians were expelled in 1755 by the British (on the fear that they would side with France during wars between these continental powers) and their replacements (mainly from the American colonies) continued and extended this tradition. The result today is a composite of salt and freshwater marsh, along with protected farmland, interwoven by a natural and manmade network of channels and canals.

When I attended Acadia University in the early 1970s, I was well aware of the Minas Basin. Its ever changing panorama of water and mud, stretching across to Blomidon, would welcome me as I descended the hill into Avonport, whenever I returned from a weekend home. But the Annapolis Valley was farming country, the best in the province and for the most part I had a land-centred view of my post secondary world. The long warm seasons allowed for everything from traditional vegetable crops and apple orchards to the more exotic tobacco and wine grapes. Except for an occasional hike to Cape Split and a meander along the dikes, the Minas Basin with its rich sediments and salt marshes did little to entice me. The quaint little fishing coves, so ubiquitous along the Atlantic coast, were nowhere to be seen. It was a perception supported by Wolfville's original name: Mud Creek.

However, time and experience have lent a broader view, and the Minas Basin has become far more appealing than I had earlier imagined. And today, with my sea kayak and a better understanding of tides, I have the found the freedom to explore this engaging world of mud flats and meandering channels; sand banks, and salt marshes, and stratified bedrock cliffs. I can observe the thousands of shore birds that pass this way during the migration, search for ancient fossils and drowned forests, and uncover the previously obscure signs of the Natives and early Acadians. Of course, I can also relax on the massive sand flats far from the summer bustle,

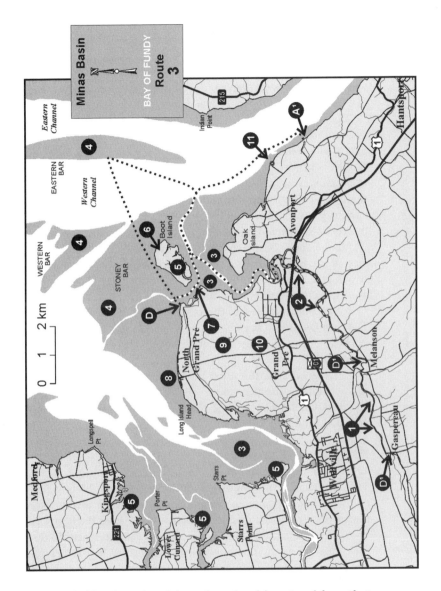

surrounded by the colourful patchwork of forest and farm that spreads out over the hills and into the horizon.

SAFETY CONSIDERATIONS:

At high water you can put in about anywhere you find access to the coast. However, at other times because of the extreme tidal range and the gently sloping nature of this shoreline, options for landing/launching are limited. If you are not using the suggested departure points be careful to accurately predict what the water level will be when you return, or you may find yourself knee deep in ooze and a long way to walk and drag.

As always, obtain an accurate weather forecast before setting out—an unexpected squall in the Minas Basin can be particularly nasty. The shallow and often fast-moving water can build up rapidly with the wind. Determine the direction of the current (especially a consideration in narrow channels at peak flow) and the times of high and low water. A relaxing stroll on the sand bank might turn into a heated rush back to the boat (or absence thereof) if you should miscalculate the incoming tide.

In the upper Gaspereau the flow is fast and there are obstacles on route, most notably the numerous large beams (used for fishing) which extend out from the edge a third of the way across. If you don't anticipate and react accordingly you may find yourself carried into, or under, one of these, resulting in a possible capsize. The river bed is also strewn with rocks and debris, which interrupt the flow (of both the water and your kayak). This section is not recommended for paddlers unfamiliar with fast moving water.

That being said, the water in the Basin is usually quite warm at the height of summer and if you should miscalculate the tide and get stuck on a flat or in a channel, remain patient (and with your boat) and wait until it rises and floats you off.

POINTS OF INTEREST:

1. Upper Gaspereau River
This stretch of river, almost down to the bridge at Melanson is non-tidal. In a dry summer there is insufficient water except when the power corporation decides to release water from the upstream dam. The locals (and others) make use of these releases to don their inner tubes and float down with the current. The initial tunnel effect, produced by large, lush overhanging oak and elm, eventually gives way to farm and field near Melanson. Protruding from the banks are large beams that are used during the spring migration of the gaspereau (also known as alewives—and kayaks!) for attaching the nets. (see Safety Considerations).

2. Lower Gaspereau River
The river is tidal until shortly above the bridge at Melanson. At high water, you have a clear view of the flooded salt marshes and

the adjoining countryside (mostly farmland) but as you sink with the tide your perspective changes rapidly, and your view plan includes a canyon flanked by glistening mud and dikes. A few aboiteaux are built into the dykes. These large, one-way valves allow the freshwater trapped inside the dyked land to escape when the tide drops but prevents salt water from entering when the tide returns. Numerous bird species are found here including hawks, ducks, Osprey, Bald Eagles.

3. Mud Flats

The inner banks of the basin are mostly mud; a thick and dense ooze that can crawl up to your knees if improper timing causes you to launch or land in such areas.

Weir fishing is still practised in the Bay of Fundy.

4. Sand banks

Further out in the basin sand banks replace mud flats. These vast plains are devoid of the throngs, even in the peak of season and when the basin empties, you can land and relax or wander with firm footing.

5. Salt marsh

Separating dry land from the mud flats, along much of the sheltered shoreline, are the salt marshes. These fertile areas are flooded twice a day and provide shelter and forage for small fish. Before the dykes were constructed, salt marshes covered a much larger area than today.

6. Boot Island

When the Acadians arrived, this wasn't an island at all but the tip, or "le bout," of a headland that thrust into the Minas Basin. However, the rising sea level has taken its toll and a passage (the Guzzle) has separated Boot Island from the mainland for over a century. The island continues to fritter away and large clumps of grass topped clay have broken from the edges. Inhabited and farmed until the early 1900s, the island is now deserted, except for the herons, gulls, and cormorants—and a crow roost in winter. The large salt marsh on the south was once dykeland. The Mi'kmaq named the island and surroundings "Kadebunegek" or clam diggings.

7. The Guzzle

This channel between Boot Island and the mainland has existed for almost two centuries and has gradually widened over time. Not so long ago, at low tide, you could easily ford the passage and farmers could cross with a wagon of hay pulled by a team of oxen. Although its width is determined by the height of the tide, it is always plenty deep for canoes and kayaks. Look carefully on the bordering flats and you may notice the tree trunks from an ancient forest that once covered this area before rising seas and subsiding land inundated it thousands of years ago.

8. Evangeline Beach

This gently sloping beach, where the ebbing tide uncovers over a kilometre of sand and boulder, is a popular summer destination. Cottages and trailers line the shore and fill the woods. The name originates with the epic poem by Longfellow on the expulsion of the Acadians.

9 Dykeland

When the Acadians arrived in the 1600s they settled adjacent the coastal marshes, and harvested salt grass and hay for their cattle. Gradually, they built extensive dyke systems, which excluded the sea water and produced large acreages of fertile soil. Many of these original dykes remain, reinforced and heightened over time. This area near Grand Pré has 28,000 feet of dikes enclosing over 3000 acres that are under sea level. Other dykes, called running dykes, follow the meanderings of the Cornwallis and Gaspereau Rivers (among others).

10 Grand Pré

French settlers arrived in this area in the early 1600s and by the mid 1700's the population had reached several hundred. From 1713 onward, mainland Nova Scotia came under British rule but the Acadian population continued to grow. The local Acadian inhabitants were deported in 1755, an event immortalized in American poet Henry Wordsworth Longfellow's epic poem "Evangeline." Longfellow never visited the place, but the Evangeline name is found in various places and tourist accommodations. It was in nearby Horton Landing that the "Planters" (from the American colonies) arrived to take over the vacant Acadian properties. Parks Canada has built a memorial to this event.

11. Horton Bluff

Around 350 million years ago, coarse sediments, eroding from the barren mountain regions, collected in valleys. The shallow lakes and winding rivers were full of fish, amphibians and reptiles and bordered by rudimentary fern-like forests. Birds and mammals were absent. In some places over a thousand feet of gravel, sand and silt collected resulting, in time, in these textured, stratified cliffs. They have given the name to the early Carboniferous strata (Horton). Among the rockfalls at the base of the cliffs (here and elsewhere along this shore) you will be able to find fossils from that period.

4

THE SHUBENACADIE RIVER

DEPARTURE POINT:

Maitland Wharf Ruins

Exit 10 (Shubenacadie) on Route 102 and continue north towards Maitland on Route 215. The wharf ruins are located shortly before the W. D. Lawrence House Museum at the Dawson Dowell Park (parking available). Approximately 95 km (59 mi.) from Halifax.

Note: Since you will be launching at or near low water you will need to carry the boats over rocks coated with a very slippery veneer of mud. Use extreme caution.

ARRIVAL POINT:

Rines Creek. Also on Route 215, approximately 5 km (3 mi.) north of Exit 10.

TRIP LENGTH:

Three to five hours, 28 km (18 mi.).

CHARTS AND MAPS:

Topographical maps: 11/E/3,6
Marine chart: None available
Canoe maps: Shubenacadie Canal and River System

ROUTE DESCRIPTION:

The Shubenacadie River, Nova Scotia's largest, begins at Grand Lake (also called Shubenacadie Lake) and meanders north towards Maitland, 78 km (48 mi.) away, where it empties into Cobequid Bay. Although not commonly thought of as coastal, the Shubenacadie River is tidal for about two-thirds of its length, up to Milford. It is a unique composite of marine and fresh water, offering an unusual and at times thrilling paddling tour.

Unlike most Nova Scotia rivers, the lower Shubenacadie doesn't dry up in late spring. Its volume depends more on the phases of the moon than the seasonal precipitation. The currents are mainly tidal driven, vary in strength and direction, and can create considerable turbulence (see Safety Considerations). The river courses through soft sedimentary strata, zigzagging often due to several traverse faults, and collecting water from a number of tributaries, the Stewiacke being the most important. The

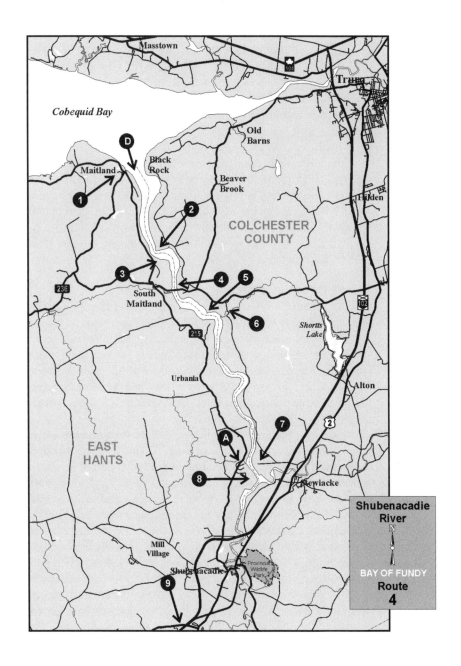

initial cliffs of sandstone, gypsum, and limestone yield further inland to rolling hills, mud flats, salt marsh, and dyked farmland. The water is relatively warm for the Bay of Fundy because it rolls in over the flats, which heat the water but it is extremely turbid. The warmer climate of the interior and the richer soil support a vegetation that is lush compared with the ragged coniferous forest that adorns most of the exposed coastline.

The Shubenacadie River is a major segment of an inland waterway that linked Halifax Harbour with the Minas Basin in the nineteenth century. The system of natural lakes and rivers, combined with canals, locks, and cable railways, was finished in 1861 but abandoned by 1870, lost to the steam railways. Today, reconstruction is under way, and with a few portages, you can now paddle the entire distance by canoe or kayak.

SAFETY CONSIDERATIONS:

The Shubenacadie River is distinct, unlike either the open coastline or most other inland rivers, and its challenges deserve special attention. The major concern is the current, which can be very strong and create considerable turbulence, including standing waves, back eddies, and opposing streams with sharp boundaries. Of particular note are those areas of the river bed that bend or funnel the water (e.g., Eagles Nest and Anthony's Nose, although not restricted to here).

The depth of the river fluctuates with the tides and it is often very shallow, even for a kayak or canoe. Channels disappear and form as the rising water floods the flats. The height of the waves and the direction of the flow can change radically in a very short period of time, and reading the water is a complicated art. While these features can be challenging for the experienced paddler, it may confuse and quickly overwhelm a novice. Watch for all sorts of debris that might follow you up the river, particularly large waterlogged beams. Note, too, that the cliffs along the lower section will prevent an easy take out should you have to cut your voyage short.

Once the initial tidal bore has passed, things don't calm down for a while but the rough spots can usually be anticipated in advance and avoided by hugging one shore or the other. Of course, the skilful adventurer will seek out just these segments. If in doubt you should first choose the lowest, or neap, tides and second, depart one or two hours after the initial tidal bore has passed, although you may end up bucking some current at the end of the journey, as the water again changes direction with the tide. You may want to discuss the route with someone who has done it before, or consider taking a commercial rafting trip (Shubenacadie River Runners, next to the put in: 1-800-856-5061; Shubenacadie Adventures Tours: 1888-878-8687; Tidal Bore Rafting 1-800-565-7238).

Some factors on the Shubenacadie actually reduce risks associated with much of Nova Scotia coastal paddling. Perhaps most importantly, the water is relatively warm during the summer and early fall. The normally cold Fundy waters have a chance to heat up while crossing the expansive flats at the head of Cobequid Bay. In addition, the bottom is sandy, the shoreline is close, and the current carries you inland, not out to sea.

Note: The tidal bore is the famous wall of water that precedes the incoming tide, which tourism officials would have us believe is worth a trip from New Zealand. However, the bore is often what the name implies, and it seldom exceeds a few centimetres. At Maitland it is usually imperceptible. You don't need to worry about being caught in its leading edge and cartwheeling up river. The turbulence that will occur—and it can be considerable—is produced by the huge volume of water that follows the initial bore and is constricted and bent by the river channel.

For the expert white water paddlers looking for surf waves and chaotic water, the best places are neither the neaps (when you might be disappointed) nor the extreme springs (when you will probably be overwhelmed by the sheer volume and speed of the current). Choose an intermediate level and launch just prior to the arrival of the bore at Maitland (the rafting companies can let you know when to expect it). Be forewarned that the paddling environment will change radically and rapidly and you will need to have your wits about you. Your bracing and rolling skills should be well honed and, should you flip, you will be in darkness since the swirling mud will totally block the sunlight. The exciting parts end just past Anthony's Nose and a good take out (if you don't fancy the smooth paddling on rest of the river) is at Green Creek, on the east bank. The run time will be about three hours. The biggest concern on a good day may be the motorized rafts (of which there are an increasing number) that will be sharing the same spots. Although they are conscientious about avoiding paddlers, this is a fast moving milieu.

POINTS OF INTEREST:

1. The W. D. Lawrence House

This is now part of the Nova Scotia Museum complex. It describes an era in the nineteenth century when the province was a major shipbuilding region and its vessels dominated the world's oceans. It was here, or more precisely, at the former shipyard next to the wharf ruins at the departure point, that the largest wooden ship in Canada was built in 1874—the *William D. Lawrence*.

2. Eagles Nest Point

A 60 m (200 ft.) bluff of reddish brown and grey sandstone, which was formed by a prominent transverse fault—one of several that alter the direction of the river. As the name implies, Bald Eagles make this their home.

3. Gypsum Quarry

A quarry located opposite Eagles Nest Point that is no longer in operation. The material was excavated and loaded into ocean freighters.

4. Green Oaks

Here a highway bridge spans the river alongside the large stone pillars that once supported a railway. Although there is plenty of space between these support structures, you should be careful. The tidal current hits them with considerable force. This is the first spot where you can easily take out.

The upper reaches of the Bay of Fundy glisten when the ebb tide uncovers enormous mud flats.

5. **Anthony's Nose**

Here 15 m (15 ft.) of hardened limestone jut into the river along another fault. Standing waves and strong currents can develop in this area. Exciting!

6. **Green Creek**

At this break in the river escarpment you will note the remains of an aboiteau at low to mid tide. Operational until a decade ago, this one-way gate developed by the Acadians allowed fresh water to flow out while preventing the sea water from entering the stream valley. The meadowland, which extends a distance inland, then provided excellent farmland. For those interested in running only the rough portions of the river, the take out is by the bridge.

7. **Fort Ellis**

At the junction with the Stewiake River, Fort Ellis once sat atop a high knoll with a commanding view of the Shubenacadie River. The old British fort has long since fallen to the weather and the plough, but recent archaeological excavations have unearthed remains of an even earlier Acadian homestead. It was one of their few inland settlements. Today, it is still farmed and is marked by a prominent grain silo.

8. **Dykes**

Cliffs have given way to mud banks and pasture, and dykes protect cultivated fields from flooding.

9. **Milford Station**

After meandering through a shallow flood plain, the last remnants of tidal water reach this station.

FIVE ISLANDS ⟞⟋

DEPARTURE POINT:
Five Islands Provincial Park
Exit 11 (Glenholme) on Route 104 and continue west on Route 2 to Five Islands Provincial Park (camping, toilets, drinking water, but no showers). An alternative departure point is Lower Economy (e.g., Sand Point Campground). Note: Since both Five Islands and Lower Economy have gently sloping mud/sand shores combined with extreme tides, it is important to plan your departure and arrival within a couple of hours of high water.

ARRIVAL POINT:
Same as the departure point.

TRIP LENGTH:
Day-long or weekend, 16 km to 20 km (10 mi. to 12 mi.). With fine weather, it is possible to round the entire archipelago in just one day. However, to do it justice you should allow yourself at least two days. You can either camp at the provincial park or on Moose Island.

CHARTS AND MAPS:
Topographical map: 21/H/8
Marine chart: None available
Geological map: The Cobequid Highlands (82-7) Nova Scotia Department of Natural Resources

ROUTE DESCRIPTION:
The highway voyager will catch but a fleeting glimpse of these Five Islands of Mi'kmaq legend. You can't drive out to them, there is no ferry, and in the spring they are often hidden in fog, and are always shrouded in a mystery that involves buried treasure and murder. Except for clam diggers, few have cause to venture close to their shores.

However, this is a geological fantasy land. Imposing black basalt contrasts with deep red sandstone; vertical, often unassailable, cliffs descend onto soft sand and mud flats; and rock spires, caves, and arches adorn the perimeter. Add to this a land- and seascape that is continually transformed by 12 m (40 ft.) tides, and

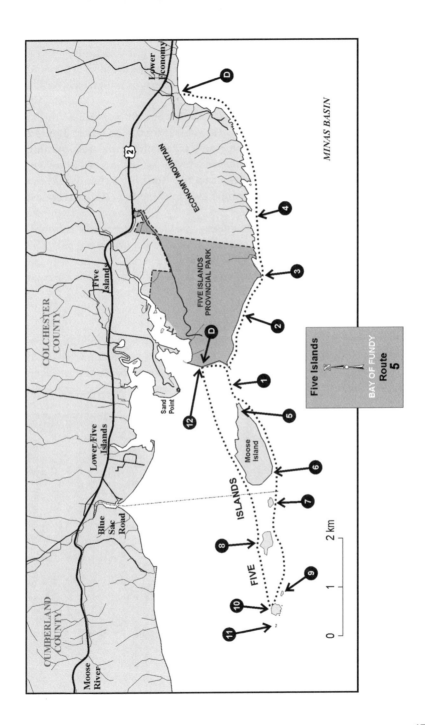

you have a story that few places can equal. If you are lucky, you might discover semi-precious stones, such as jasper, agate, and amethyst, embedded in the volcanic basalt, or even fossils on the park beach.

Tiny dinosaurs once roamed this ancient rift valley until a cataclysm wiped them out, over 200 million years ago. At McCoy's Brook on the mainland, palaeontologists are searching for clues to this mass extinction. Maybe you will discover the footprint of a dinosaur or ancient reptile. You will certainly spot the sea birds and seals, and probably one of the Bald Eagles that nest in the area.

If the weather doesn't allow a paddling trip you might consider a hike from Lower Economy around to the provincial park (2-3 hr). The cliffs, caves, and waterfalls are stunning. Once, I hiked and paddled this section on the same day and it offered a great contrast.

The Bay waters have eaten through the tip of Long Island.

SAFETY CONSIDERATIONS:

Pay particular attention to the tides and currents around the Five Islands. Their speed and direction can seldom be predicted accurately. They are usually the trickiest in the narrow passages, such as between Moose Island and the mainland, and around headlands.

Navigate these spots with caution and always anticipate where you could land if a problem should arise—much of the shoreline is inaccessible at high water. Be wary of the wind, especially when it flows against the currents. Squalls can move in rapidly and the wind often picks up with the incoming tide. A tranquil surface can rapidly turn into unmanageable standing waves. In summer the temperature of the Minas Basin is not usually as cold as the mouth of the Bay of Fundy. Sometimes in can actually be rather warm, but don't count on it.

Remember that the tide rises rapidly. A stroll from Long Island to Pinnacle Island on the connecting sand bar, or over other tidal flats, might be a short one indeed. You could find yourself surrounded and cut off from shore without realizing it. The hike from Lower Economy to the park (about 2-3 hrs) is also only possible at low water, so time your trip accordingly. Bring some sturdy hiking boots if you want to explore on foot; there is plenty of sharp, angular basalt rock. It may be tempting to climb up to the top of the islands, but be extremely cautious. Egg and Diamond Islands are inaccessible without aids, and the others, except for the eastern tip of Moose Island, can be difficult and dangerous. Be particularly wary of any ropes dangling over the edges. These may have been around for years and are only waiting for a tug to break.

The only certain campsite is on the eastern tip of Moose Island and even here you must bring the boats up over a ledge for security. Other places might look inviting at low tide, but treat them with caution, especially during a full moon.

POINTS OF INTEREST:
1. Two Hour Rock and The Old Wife
The former only appears a couple of hours prior to low water, and the latter is always partially exposed. Both can add to the turbulence in this passage, where the currents are already strong. Be cautious.
2. Red sandstone cliff
This is a spectacular section, surmounted by black basalt. Greyish white limestone trickles down the moraine, a reminder of a former inland sea.
3. "Petrified" sand dunes
Where the vertical face of Red Head juts into the bay, be wary of currents. This is one of our best examples of petrified sand dunes in the province with the layering of the ancient sand clearly evident.

4. Economy Mountain

The cliffs here are entirely Triassic sandstone and have been eroded into a ragged sequence of caves, coves, and waterfalls, ideal for
poking around at high water.

5. Moose Island

Named for its resemblance to the hump of a moose emerging
from the water, it is the largest of the islands and the only one to
have been inhabited. It was deserted over a century ago after a
mysterious death there. White spruce and paper birch cover most
of the original fields. Camping is no problem, but finding a site in
pristine shape is another matter. Lack of a road or bridge hasn't
kept the party crowd away. The south shore might yield semi-precious stones; the north side borders extensive flats, frequented by
professional clam diggers.

6. Sandstone strata

The distinctive horizontal sandstone strata, with alternating red
and grey bands, indicates an ancient climate with succeeding dry
(oxidized reds) and wet (reduced greys) periods. Some geologists
believe that this cycle is linked to the earth's twenty-five-thou-
sand-year wobble about its axis.

7. Diamond Island

This island is rimmed by 30 m (100 ft.), vertical cliffs. Don't plan
on reaching the plateau of this tiny fortress. During low tide a
basalt ledge allows you to walk around the island.

8. Long Island

The plateau of this island can be reached from the small cove on
the north side. Some climbing skills and a safety rope will help.
Legend tells of pirates burying their booty on top and a few locals
have searched for it, without success. At the western tip, the tides
have worn an arch through the basalt.

9. Egg Island

Made of solid sandstone and the smallest of the five islands, it,
too, is unassailable, at least with the skill and equipment that I
usually bring on a kayak tour. The grassy summit is home to gull
and cormorant colonies. The latter are likely linked to the demise
of the bleached stumps that litter the top.

10. Pinnacle Island

Originally called Cathedral Island because of huge spires that
once flanked its perimeter, the ravages of storm and tide have
since removed most of them. With agility and good boots, you can
scramble up to the plateau from the cove on the west side. The

view is great! During neap tide there is space to pitch a tent on the east beach, but it is often covered following the full moon. At low tide you can walk around the entire island in a couple of hours.

11. Pinnacle Rock

Undoubtedly attached to the main island years ago, it now stands alone, isolated by high water.

12. Dinosaur and reptilian footprints

These have been found preserved in the loose rock at the base of the park. Each spring new fragments fall to the beach from the overhanging cliffs

6

CAPE CHIGNECTO

DEPARTURE POINT:
West Advocate–Cape Chignecto Provincial Park
Exit 11 at Glenholme, Route 104. Follow Route 2 until Parrsboro and then continue on Route 209 to West Advocate. Put in at Red Rocks, the end of the gravel road (Provincial Park entrance). Approximately 240 km (149 mi.) from Halifax. There is now a per diem entrance fee and a campsite charge.

ARRIVAL POINT:
Apple River, where, at high tide you can paddle right up to the wharf. Usually, you won't get beyond Apple River Bay. Therefore, the best place to leave your car is in West Apple River, although, it will be a long carry, even here, should you arrive at low tide. An alternative arrival point is at Spicers Cove. Depending upon wind direction you may wish to reverse the route direction and begin at Apple River or Spicers Cove.

TRIP LENGTH:
Two to three days, 30 km (19 mi.). This route can be completed in a couple of days, but three to four days will give you more time to explore and provide some leeway in case of poor weather. If you become stormbound, the chances of exiting en route are very limited.

CHARTS AND MAPS:
Topographical map: 21/H/7
Marine chart: None available
Geological map: Cobequid Highlands (82-6) Nova Scotia Department of Natural Resources

ROUTE DESCRIPTION:
Cape Chignecto is the western extremity of the Cobequid Mountains, and its southern escarpment is the most obvious sign of the fault line that runs the width of the province, dividing Nova Scotia into two fundamentally distinct geographical regions. Its weathered cliffs contain a diversity of formations seldom found in such a compact area. Precambrian gneiss, schist, and slate are intruded by the granites and clothed by the recent sandstones and conglomerates,

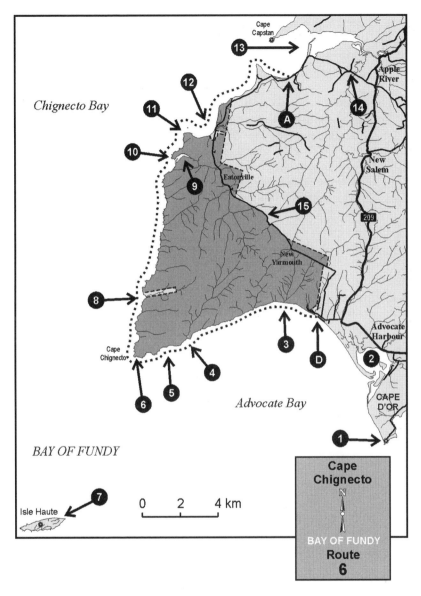

Cape Capstan

Chignecto Bay

Apple River

New Salem

Eatonville

209

New Yarmouth

Advocate Harbour

Cape Chignecto

Advocate Bay

CAPE D'OR

BAY OF FUNDY

Isle Haute

0   2   4 km

Cape Chignecto

N

BAY OF FUNDY
Route 6

all intermixed in a myriad of colours, textures, and forms.

This imposing scenery is rendered more striking by over 12 m (40 ft.) tides that are constantly remoulding the shoreline. Differential erosion has produced amazing pinnacles, arches, and sea caves. The deep green rockweeds are at eye level one moment and high above your head a few hours later. Old wharf pilings appear and then vanish, shoals become islands, and islands become mainland. It is a strange world, especially for those used to a more moderate tidal differential along the Atlantic coast. The southern escarpment overlooks the highest cliffs on mainland Nova Scotia, over 200 m (700 ft.) in some places. On the western shore, the elevation is somewhat less, but cliffs and pocket beaches continue to the gentle incline in Apple River Bay. The entire coastline is a jagged combination of shoals and rock spires inset with tiny coves and waterfalls. Seals are common, as are sea birds, such as cormorants and guillemots, and you will probably spot Bald Eagles gliding in the updrafts. There are several small spots, which provide for a lunch stop, or longer if the weather dictates. Refugee Cove and Eatonville are the only two major breaks in this often impenetrable escarpment. These former lumbering and shipbuilding centres now offer the most idyllic in wilderness camping.

This route has been one of my favourite. It is a region of the province seldom seen by either tourists or Nova Scotians, making its unique beauty all the more appealing. However, recently, it has been designated as a provincial wilderness park and a perimeter trail has been constructed (i.e., it is now less of a wilderness) and several questionable regulations have curtailed enjoyment of the park. Camping is limited and, as of this writing, campfires are not permitted, even on the vast expanses of cobble beach that border the cape (probably one of the least intrusive and safest spots in the province on which to have a campfire).

SAFETY CONSIDERATIONS:
Due to the extreme tides and the exposed shoreline, you must be cautious on this route. Set out only with a favourable forecast. If you become stormbound, your only option may be to wait it out. On the other hand, since the route parallels the shore, you can land quickly if conditions dictate. The cliffs are steep, but there are many places with small beaches above the high water mark.

The tidal currents slow down considerably near the shore, and unless there is wind, they should pose little problem. However, be wary of submerged shoals and islets and any promontories, as they all lead to localized acceleration. Wind will be your main concern. It can whip up standing waves in minutes and often accompanies the incoming tide. Stay ashore and wait it out if in doubt.

Control any temptation to scale the cliffs, unless you know what you are doing. Although much of the rock is granite, it is brittle and loose. Also be careful on the blankets of seaweed; they cover large areas and are slippery.

POINTS OF INTEREST:

1. Cape d'Or

Golden Cape (the English translation) was named by French explorers for its copper containing rock, which glistens a brilliant golden yellow in the late afternoon sun. A mine operated here until the early part of this century. The tidal currents around the cape are among the most spectacular in the entire Bay of Fundy. The lighthouse has been automated and has been renovated into a tourist accommodation.

2. Advocate Harbour

This harbour empties at low tide. Its entrance is flanked by two sand spits, kept open by the river. The abundant sand and cobblestone come from outwash deposits, which are debris laid down by rivers flowing out from the Ice Age glaciers. The underlying bedrock is the relatively young and soft Triassic sandstone.

3. Siltstones and sandstones

The undulating layers of ash-grey siltstones and sandstones near West Advocate testify to the power of crustal movement.

4. Refugee Cove

Acadians from Belleisle, near Annapolis Royal, fled to this obscure little cove in 1755 to escape deportation. With the help of natives, they eventually made it to the more secure Acadian settlements in New Brunswick. The cove remained deserted until the late 1800s, when, like most other harbours in the Bay of Fundy, it was the site of a lumbering operation for the booming shipbuilding industry. The remains of a brick furnace, which produced the steam to drive the sawmill, and the dam, which served the holding pond, are still evident, although the cove has been uninhabited for decades. Poison Ivy grows on the bar.

5. French Lookout

Used by the Acadian refugees to spot British warships searching for those who had escaped the initial deportation, it can be reached from Refugee Cove by the coastal trail. The rusty granite escarpment, intruded by contrasting black diabase dykes, plunges vertically into the bay. This shoreline has the highest actively eroding cliffs in the province-200 m (700 ft.).

Three Sisters:
High water

6. The Devils Slide

The western extremity of the Cobequid Mountains enters the bay at Cape Chignecto. The Devils Slide, an enormous incline excised from the granite, lies just to the east. Round the cape with caution, since water conditions may differ considerably on the other side. In calm weather, the currents run parallel to both shores and are not usually very strong.

7. Isle Haute

High Island (the English translation) lies 8 km (5 mi.) southwest of Cape Chignecto and is the only island in this region of the bay. It is rimmed by sheer basalt cliffs over 90 m (300 ft.) and accessible from a bar on the eastern end. It is also a legacy of the molten magma, which flowed into the faults and fissures formed during the break-up of Pangea and out over the surface to cover the entire rift valley. Isle Haute was a summer station for the Mi'kmaq and artifacts have been unearthed near the pond at the eastern tip. Old coins have been discovered, lending credence to tales of treasure. I don't recommend paddling to Isle Haute, unless you are experienced and knowledgeable about the Fundy tides—a change in weather could leave you stranded for days.

8. Big Bald Rock Brook

This brook flows through a series of bathtub-size pools before disappearing under a steep cobblestone beach. The stream is cold regardless of the time of year. The picturesque cove is flanked by granite bedrock, with a dense covering of barnacles and rockweed. It offers a sheltered stop, one of several along the western shore.

9. Eatonville

This is the largest river valley on Route 6. During the later part of the eighteenth century, it was a prosperous logging community with a large wharf and mill, a road leading into the interior, and many homes. It even had a school. Some of the largest sailing vessels built in the Bay of Fundy came from the Eatonville yards. A wooden tramway, using horse-drawn carriages, brought the logs down from the plateau. The main village was located further inland, but all that remain now are overgrown fields.

The mill closed about 1920, but ruins are still evident. Shifting sand has buried most of the wharf, but the cribbing that supported the tramway is still there, as are huge beams and rusting hardware scattered about the barrier beach. Just above the high tide, driftwood of all sizes and origins attest to the violence of the storms. Gooseberries thrive on the sand and gravel bar.

10. Three Sisters

North of the harbour entrance stand the Three Sisters, island spires at high tide and algae-draped rock pinnacles six hours later. Depending on the water level, you can either hike among a moonscape of caves, arches, and spires or paddle into a seascape that rivals anything in eastern Canada.

Three Sisters: Low water

11. Squally Point

When the ice sheet made its final retreat twelve thousand years ago, the earth's crust, depressed by the enormous weight of the glaciers, rebounded. The former shoreline is marked in some areas by raised beaches. This one on Squally Point is the highest in the province.

12. Spicers Cove

Here we leave the igneous rock behind and paddle by a huge arch of sandstone and conglomerate. Near the middle of the cove are some coal-bearing sedimentary strata. At the western edge is the sharp boundary between the igneous rhyolite and conglomerate. This is an optional take out spot, and the shore road connects with West Apple River.

13. Apple River Bay

For scenery, this bay is as far away as you can get from the southern granite escarpment. The sandstone outcrops and the shallow basin are reminiscent of the upper reaches of the Bay of Fundy. Arrive at low tide and you will be greeted by an extensive flat of slippery ooze. The Bar, a sandy indentation into Apple River Bay, is one of the few areas in the Bay of Fundy with well-developed sand dunes.

14. South Branch Apple River

You can wash all that mud off here. This is also a launching site, at high water, for a paddle in the reverse direction .

15. Eatonville road

The original road was neglected for decades, with the bridges out and alders claiming the bed. However, a local citizens' group has recently undertaken the repair and upkeep. The former pulp company roads that crisscross the plateau are in better shape but unmarked, and it is easy to get lost.

COASTAL PADDLING ROUTES
OF CAPE BRETON ISLAND

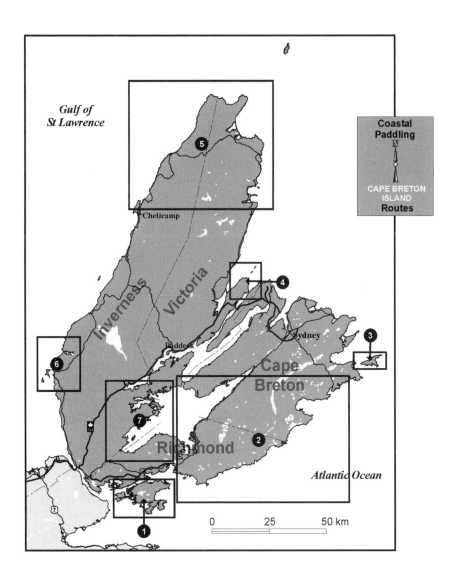

INTRODUCTION

I peered from under my hat at the magical forms evolving overhead, visions of childhood fairy tales. The charging steeds, legendary sea creatures, and medieval castles with intricate turrets reaching into the sky took shape, disappeared, then reformed in the sky before vanishing into the deep blue background. I found myself relaxing for the first time in days, allowing the sun's warmth to soak into my body—there were few warnings of UV rays in 1980. The nagging back pains had finally dissipated, along with the seasonal fog, and the extended stretch of fine weather had allowed us to make up for lost storm days. We could now appreciate our surroundings. Although only a few hours by car from Tangier, the tip of Cape Breton Island could have belonged to another province, or country, given the differences. The salt-laden spruce near my home, coating a low relief of irregular boulders, had become a vague memory under these lofty highlands, draped in lush hardwoods and cut by valleys, streams, and waterfalls.

We knew that soon the current would increase and fight through the jagged shoals off Cape North. We packed up our scattered gear from the light station lawn, loaded the canoe, and launched into the swirling waters of the Cabot Strait. It was already mid-July and we still had over two months of travelling. We reached the cape quickly, but the expectation of wind and strong currents on the other side made us apprehensive. The Gulf of St. Lawrence is in constant motion, escaping to the ocean, and our early days in the voyage had taught us what to expect from protruding headlands. This one was especially prominent and we clipped on our spray deck. We were prepared—or so we thought.

Suddenly, amidst a blanket of brilliant white foam dancing and rolling over Bay St. Lawrence, and directly in front of our canoe, smooth dark shapes headed towards us, sparkling rays glancing off black backs. All at once, the swimming forms surrounded us. They rushed beside and under the boat, and sometimes, it seemed they would fly over it too, often less than a paddle's length away. The sea was aboil. The waves were cresting and ominous darkened cliffs forbade a landing. I was petrified, not knowing what to expect and fearing the worse.

Then, just as quickly as it began, it was over. Our fear turned to relief, then to awe, and finally to disappointment as these Pilot

Whales disappeared, pursuing a school of mackerel down the coast. After such a rush of conflicting emotions, we were drained, and since the wind was continuing to pick up, we landed as soon as we could find a scrap of beach. Our journey around Cape Breton Island would have to wait until the next day.

The High Capes on the northern tip of Cape Breton Island are reminiscent of the Scottish highlands.

My circumnavigation of Nova Scotia ended over a decade ago, but the vivid memories of those Pilot Whales will be forever etched in my memory. There were other surprises too, of course. Cape Breton is magnificent, and its geological and biological melange has drawn me back many times.

Cape Breton Island lies at the northeastern end of Nova Scotia. It is an irregular shaped triangle, less than 150 km (93 mi.) through the widest section, but has a rambling shoreline that exceeds 2,000 km (1,200 mi.). A causeway over the Strait of Canso links it to the mainland. Cape Breton Island separates the Gulf of St. Lawrence from the Atlantic Ocean, and its geology and topography vary dramatically from one side to the other. The ancient volcanic rock of the eastern shores has formed a string of submerged shoals, interrupted by broad, exposed beaches with few sheltering inlets, a good reason why divers search this area for wrecks. Fishing communities have developed in some relatively protected harbours, such as Forchu, Louisbourg, Garbarus, and

Main-à-Dieu. Abundant drumlin material supplies the sediment for the baymouth bars that close off the inlets. Offshore islands, so common along the Eastern Shore of the mainland, are rare. Otherwise, the climate and vegetation is similar. The water is cold most of the year, resulting in a constant threat of fog, even well into the summer. The landscape has a stark appeal but it is only for the experienced paddler.

On the western coast of Cape Breton, the dearth of islands also applies, but that is where the similarity ends between the two shores. The coastline is relatively linear, and with the exception of Port Hood and Chéticamp, the gulf harbours of Cape Breton are narrow river mouths, which often require dredging. Strong currents flowing over sand bars at the entrances can produce chaotic conditions. Rocky shoals are not as common. The water temperature is usually quite warm in summer, often exceeding 18°C (65°F), more reminiscent of Prince Edward Island than the Atlantic coast, and fog is rare. The highlight of this shore is the Highland region, beginning at the National Park in Chéticamp and continuing around the northern tip. Ancient bedrock has thrust up through a layered carpet of sedimentary strata. The oldest rock is over 1 billion years old, a tiny segment of the Canadian shield tucked into the Maritimes. The youngest rock dates from the Carboniferous era of fern forest and evaporating seas. Erosion has since carved them down to under 540 m (1,800 ft.), but they are still impressive when seen erupting vertically from the gulf waters—a powerful combination of sheer cliffs, incised valleys, sea caves, and pinnacles. This is one of the most rugged and impressive coastal areas in all of North America.

Hiking is a natural adjunct to a paddling tour and the perfect option when stormbound. A climb up to the denuded plateau highlights the undulating sequence of cliffs and coves weaving up the coast. However, good landing spots are scarce, and with the prevailing winds coming from the west (i.e., on shore), caution and experience are needed.

Unique to Cape Breton Island is the Bras d'Or Lake. This is a large saltwater basin occupying much of the interior and it is essentially landlocked, open to the sea via two narrow passages and the canal at St. Peters. This lake holds the warmest of all Nova Scotia's coastal waters. In winter, though, large expanses become a solid sheet of ice. It is the preferred realm of the sailor, sheltered from the storms and fog of the open Atlantic Ocean, although the long fetch in some sections can result in an acute chop. Well-appointed marinas and small villages share the surrounding rolling hills with rich deciduous forest and open farmland. If empty wilderness is your destination, then you may have to look elsewhere, although the paddler can usually find some undisturbed shoreline, even on the Bras d'Or Lake.

Tidal range around Cape Breton is modest—0.6 m to 1 m (2 ft. to 4 ft.) in the gulf and 0.9 m to 2 m (3 ft. to 6 ft.) on the Atlantic, and negligible in the Bras d'Or Lakes. The currents are light, except around prominent headlands and in narrow passages, such as Cape North or between Scatarie Island and Main-à-Dieu; here, when combined with opposing winds, they can be treacherous. The ocean currents, usually counterclockwise, predominate over tidal flow in the Gulf of St. Lawrence.

Groups of pilot whales pursue schools of squid and mackerel along the Highland coastline.

The Cape Breton coastline is home to an assortment of sea birds and marine mammals, some of which are seldom encountered elsewhere in the province. This is the southern limit of the Black-legged Kittiwake, which nests at only a few places along the eastern shore, and the site of Nova Scotia's only significant Atlantic Puffin colony—the Bird Islands, not to be confused with the Bird Islands on the Eastern Shore of the province. Bald Eagles are common in the Bras d'Or Lake and along the Cape Breton Highlands, where Pilot Whales pursue mackerel and squid—a sure sight in the late summer. Larger whales, such as Minke, Humpback, or Fin, are occasionally spotted further offshore. Both the Grey and Harbour Seals frequent the shoals. There are no exotic large mammals inland, but you may catch sight of black bear, deer, or moose in the Highlands. There have also been unconfirmed reports of cougar.

The human history of Cape Breton dates to the last ice age, when indigenous peoples in the south followed the retreating glaciers into the area. Little is known about these early inhabitants, and they eventually disappeared. The ancestors of the present Mi'kmaq settled the region a couple thousand years ago, and their descendants still live in several communities on the shores of the Bras d'Or Lake. The first incursions of the Europeans are obscure. Myth has it that a group of Irish monks, prone to wander the North Atlantic in search of converts, were the first to find their way here. That may be fanciful thinking, for there is no evidence to support this romantic theory; nor is there evidence to support the claim that the Vikings, or later John Cabot visited.

What is known for certain is that the French and English disputed "ownership" of this territory, along with the rest of North America, for well over a century. The latter eventually won out with the capture of the fortress of Louisbourg and evicted the French inhabitants. The reconstruction of this fortress, the most ambitious on the continent, depicts accurately the life of those times. Following the expulsion of the French, Britain encouraged immigration to the island which was accelerated by the "clearances" in Scotland. Powerless tenants were evicted from the Highlands to make way for large sheep farms. Many of the immigrants ended up on New Scotland's shores, where they have left a lasting imprint in the place names, such as MacDonald Glen, Inverness, and Loch Lomond, and in the continuing popularity of traditional Celtic music. Gaelic is still spoken by a few of the older folk and is taught at a local college.

Many of the dispersed Acadians also made their way back, settling on the rocky shores spurned by others. Isolation has preserved their language, and in communities such as Isle Madame and Chéticamp, a bountiful ocean led to prosperity, until the recent collapse of the Atlantic fishery.

Coal was discovered around the island and mined in thick

seams that ran well out under the ocean. Iron was smelted, and an industrial economy developed around the deep-water port of Sydney—the province's third largest city with a population of about 26,000. Changing economic patterns have left a legacy of unemployment and industrial pollution, which have burdened the island for decades.

Vertical marble cliffs near Cape North.

Tourism is offered as a hope for the future as more visitors arrive each summer to sample the island's diverse and accessible fare. No less an illuminary than Alexander Graham Bell chose Baddeck, overlooking the Bras d'Or Lake, to spend his summers and conduct much of his research. Although he had travelled the globe, he found that Cape Breton "out rivaled them all." However, the seasonal employment provided by this industry will not compensate for lost jobs in the resource sector.

Due to the dramatic variations in coastal features, climate and water conditions, a detailed discussion of these is reserved for the specific routes that follow: Isle Madame, the East Coast, Scatarie Island, the Bird Islands, the Highlands, Mabou/Port Hood, and the Bras d'Or Lake.

ISLE MADAME 1

DEPARTURE POINT:
Petit-de-Grat
On crossing the Canso Causeway, turn right onto Route 4, which becomes Route 104. Take Exit 46 and continue south on Route 320. After crossing bridge to Isle Madame, follow the signs to Petit-de-Grat. Put in at the Government Wharf. Approximately 325 km (200 mi.) from Halifax. Note: This is only one of many possible departure spots around Isle Madame. Others include West Arichat, Pondville Beach and D'Escousse (opposite a historic bed and breakfast).

ARRIVAL POINT:
Same as the departure points.

TRIP LENGTH:
Circumnavigating the whole island would take three to six days, 85 km (53 mi.), not all of it interesting. A far more appealing option would be a day-long to overnight paddle in segments such as Arichat Harbour, or around Petit-de-Grat Island, 17 km (11 mi.).

CHARTS AND MAPS:
Topographical maps: 11/F/6,7,l0,11
Marine charts: St. Peters Bay to Strait of Canso (#4308: 37,500)
Note: Unfortunately, Isle Madame is not included on a single topo map but appears in bits and pieces on several topo maps.

ROUTE DESCRIPTION:
Situated off the southeastern tip of Cape Breton Island, Isle Madame and its irregular outline of shoals, islets, headlands, and inlets are well removed from the more travelled roads, which carry visitors to the Highlands or to the Fortress of Louisbourg. The area was settled by French from Louisbourg about 1720 but was visited by European fishermen for decades, if not centuries, prior to this, and its name recalls one of the titles of the Queen of France. These early inhabitants were expelled following the fall of Louisbourg in 1758, and the island was deserted for a time.

Many of the Acadians returned, and this is one of the few areas in the province where French is still spoken. Until 1928, you had to rely on a boat to reach the island. Modern communications, however, are gradually prying open this close-knit community to the dominant English speaking North American society.

This neglected part of the province is less than a half-hour's drive from the Bras d'Or Lake but could scarcely be more different. Absent are the rolling hills and lush hardwoods that surround the lake. Gone, too, is the warm salt water. This is a rugged landscape, enveloped by the cold- and fog- producing North Atlantic Ocean. It is cloaked in stunted conifers, shallow lakes, and acid bogs. Actively eroding drumlins, a legacy of an ice sheet that once covered the area to a depth of over 1 km (0.6 mi.), offer a contrast to the surface bedrock, providing ample material for the islands, spits, barachois, and beaches that define the perimeter of Isle Madame. Marginally more productive, these hills often serve as the only farmland in the region.

The road closely follows the shore where the fishermen settled, and it is difficult to escape the signs and lights of habitation. Even in seemingly remote sectors, trails often permit access. Only on the small islands can you be assured of peace and isolation, at least from the ubiquitous ATV's, which seem able to travel everywhere. Fortunately, there are plenty of these outposts, such as Crichton, Jerseyman, and Green Islands. Should you require supplies while en route, a convenience store is never far away. Most of the island is private so use discretion if camping. Green Island and the Mackerel Cove shore is public.

Isle Madame offers an intimate view of life in a coastal fishing community, of how things were and what they have become. Small fishing boats float alongside huge ocean draggers; colourful four-square dwellings sit next to modern bungalows—and a once prosperous fishery is now in decline.

Safety Considerations:

The waters encompassing this route vary, from sheltered islets bounded by sandy shores between Janvrin Island and Isle Madame to the exposed rocky coast off Petit-de-Grat Island. Potential risks can change radically between such areas, so this should be accommodated when planning a tour. Remember, too, that the water remains cold throughout the season, and fog is common, especially in spring and early summer. Local motorboat activity is also greater than in the more isolated routes.

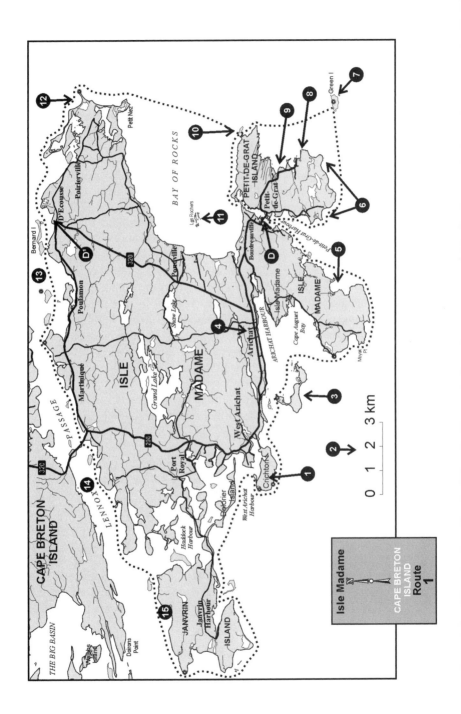

Isle Madame

CAPE BRETON ISLAND
Route
1

POINTS OF INTEREST:

1. Crichton Island

This island is connected to Isle Madame by a deteriorating breakwater, which contrary to indications on the topographical map, does not incorporate a bridge. So, a short portage will be necessary when passing this way. Car access has long since been impossible, and the farm on the island is deserted, only foundations and an old orchard remain. Open fields line the sheltered northern shoreline, while shoals and barachois face the bay.

2. Cerberus Rock

Lying just below the water, 5 km (3 mi.) south of Crichton Island, this hidden shoal guards the entrance to the Strait of Canso. It is a constant menace to the huge tankers on their way to the oil storage facilities at Port Tupper. The Arrow collided with this reef in 1970 and sank, resulting in Eastern Canada's worst oil spill ever. Large areas of coastline were polluted, and numerous birds and marine mammals were killed. Fortunately, time and the high-energy Atlantic Ocean have removed most traces of this incident.

Chedabucto Bay, the largest on the Atlantic coast, was originally part of an ancient river system, which flowed northeast into the St. Lawrence during the Triassic/Cretaceous era. Tilting and submergence of the earth's crust created the bay and the strait. The southern boundary of the bay marks the Chedabucto fault, which extends across the province and out into the Bay of Fundy off Cape Chignecto.

3. Jerseyman Island

Actually three islands connected by narrow sand/cobble tombolos, it got its name from the Jersey traders who settled here in the late 1700s. These French speaking British citizens from the Channel Islands were adept at exploiting the fish marketing business, and also, some would say, adept at exploiting local fishermen. The Jersey men were active in many parts of Atlantic Canada. When the island was attacked by American privateer John Paul Jones, the inhabitants resettled on Isle Madame. Off the northern side of the island are the pens of the largest finfish (steelhead) farm in North America. By mid-August there is a good chance to spot Pilot Whales in Arichat Harbour.

4. Arichat

One of the oldest communities in Nova Scotia, it is also the largest on Isle Madame with a population of about 900 and is the county seat. Arichat was a prosperous port of call in the 1800s, when shipbuilding yards and factories lined its waterfront. With the present decline in the fishery, things are quieter.

5. Mackerel Cove

The site of an early Acadian village, it was abandoned in the 1920s, when the inhabitants moved to the more hospitable and serviced Petit-de-Grat and Arichat. Intriguing stone fences and foundations remain, and the wreck of a schooner is scattered along the beach. This is a good campsite. North of Mackerel Cove is another isolated harbour, the Great Barachois, and a stopping spot for migrating sea birds. This shallow basin is protected by Spider Island and a number of reefs. Caution is advised when entering, as there is surf in rough weather. A nature trail is being constructed linking Mackerel Cove (and eventually Cape Augel) to Petit-de-Grat.

6. Red Head

The highest drumlins on these islands, over 30 m (100 ft.) are eroding into the sea here. The undulating topography was stripped long ago of its forest cover, yielding fuel and pasture. At the base of this moorlike landscape are outcrops of Precambrian volcanic rock.

Soft drumlins are rapidly eroding into the sea.

7. Green Island

This is a tiny islet of resistant bedrock less than a kilometre in circumference. During our "trek" around the province in 1980, a violent storm stranded us here, while waves and windswept spray washed the island. We found refuge in the lighthouse keeper's home, where a well-appointed stereo and ample quantities of rum deadened the blast of the foghorn. Today, the mood has changed. The houses have been boarded up and the keepers have left. Green Island still offers a superb camping spot, although its rocky girdle demands caution and calm weather.

8. Rusty-red granite

The low headland just south of the Petite Anse is striking and would be more aptly named Red Head than the bleached drumlin a short distance away. Perhaps the cartographer made a mistake— Ottawa is far away. The assorted structures overlooking the cliffs, varying from stone to metal drums to wood, are hunting blinds.

9. Petite Anse

One of the most picturesque coastal villages in the province, it resembles a Newfoundland outport. Its colourful houses nestle close together along the exposed rock bordering a winding roadway.

10. Gros Nez

This is the site of a gull colony. Because of the presence of humans around most of Isle Madame, there are relatively few spots that provide the isolation needed by nesting sea birds.

11. Rock Islets

A short distance off Pondville beach is this compact collection of rocks and reefs. Numerous seals congregate here in summer.

12. Cap La Ronde

Here is another good example of the drumlin topography exhibited throughout the island. The rounded hills were cleared for farms, and unlike the modest homes in the nearby fishing villages, imposing farmhouses overlook the ocean here. The abundant local sediments have been shaped by the ocean waves and currents into sand spits and barrier beaches, sheltering saltwater lagoons and marshes. The light tower on Cap La Ronde will soon become another victim of the insatiable power of the sea as glacial till is undermined. If you poke in the Goulet and around Potato Island note the tide or you could be left aground.

13. D'Escousse Harbour and Poulamon Bay

These have several low-lying, forested islands, which add to the relative shelter of the north shore of Isle Madame. A number of shellfish (mussels and scallops) aquaculture sites are found along this shore. A historic bed and breakfast at the water's edge in D'Escousse is an alternative departure point or a possible accommodation en route.

14. Lennox Passage

This is the narrow channel that separates Isle Madame from Cape Breton Island. Originally a ferry at Grandique Point linked the two, but a bridge was constructed sixty-five years ago. A modern causeway/drawbridge now carries traffic to and from the island. The southwest lie of the passage funnels the prevailing winds. Be cautious of the currents under the bridge.

15. Janvrin Island

This island got its name from one of the Jersey traders. It is underlain by much softer sedimentary rock than Isle Madame or Petit-de-Grat Island. It is relatively sheltered, and sand beaches surround much of its perimeter. Lagoon and ponds back many of the coves and headlands. The shores are strewn with eel grass in addition to the ubiquitous seaweed, emphasizing the abundance of sheltered water in the area. The topography is low and this section is not as interesting as other parts of the island. The roadway links Janvrin to Isle Madame via two smaller islands. Note that there are two causeways and only one bridge.

THE SOUTHEAST COAST

DEPARTURE POINT:
Point Michaud Beach
On crossing the Canso Causeway follow Route 104 to St. Peters. Continue on Route 247 to Point Michaud where you can launch from the beach. Approximately 320 km (199 mi.) from Halifax. An alternative departure point is the bridge at Grand River.

ARRIVAL POINT:
Louisbourg. For this trip you will definitely need to leave a car at your destination, approximately 140 km (87 mi.) away from the departure point. There is no public transportation between Louisbourg and Port Michaud and precious little traffic, should you attempt to hitchhike.

TRIP LENGTH:
Four days to a week, 75 km (47 mi.).

CHARTS AND MAPS:
Topographical maps: 11 F/9,10,16; 11 G/3
Marine charts: Red Point-Guyon Island (#4374: 75,000); Guyon Island-Flint Island (#4375: 75,700)

ROUTE DESCRIPTION:
Although Cape Breton seems to draw the majority of Nova Scotia tourists, the southeastern coastline is rarely one of their destinations. It is unpopulated, untravelled, and for the most part unknown even to those who are native to the province. Much of the coastal roadways are unpaved, which also tends to deter today's traveller, although upgrading is now under way, and there is a noticeable lack of visitor services. Most traffic on the eastern part of Cape Breton sticks to Route 4, along Bras d'Or Lake.

Few coastal paddlers attempt this route. It is rocky, exposed to the wrath of the open ocean over much of its length, and susceptible to dense fog well into the summer months. However, it is this very isolation that will draw the adventuresome paddler to this region of contrasts. The dark, volcanic rock which underlies this shore resists the sea, but the overlying loose drumlins are a

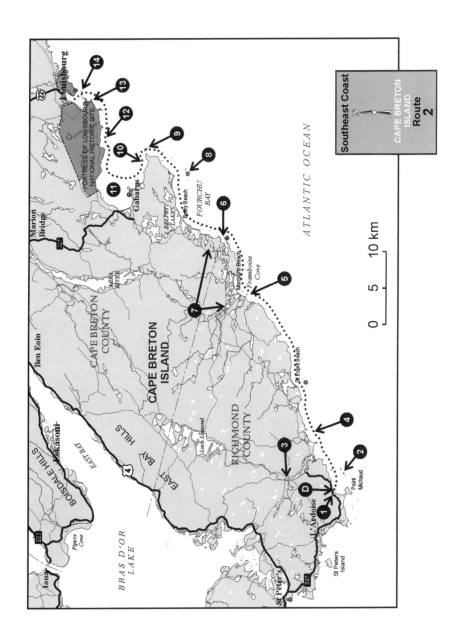

major source of sediment. Unlike the Eastern Shore of the mainland, defined by a ragged indented profile, the sand and cobble left by the ice sheets have been distributed the length of this shoreline, straightening it by forming spits over the mouths of bays and harbours. Here we find some of the most extensive beaches along the Atlantic coast of Nova Scotia.

Above these bays and beaches lies a low relief of stunted forest, extensive bog, and a wealth of interconnecting lakes, streams, and marshes. In fact, you can paddle parallel to much of the coast through this inland maze. The soils are cool and wet and marine exposure severe. This is not good farming country, although the abundant drumlin material is more conducive to agriculture than along the mainland coast. In the 1800s Scots settled the area and sheep farming was extensive, but most of these early farms have long since been abandoned. Numerous oldfields follow the edge of the eroding cliffs (good deer habitat), as do early roads and trails. Rock piles and stone foundations are easily found. White spruce grows along the coast, with balsam fir inland (spruce budworm is endemic), and black spruce and larch in the depressions. The better drained headlands support a dense heath cover, especially crowberry.

There is little boat traffic these days. The inshore fishery has fallen on hard times. Even the larger vessels from Forchu, Gabarus, and Louisbourg have been tied up or sold. The fish are gone and the cod and haddock fishery have been closed here. An already isolated shore will become even more isolated as people continue to move away. Even the lighthouse keepers have been replaced by automation.

However, other coastal life continues to prosper. Both Harbour and Grey Seals are common, and this is a staging area for migratory waterfowl and shorebirds. It boasts one of the few Black-legged Kittiwake colonies in Nova Scotia, and the most southerly. Gulls, cormorants, guillemots, and Eider Ducks also nest along this shore. At the end of this route the Fortress of Louisbourg awaits, the largest historical reconstruction in North America.

SAFETY CONSIDERATIONS:
I distinctly remember the afternoon in 1980 as we set out from Point Michaud Beach on the southeast coast. The sea was placid, the visibility almost limitless. Offshore, a curtain of dense sea fog glowed in the sunlight, having moved little the entire day. We

were confident that the fog wouldn't bother us before we reached our destination. How wrong we were! Scarcely had we passed the Basque Islands, when a brisk onshore breeze displaced the calm, and it was only minutes before we were shrouded in obscurity.

We couldn't continue under such conditions, so we headed towards the shelter of L'Archeveque Cove. However, en route we had to thread the shoals off Black Point, where we were rapidly surrounded by screaming gulls and breaking waves. Our stomachs were tied in knots, and what had been an enjoyable paddle only minutes earlier, had turned into a terrifying confusion. We cautiously poked our way along, and by the time we reached the safety of L'Archeveque we were both physically and mentally exhausted. While we set up our tent, the wind changed direction and pushed the fog back out to sea. Low sunlight blanketed the scene in rich reddish hues, and the coastal waters were calm once more.

A fringe of jagged shoals along the eastern coast of Cape Breton demand vigilance of the coastal paddler.

That early experience taught me the essential lesson about this coastline. The water is cold and the fog is frequent until well into summer. However, unlike the Eastern Shore, these waters lack the protective island archipelago. In its place is an uninterrupted string of shoals, reefs, and headlands cutting through the water like a row of jagged teeth. It's as if the sea level of the Eastern Shore had risen by a few metres, obliterating all the islands, leaving a lethal imprint just under the surface. Extreme caution is advised. Even in apparently calm conditions, a gentle swell emanating from an earlier storm can erupt without warning over an unseen shoal. Sometimes several minutes can elapse between such incidents. Anticipating this possibility, while surveying the path ahead, is essential. Such unexpected roughness, along with the dearth of sheltered harbours and coves, a rocky shoreline, and barrier beaches which are exposed to a breaking surf, converge here for all the ingredients of a risky paddle. Although you might well paddle several days under calm conditions and wonder what the fuss is about, the ocean could suddenly turn against you.

POINTS OF INTEREST:

1. Point Michaud Beach
This is an impressive, hard-packed sand beach over 2 km (1.3 mi.) long. It is backed by sand dunes and large cranberry bogs. The beach is a provincial day-use park with change houses and pit toilets.

2. The Basque Islands
These are a tiny collection of grass-covered islets less than 2 km (1.3 mi.) off Point Michaud Beach. They have the only Eider Duck colony on this shore (other than one on Scatarie Island), and it is one of only three known Grey Seal breeding colonies in Nova Scotia. Breeding season runs from February to the end of March.

3. Grand River
This is a narrow, rapid-moving stream until it reaches the tiny village of the same name, where it widens and slows considerably, becoming a drowned estuary. During the days of sail, coastal schooners would travel inland to pick up supplies and take on cargo. For the 5 km (3 mi.) or so until it empties into the ocean, the river is flanked by fields and farms. Be cautious at the river mouth. Where the fast-flowing channel meets the ocean swell, turbulence can result, especially standing waves with an onshore wind.

4. L'Archeveque
Like many places along this shore, this one owes its name to the French who inhabited "Ile Royale" (as Cape Breton was then called) until 1758. This picturesque cove, with unpainted sheds, stagings and wharves, and hauled-up and sun-weathered fishing boats, is now a relic of times long past. A narrow channel leads to a bluff overlooking the ocean, and the shoals. L'Archeveque was

once an active community of over a hundred people, with a lobster cannery and a church. Today there are no houses and the cove is usually silent.

5. Red Cape

This cape forms a steep wall of rapidly eroding sand and gravel. Deep vertical fissures mark the paths of countless tiny streams, which carry the loose glacial debris into the sea. Clods of grass hanging over the edge and scattered along the bank emphasize how rapidly this process is occurring. From the view on top, it is readily apparent where this material is transported: onto the beaches of Framboise Cove. (Framboise means "raspberry" in French, and like many other place-names in eastern Cape Breton, it stems from the French occupation prior to 1758. Scottish Highlanders settled the area in the early nineteenth century.)

Although larger than most local drumlins, this one presents an obvious example of the coastal processes at work from Point Michaud to Gabarus. Over ten beaches have filled what were once bays between headlands. Many are in the form of spits, kept open by large streams, while others completely seal off the bays, creating sheltered lagoons. The net effect has been to straighten an original irregular shoreline. The extent and speed of this modification is illustrated by the stands of coastal spruce that have been invaded and killed by moving sands, and the presence of river outlets not indicated on the maps. This contrast with the Eastern Shore on the mainland emphasizes the role of the Ice Age in determining the shape of our Atlantic shoreline.

6. Forchu

This is a tiny fishing village straddling the narrow harbour, which cuts extremely resistant and highly deformed Precambrian volcanic bedrock. This port has seen better days. It was once an important coastal settlement with a population of about one thousand people. These days, less than a hundred inhabitants remain in a deteriorating environment. The name Forchu is derived from the French "fourchette," meaning "fork" and referring to the shape of the harbour. Strewn on the rocks just south of Forchu Head are the twisted, rusting remains of the Iceland II, a stern trawler wrecked in 1967 with the loss of ten lives.

7. Lakes

Most of this shore is relatively even, dipping gently into the sea. The surface is covered with irregular lakes and wandering streams, the result of the glacial deposits that have completely altered the original drainage pattern of numerous northeast-southwest faults. These lakes usually enter the sea via narrow, often fast-flowing streams. They are tidal, especially where the entrances are large, and there is a steady gradation of salt to fresh water as you range inland. They are also at times extremely shallow—often they can be navigated only during high tide—and may form large areas of salt marsh, for example, opposite Framboise Cove. This is excellent bird habitat with nesting Black Ducks, mergansers, and loons.

Should weather or sea state prohibit a continuation along the coast, or for a change of environment, exploring this inland waterway is an alternative. In some sections, for example between Framboise Cove and Forchu Bay, you can enter at one point and exit at another, several kilometres further up the shore, albeit with a little portaging. The possibility also exists to take out on the highway that runs along these lakes.

8.   Guyon Island

This is a treeless, irregular islet surrounded by a multitude of shoals. It is less than 2 km (1 mi.) off Winging Point, the apex of a long cobble beach extending several kilometres from Belfry Lake to Cape Gabarus. The lighthouse keepers' houses are still standing as of 1997 but are boarded up. Due to the local abundance of shoals, particular caution is advised until you round Cape Gabarus into Gull Cove.

9.   Green Island

This is a tiny rocky outcrop less than a kilometre off Cape Gabarus, guarded by a scattering of shoals. A sparse coating of grasses and coastal plants has a good dash of sea bird guano in season. This is an important nesting site for the Great Cormorant, which is more common here than the smaller Double-crested type, unlike along the Eastern Shore. It is also the southernmost nesting colony of the Black-legged Kittiwake, although this sea bird has been gradually extending its range and may soon show up further south.

10. Gull Cove

This is an abandoned fishing village that can now only be reached from the sea or a 5 km (3 mi.) hike from Gabarus. The fields are dotted with the foundations of former houses—some of which were later hauled over frozen bogs and lakes to a new settlement inland—and, on occasion, by cattle and horses that are brought in to graze on the open pasture. The exposed shore, with cliffs and a cobble beach will prevent landing during northerly and easterly winds.

11. Gabarus Bay

This is the largest along this coast and the only stretch where sea cliffs are found, over 30 m (100 ft.) in some spots. This represents a break in the nature of the coast. South of Gabarus we find the numerous bays protected by sand and cobble spits and beaches. North of here, a rocky shoreline with cobble and boulder beaches dominates—a direct function of the decrease in drumlin source material.

12. Kennington Cove

In June 1758, a force of twenty-seven thousand British put ashore at Kennington Cove. They dragged their heavy guns over rock and through woods and bogs to attack Fortress Louisbourg from the rear.

13. Louisbourg

The Fortress of Louisbourg National Historic Site commemorates a pivotal period in Canadian history, when the British defeated the French and gained control of all that was to become Nova Scotia.

Following the Treaty of Utrecht in 1713, the French had been driven from the south coast of Newfoundland and left with the islands in the Gulf of St. Lawrence, including Cape Breton Island. Fish, particularly codfish, was an indispensable commodity when famine still ravaged Europe and the French were in search of a new location from which to defend their interests in the area. The ice-free port of "English Harbour," which they renamed in honour of Louis XIV, the Sun King, provided access to fish and a good fort site. For thirty years, the port prospered, becoming the fourth busiest in North America, after New York, Boston, and Philadelphia, and traded with the West Indies, New England, and Europe.

However, when hostilities broke out again between these two European powers in 1745, as they did with considerable regularity during this era, the New Englanders attacked and succeeded in capturing Louisbourg.

The town was returned to the French with the signing of a peace treaty, but with renewed hostilities, it was besieged and captured once again, under the command of James Wolfe. This time, not about to risk a possible return to France, the British blew up the town and its fortification, stone by stone. The ruins were left mostly undisturbed until 1961, when the federal government began the largest historical reconstruction in North America.

Over the years these windswept fields have been transformed

into a moment in history—the summer of 1744. The restoration has been thorough and meticulous, using the original plans that were preserved in the French archives. Local residents find summer work as soldiers, bakers, housemaids, officers, and children, all clothed in traditional garb and engaged in normal activities of the period. To visit the fortress you are expected to take the bus, which connects the visitor centre with the site, although I've landed at the gates themselves and wandered about unaccosted. Regulations and their enforcement do change with time, so be discreet if landing unofficially, or check ahead of your arrival for what is acceptable.

The modern town of Louisbourg, with a population over 1,000—the largest on this coast, has always relied on the fishery, and its fortunes have paralleled those of the industry in larger centres. The current fishery moratorium has been devastating for the area, closing the processing plant and putting many people out of work. Tourism has taken up the slack somewhat and accommodation is plentiful, especially bed and breakfasts, but be sure to reserve in advance during July and August.

14. Louisbourg Harbour

It is guarded by three islands and numerous shoals. Battery Island was heavily fortified during the French reign. Shipwrecks litter the ocean floor. One, Le Chameau, sunk with the payload for the French garrison. It was recovered in the 1960s, yielding the largest haul ever from a wreck off the Nova Scotia coast. In the early 1800s the Astrea, an Irish immigrant ship, ran aground with the loss of over five hundred lives. Lighthouse Point, on the northern entrance to the harbour, is the sight of the first lighthouse in Canada (1733). The British captured the point during the siege of Louisbourg and used the position to bombard Battery Island. Remains of the original foundation have been unearthed and stabilized.

SCATARIE ISLAND ⟶ 3

DEPARTURE POINT:
Main-à-Dieu Harbour
From Sydney take Route 22 towards Louisbourg. Turn left at Catalone and follow signs to Main-à-Dieu. You can put in from the beach at Burkes Point, on the east side of the harbour. Approximately 35 km (22 mi.) from Sydney, 465 km (289 mi.) from Halifax.

ARRIVAL POINT:
Same as the departure point. Alternatively, continue on to Louisbourg for an extended tour.

TRIP LENGTH:
Two to three days, 35 km (22 mi.). Add a day or two if you plan to take out in Louisbourg, 70 km (43 mi.).

CHARTS AND MAPS:
Topographical map: 11/J/4; 11/G/13 (Louisbourg)
Marine chart: Guyon Island to Flint Island (#4375: 75,000)

ROUTE DESCRIPTION:
Scatarie Island juts into the Atlantic Ocean off the eastern part of the province. It is one of our largest offshore islands, over 10 km (6 mi.) in length, but one of the least known. When I first paddled by, during my circumnavigation in 1980, Scatarie was obscured by the early summer fog and I saw little. It remained an enigma until a few years ago, when a friend and I (and Hurricane Bob) chose to visit this remote coastal outpost.

Scatarie is an ancient bedrock outcrop, guarded by an irregular pattern of shoals, or "sunkers" as they are called in local parlance. It is a raw world, and not a very pleasant landfall to many early visitors from across the ocean. Only Sable Island and St. Pauls Island have claimed more sailors' lives. Sheltered harbours are nonexistent, vegetation is impoverished, and the cold Atlantic fog and winds are ever present, especially during winter and spring.

In spite of this stark picture, Scatarie Island did have its share of human visitors and for a time it even had permanent settlement. Today, it is deserted and the light stations are automated. However, that desolate nature, which eventually drove off the inhabitants, now appeals to many of us who spend our lives pampered by city existence. Scatarie's ragged shoreline offers plenty to explore; its geology is varied and colourful. Much of the interior is covered in a dense mat of White Spruce, but the open perimeter offers some of the best coastal hiking in Atlantic Canada.

SAFETY CONSIDERATIONS:

Scatarie Island has had its share of wrecks, with good reason. Persistent fog, winds, and currents combine with a rocky shoreline fringed with shoals to create a deadly mixture. Good judgement and paddling skills are a must. When weather and water conditions deteriorate, there is no sheltered route, and you may have to land on a surf-exposed shore. Your trip might even become a hiking outing. Allow yourself an extra day or two and bring sufficient rations.

Of particular note is the Main-à-Dieu Passage. Ocean currents flowing around the island accelerate through this channel. Opposing winds can create dangerous standing waves. Obtain local advice on the conditions before departing. An alternative approach is to hire a local fisherman to carry you and your gear across. Even in calm weather, this route is not recommended for the novice paddler.

POINTS OF INTEREST:

1. Main-à-Dieu

This is the easternmost village in Nova Scotia, population 375. It is believed that the name evolved from the Mi'kmaq word for "devil" (manadoo). Paradoxically, the French translation, "hand of God," has been construed as referring to the crook of land at the tip of the peninsula. The surrounding forest was destroyed during a major fire in 1972, which also claimed the church and several houses. The inhabitants had to be evacuated by sea. Charred tree trunks still cover the hillside.

2. Main-à-Dieu Passage

This is a scant 2 km (1 mi.) across, but it must handle much of the current that flows along this edge of Cape Breton. As the water accelerates through the passage it is modified into long, undulating swells and, in opposing winds, steep, cresting waves. Choose slack water and cross during calm weather. For experienced coastal paddlers only!

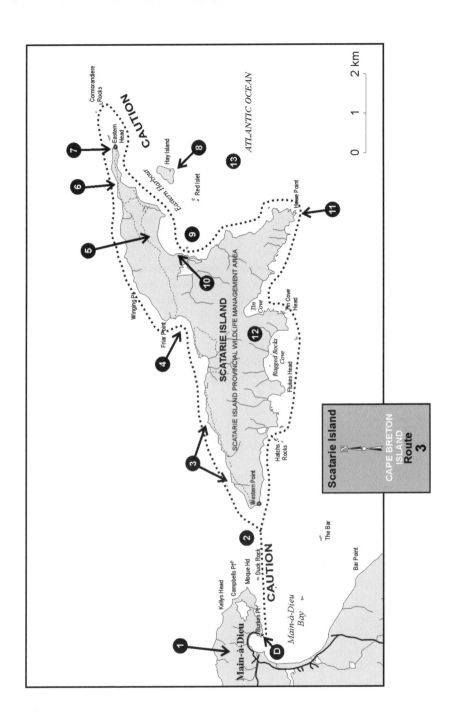

3. Hiking Trail

The shoreline of the island is ideal hiking terrain. A trail skirts the length of the northern coast, although for much of the distance, a carpet of dense crowberry permits you to wander at will, with few impediments. The province has few coastal areas, or areas of any type, for that matter, where you can hike with such freedom.

A series of cliffs are interrupted by high-energy, rocky beaches. Several small freshwater ponds have formed behind these barriers. The incessant winds are revealed by isolated, prostrate trees and a forest edge that has taken on a aerodynamic slope to deflect the onshore wind. It is often almost impossible to enter the interior woods through the dense tangle of branches.

4. Northwest Cove

This is the most accessible and sheltered landing on a generally inhospitable coastline. The crumbling concrete wharf suggests a more active past. The boat house, which served the light station, is the only remaining building in the cove—even its days are numbered.

5. Scatarie Island

The human history here probably began with native North Americans, although, it seems there was little to have attracted them. Basque and Portuguese fishermen certainly passed this way—maybe even before the voyages of Columbus—and the name of the island is thought to have originated with the Portuguese. It was possibly a whaling station. Perhaps they even made it a summer fishing base, salting and drying their catch before returning to Europe. We know that the French did just this, settling the island during the period that Louisbourg, only 20 km (12 mi.) southwest, was a bastion of French power in North America. The fortress garrison was a ready market for the islanders, and the cod were particularly prolific off its shores. A census in 1716 recorded over four hundred inhabitants and although most of these were temporary summer workers, only about a hundred men, women, and children eked out a year-round existence.

When Louisbourg fell to the British in 1758, Scatarie's inhabitants were deported. No obvious signs remain of this early period. The island stood deserted until the mid-1800s, when a life-saving station was built, and several families arrived from Newfoundland. These new settlers had it no easier than the French. In spring and summer, the fog and storms could render fishing hazardous in the shoal-infested waters. In the winter the drift ice made fishing impossible, and the boats had to be hauled up on shore to prevent them from being crushed. Added to this hardship was the isolation from mainland communities. They had to bring in nearly everything they needed to survive, including building wood, which couldn't be extracted from the stunted, twisted trees on the island. However, they persevered, and by the early part of this century, over a dozen families were firmly established, along with their own church and school. They supplemented fishing with subsistence gardening—potatoes, cabbage, and turnips were about all that would grow—and perhaps raised a few sheep and a cow.

With the advent of refrigeration and consumer demand for a fresh fish product, the islanders could no longer compete with the mainlanders who had easy access to the modern fish processing plants. The demand for salted codfish dwindled, and with it, the single reason for clinging to this rock. By the Second World War, few people remained. Now there are none. Most houses have collapsed, and the church is also gone. Only one lonely homestead, standing precariously, overlooks Hay Island.

6. Cemetery

Here lie the bodies of four men, whose boat was torpedoed during the First World War. Although they had reached the shore alive,

An abandoned homestead on Scatarie Island.

they died of exposure before the lighthouse keeper found them. The graves are marked by crosses.

7. Eastern Head

It overlooks the Cormorandière Rocks, the easternmost point in Nova Scotia, except for Sable Island. The light station dominates the tip. Its white tower is 22 m (74 ft.) above the ocean, and its warning beacon reaches out over 12 km (20 mi.). The lighthouse keepers' homes are boarded up but still standing, although that might well have changed by the time you arrive. Vandals might rearrange the plaster or the Department of Transport might burn them. Next to the tower is a small grave, bordered by a picket fence, where one of the former lighthouse keeper's children is buried. This part of Scatarie is exposed and barren. Except for grasses, there is little vegetation, and even this is dominated by shards of rock that carpet the land.

The hiking on Scatarie Island is superb.

8. Hay Island

As its name implies, this island has no tree cover. It is the nesting site for a large colony of gulls as well as Eider Ducks. Leach's Storm-Petrels nest on nearby Scatarie in underground burrows.

9. Eastern Harbour

It is little more than a shallow bed of shoals awash in surf with the slightest wind. Anticipate breakers that arise suddenly from apparently calm water. Seals are common; this is where I encountered the most seals that I have ever seen at one time—well over two hundred huge Grey Seals.

10. The Cambrian/Precambrian boundary
This boundary is exposed at the apex of Eastern Harbour. It was during this period in the earth's history that multicellular life evolved rapidly into what has been called the "Cambrian explosion." There are few places where this boundary can be seen, and it offers the potential to study a pivotal period in evolution. The rocks on Scatarie have been described as pristine, meaning they have changed little since their deposition millions of years ago.

11. Howe Point
Unlike much of the northern shoreline, this promontory is characterized by bog and kettle holes. A dominant plant is the bakeapple, a member of the raspberry family. From the vantage of the hills, you have a great view of much of the island and of the mainland.

12. Interior of Scatarie Island
Unlike the perimeter, much of the interior is forested—a tangle of spruce and fir with scarcely a deciduous tree in the entire mix. This impenetrable maze is traversed by several trails, cut during the days of human habitation and maintained by hunters. There are only a few ponds and no major streams. The island is a wildlife management area, but few large mammals make this their home. Deer survive on most of the large, forested offshore islands, but the once common red fox is gone. There are no moose or black bear. Attempts to introduce Arctic hare and ptarmigan were unsuccessful, brought to an end by the Great Horned Owl and poachers.

13. Shipwrecks
Scatarie Island is the meeting point of three major ocean currents, and in combination with the tides and winds, these produce some treacherous conditions. The ocean bottom is covered with shipwrecks—a potential pleasure for divers.

4   THE BIRD ISLANDS

DEPARTURE POINT:

Big Bras d'Or

Take Exit 14 on the Route 105 and follow signs to Big Bras d'Or. Accommodation available at a bed and breakfast or a private campground. Easy put in at the beach. Approximately 385 km (239 mi.) from Halifax.

Note: Another possible departure point is at Cape Dauphin, the shortest route to the islands. However, access from here involves a long carry down a hill over private property. First obtain permission from the owners.

ARRIVAL POINT:

Englishtown, or return to Big Bras d'Or.

You can take out at several spots near the Englishtown ferry, or at the campground on the northwest side of St. Anns Bay.

TRIP LENGTH:

Day-long or weekend, 25 km (15 mi.). From Cape Dauphin 12 km (7mi.).

CHARTS AND MAPS:

Topographical maps: 11/K/7,8

Marine chart: St. Andrews Channel-St. Anns Bay (#4277: 40,000)

ROUTE DESCRIPTION:

The Bird Islands have been aptly named. During breeding season, swarms of sea birds envelop these grassy islands in a cacophony, and they are a major destination of the avid bird-watcher. In fact, one of the islands, Hertford, has been acquired by the Nova Scotia Bird Society. The islands are the only major nesting area in Nova Scotia for the parrotlike Atlantic Puffin and one of the few breeding sites for the Black-legged Kittiwake. These are joined by Razorbills, Leach's Storm-Petrels, cormorants, guillemots, and gulls. The islands have not yet been formally protected but soon should be. Until then, paddlers are asked not to land on them before the end of the nesting season, mid-August. In any case, the noise and profuse guano, along with the difficult access to the plateau, render a casual stroll about the estate rather unpleasant.

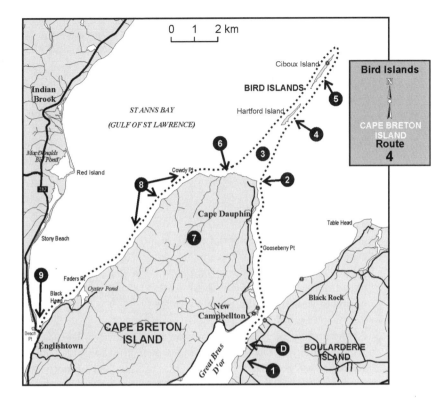

The birds and stratified rock are best viewed from the water.

The Bird Islands consist of horizontal, layered, sedimentary strata from the early Carboniferous era, which were deposited over 300 million years ago. Relatively soft and surrounded by the sea, they are eroding rapidly and much has been lost over time. Remains of early plant life are captured as fossils in the ancient sediments.

The mainland coast is a composite of several rock types of varied age and composition. The juxtaposition of granites, diorites, limestone, and sandstone are striking. A large limestone cave at the tip of Cape Dauphin has religious significance for the Mi'kmaq.

SAFETY CONSIDERATIONS:

The sea surrounding the Bird Islands is open to the elements, thus they should be visited only during calm weather. A strong southwest wind will often flow out of St. Anns Bay, gathering in momentum as it approaches the islands. Calculate sufficient time to paddle out and back, as well as for bird-watching. Camping isn't permitted on the islands during nesting season, and you should only land in an emergency. Note that there are few suitable landing spots, and even fewer good camping sites, along this route. (Refer to (9) in the Points of Interest.)

The islands are the backbone of a ledge extending out from Cape Dauphin. On the western side, the water is 40 m (131 ft.) deep, but on the east side it is only 20 m (66 ft.). Be aware of the considerable turbulence that may result when the underwater currents flow over it.

POINTS OF INTEREST:

1. Big Bras d'Or
A small village with a store, a campground, and a bed and breakfast, it is a good spot to put in. This is also the base of the Bird Island Tours, and if for any reason you don't have the desire or skill for a kayak journey in these waters, a boat tour is another option to view the bird life at close range.

2. Cape Dauphin
At the end of the New Campbellton Road, it is the closest spot from which to reach the islands. However, check with the local residents before dragging your equipment over their property. St. Anns Bay was originally called Port Dauphin after the eldest son of the king of France and was considered for their main fortifications before the French chose Louisbourg.

3. Hertford Ledge
It extends from the mainland to the islands just below the surface, with a drop of 20 m (66 ft.) on the western side. The overflow can vary from barely perceptible to very turbulent. Caution is advised.

4. Hertford Island
This is the smaller of the two islands. It is owned by the Nova Scotia Bird Society, which discourages any visits during nesting season. However, the cliffs that rim the islands are usually sufficient disincentive.

5. Ciboux Island
This island is crown land, and there are as yet no restrictions on access, although things may have changed by the time of publication. Effort is being made to place it under some kind of protection. However, regardless of its official status, you should not land until after nesting season. (In this case, not until mid-August.) Ciboux, as with Hertford, is a grassy plateau, surmounting, for the

most part, unassailable cliffs. A hefty spattering of guano whitens the landscape and scents the air during the nesting season. Gulls reside here en masse, as do Leach's Storm-Petrels, which avoid predation by building their nests at the end of tunnels and by entering and exiting them only at night. The soft, carboniferous strata forming the island is infused with assorted fossils. Preserved imprints of fronds and stems from an ancient fern forest, which once covered much of the present-day Gulf of St. Lawrence, are easily spotted in the exposed rock. The preferential erosion has produced cavities in the cliff face that provide safe havens for the puffins. Small coal veins are sandwiched between layers of sandstone, alluding to the much larger seams that have formed the industrial base of the nearby Sydneys.

The Bird Islands are the site of the only major Atlantic Puffin colony in Nova Scotia, one of two Razorbill colonies and one of a few Black-legged Kittiwake sites. These pelagic sea birds are near their southern nesting limits.

The Atlantic Puffin is a colourful sea bird that has been adopted as the official Cape Breton symbol, although it is found in only one spot on the island and totals less than fifty pairs. It is near the southernmost limit of its ranges with only one other

Black-legged Kittywakes nest in the cliff crevices of the Bird Islands.

known nesting site in Nova Scotia—Pearl Island—and a few others in New Brunswick and Maine. The bulk of the world population—several million—reside in Iceland. The puffin is easily identified by its conspicuous parrotlike beak, bright orange legs, and very rapid wing beats. Over most of its range, it nests at the end of a burrow or among the rocks. On the Bird Islands, however, they also use the naturally eroded holes in cliff faces. This has enabled them to evade the gulls, who would otherwise make short work of them. They nest in late May to early June (usually only one egg), and feed on small fish, often caught far out at sea. They sometimes arrange their catch in a neat row in their beaks when bringing them back to the nestlings.

The Razorbill, a relative of the Great Auk, which was hunted to extinction during the last century, is doing quite well in the isolation of Iceland. But only 2 per cent or 3 per cent breed in North America, and most of these in Labrador. Nova Scotia has three known nesting sites. The largest is the Bird Islands, but even here, there are probably less than one hundred nesting pairs, substantially lower than the estimated five hundred in 1925.

Presumably the Razorbills, puffins, and many other species were much more prevalent prior to the arrival of the Europeans. In addition to direct depletion due to use for food, eggs, and feathers, the introduction of cats, rats, and dogs completed the cleanup on many islands. Now that these offshore islands are reverting to their natural state, some of these sea birds may make a comeback, although the exploding gull population may keep them in check.

The Black-legged Kittiwake is a small dovelike gull that feeds far out to sea and comes to shore only to breed. It nests on narrow, rocky ledges 3 m to 8 m (10 ft. to 26 ft.) above the ocean. This is one of the only sea birds whose numbers are expanding in our region. Unknown to breed here prior to 1971, it now nests in several locations on eastern Cape Breton Island, its southernmost range. The Bird Islands site has over one hundred pairs, and this number is increasing.

6. The Fairy Hole

This is a fascinating series of connected chambers leading through the limestone into the heart of the mountain. I'm not certain how far it extends but certainly well beyond the distance that I felt comfortable with. Bring a powerful flashlight, with spare batteries, if you plan to explore.

This cave has symbolic significance for the Mi'kmaq. As legend has it, Glooscap once possessed a lodge here which he frequented. When visiting one day he noticed two maidens sitting beside the entrance. In order to impress them with his agility he jumped from his war canoe, breaking it in half. These pieces became the Bird Islands. The maidens found this somewhat amusing, which angered Glooscap so much that he turned them to stone. They remain to this day, in the form of two enormous boulders flanking the entrance. If weather or time make a paddle to the cave impossible, there is a marked trail leading to the cave from the end of the New Campbellton Road.

7. Kellys Mountain

This is hardly an alpine summit, but at 335 m (1,100 ft.) it is the highest point on the Nova Scotia segment of the Trans Canada Highway. The bulk of the mountain is ancient granite, dating from the Cambrian/Precambrian boundary. It is flanked on the eastern side by a complex mixture of sandstones, siltstones, limestone, quartzite, and numerous other rock types. Some highly deformed strata exposed on the top of the mountain may be over a billion years old. This region is significant to the Mi'kmaq as the resting place of their legendary prophet Glooscap. It is perhaps their most important religious shrine. A recent proposal to open a huge quarry in the mountain has worried and angered the Mi'kmaq, as well as nearby fishermen and tourist operators, who believe the operation will damage the Fairy Hole and detract from the natural beauty of the area—a classic conflict between development pressure and conservation.

8. Beaches and good campsites

They are scarce along the steep shores of this peninsula. However, Little Grappling Beach, Big Grappling Beach, and Sandy Beach offer a landing and a possible camping spot.

9. Englishtown

Here a car-ferry crosses a narrow constriction in St. Anns Bay. You may put in or take out near the ferry or leave from the campground on the northwest side of the bay.

5

THE HIGHLANDS ⟋⟍

DEPARTURE POINT:
La Bloc (Cape Breton Highlands National Park)
Drive to Chéticamp and continue north past the National Park Information Centre, 6 km (4 mi.). The total distance from Halifax is about 415 km (258 mi.). Overnight parking is not permitted at La Bloc and you will need to shuttle the vehicles back to the Information Centre where parking is free. Alternative departure sites, include Chéticamp Harbour and Pleasant Bay. There is a camping fee within the park (Fishing Cove) and a boat launching charge at Pleasant Bay.

ARRIVAL POINT:
Dingwall (Aspey Bay) or Ingonish. Note: Once past Pleasant Bay, the next chance to take out is at Meat Cove, a further 40 km (25 mi.)up the coast. If strong winds prevent departing from the western side you will usually be able to leave from the Ingonish side.

TRIP LENGTH:
Six to ten days, 85 km to 105 km (53 mi. to 65 mi.)
Note: It is certainly not obligatory to complete the entire route. Several enjoyable day-long and overnight options exist such as between Cheticamp and Pleasant Bay (overnight in Fishing Cove), North Pond, Meat Cove-Cape St. Lawrence, and Ingonish Harbour.

CHARTS AND MAPS:
Topographical maps: 11/K/10,15,16; 11/N/1,2
Marine charts: Chéticamp to Cape St. Lawrence (#4464: 74,500); Cape Smoky to St. Paul Island (#4363: 74,500) Although the total cost of the marine charts (roughly $40 Canadian) is about half the cost for the topographical maps, the latter are larger scale and indispensable for hiking.

ROUTE DESCRIPTION:
The Cape Breton Highlands have long been the favorite destination for visitors to Nova Scotia, often to the chagrin of those clamouring for more attention in the rest of the province. However, its tourist status is well deserved. The Cabot Trail, named for the fifteenth-century Venetian captain, John Cabot, who may, or may

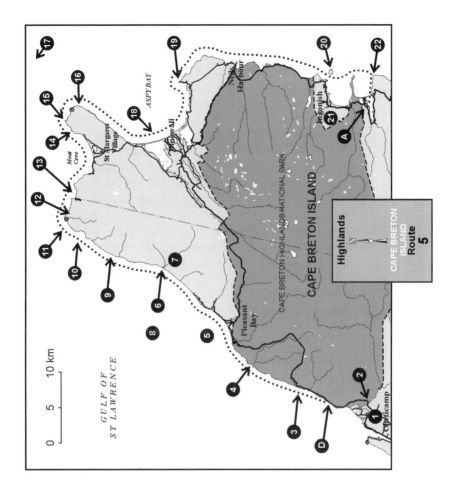

not, have visited these shores is a scenic drive that rivals any on the continent. Its winding path clings to a rugged terrain separating the Gulf of St. Lawrence from the Atlantic Ocean, where an ancient plateau erupts from the sea.

The rich hardwood forest flanking the Highlands belies the fact that it is much further north than the stunted woods surrounding my abode on the Eastern Shore. In fall, the colours are gorgeous. Only up on the barrens, out of sight from the coast, do budworm-denuded conifers betray a harsher climate and impoverished soils. These are claimed by the furtive lynx and the largest moose population in the province.

The shoreline is relatively linear, with no sheltering islands—

St. Paul Island is 15 km (9 mi.) offshore. Ancient, igneous bedrock alternates with deformed sedimentary strata to create the imposing cliffs that slide under the gulf waters in enormous sheets. Sea caves, arches, and overhanging crescent amphitheatres are carved into the escarpment. Shoals and spires litter the perimeter. From the perspective of the paddler, you will touch a geological variety that car campers only dream of. Wildlife flourishes. Bald Eagles peer from protected vantage points, seals sunbathe on the numerous reefs, and most impressive of all, the Pilot Whales range close to shore in pursuit of mackerel and squid. Occasionally you will also spot Black bears rambling along the cleared slopes.

This is also one of the few areas in Nova Scotia where hiking is a natural adjunct to a coastal paddling tour. Reminiscent of northern Scotland, with which the Cape Breton Highlands share earth history, much of the terrain is naturally denuded, and your ramblings are often unobstructed by the thick forest that is common along other shores. The views from the top are exceptional. This is one of the most imposing coastal regions in eastern North America.

Permanent European settlers were late in arriving to this inhospitable region. Even by the latter half of the 1700s, at a time when cities were sprouting along much of the eastern seaboard, this isolated place remained quasi-deserted. Accounts by shipwreck survivors paint images of a stark and unforgiving wilderness. One particularly vivid narrative (Castaway on Cape Breton, see Appendix) relates how a vessel foundered south of Chéticamp while en route to New York, during the American Revolution. Left with few provisions and a leaky lifeboat (and certainly no high tech overgarments) a tiny band of survivors sailed, rowed, and dragged their flimsy craft around the tip of the island in midwinter! The gulf pack ice crushed against the jagged shoreline, prodded by the extreme winds and biting cold that crept into the crevices of their inadequate clothing and froze their extremities. They struggled to St. Anns Bay, covering the entire highlands, before they encountered the first native encampment, and safety.

Settlers eventually did arrive: Acadians returning from exile, Loyalists fleeing defeat at the hands of the Yankees, and Scottish sharecroppers driven off their lands by British barons and their sheep. These late arrivals grasped any piece of land where they could drag a boat on shore and survived by fishing and some farming. It was a harsh existence, which we tend to romanticize

Impressive waterfalls tumble over the Highland cliffs onto the Gulf of St. Lawrence.

these days, and when better opportunities arose elsewhere, they took them.

By the time construction began on the Cabot Trail in the 1920s, some of the more isolated outposts, such as Fishing Cove, had already been abandoned. Today, much of the Highlands have been designated a National Park, and a few small communities cluster on the perimeter. Chéticamp and Ingonish are the largest.

SAFETY CONSIDERATIONS:

The Highlands route has advantages and disadvantages for safety. On the down side, its exposed shore provides few significant breaks in the escarpment, and when they do occur, as at Pollet Cove, they seldom offer anything more inviting to a weary paddler than a surf-washed cobble beach. Even during calm weather, extra care in landing is usually needed. The sheltered harbours, such as Pleasant Bay, Bay St. Lawrence, and Dingwall, are well separated. An offshore island belt, like that on the Eastern Shore, is absent.

The tidal range along this route is modest, under 3 m (10 ft.) and the resultant currents are minimal. However, ocean currents due to the counterclockwise flow of the gulf waters can be challenging in places. These exit into the Atlantic around the tip of the Highlands, such as Cape St. Lawrence and Cape North and can attain several knots. Unlike the tidal currents, they are dependent upon factors that aren't easily predictable—pressure areas, distant storms, and so on—and can be complicated by local winds and back eddies. Use caution in these areas.

While the maps may indicate an almost continuous scarp outside the major valleys, small beaches do exist which can serve as a haven in an emergency. (Note the upper storm line so as not to get trapped by a rising flood tide.) However, your only escape will still have to be by sea. Poor weather in this region means staying put, so include extra rations for those storm days. An exit overland will be blocked by either a vertical wall, a gully of brittle rock, or an algae-covered stream bed. Should you reach the plateau, you will then be met by a featureless terrain of bog and dense fir—a hiker's nightmare.

On the up side, the relatively warm seasonal water temperature, which can exceed 20°C (68°F), provides a welcome safety buffer. In fact, the gulf is consistently warmer than the streams draining the plateau. Even after rounding Cape North and into Aspy Bay the ocean temperature is still largely influenced by the gulf. As a result, fog is rare. Unlike on the Atlantic coastal islands, fresh water is abundant along with the attendant shower and washing "facilities."

Major summer storms are infrequent, and when they do occur they usually pass through quickly, and a rough sea dies almost simultaneously with the wind. There are periods in midseason when the ocean is calm for days. The prevailing southwesterly winds can help you up the western shore, but they will also create a chop and you should be comfortable with a following sea. Sometimes a persistent blow will force you to switch the departure point to the Ingonish side of the peninsula, although this has happened only in about 10 per cent of my trips. Be particularly wary in places where winds interact with the current. Towards the end of summer expect a more frequent and stronger northerly flow. Several rivers and innumerable streams provide abundant fresh water even in the driest of summers. Boiling is advised, especially in valleys where livestock is pastured.

Calcite seams intertwine with the layers of slate and sandstone near Meat Cove.

POINTS OF INTEREST:

1. Chéticamp

It is the largest Acadian village in Nova Scotia—nearly 3,000 inhabitants including the surrounding hamlets—and French remains the predominate language. It was settled well after control of the island had been gained by the English with the capture of the Fortress of Louisbourg in 1758. The Acadians, who had been deported, or who had eluded capture, and subsequently returned, sought out remote coastlines where isolation would reduce potential harassment by the British. According to one story, they landed on Chéticamp Island before 1760 and moved up on the plateau, out of sight.

However, survivors of a wreck in 1780 found no sign of any permanent settlement. The first recorded settlement was in 1786.

Chéticamp is a service centre with several food and hardware stores, gas stations, and ample accommodation; however, advance reservation is essential during July and August. The holiday bustle and Acadian ambience make this an attractive destination and the newly renovated waterfront adds to the appeal. Whale-watching tours are available.

The coastal plain between the Highlands and the gulf was originally a lush forest of sugar maple, pine, and oak and, as early as the mid-1600s, it was heavily logged for the European navies. Much of it had already disappeared before the Acadians settled; none of the original forest remains today. The rolling topography consists mostly of windswept fields and conifer woods.

2. Cape Breton Highlands National Park Visitor Reception Centre

It has excellent displays on the natural and human history of the park—the oldest in Eastern Canada, declared in 1936—and a well-stocked book store specializing in nature themes—from whales to forest ecology, from bog flora to the highland geology. Park staff are knowledgeable. The campground is well laid out with wooded sites, picnic shelters, hot showers, and a laundromat.

Prior to launching, you require a camping permit for Fishing Cove—reserve early since space is limited and taken mainly by backpackers who hike down from the Cabot Trail. Tel. (902) 224-2306 summer; (902) 425-3436 winter. Expect some questions about your paddling experience, although there are as yet no rules specifically governing paddling along park boundaries.

La Bloc is an excellent departure point; easily accessible, with a gentle cobble shore, adjacent picnic tables, and toilet facilities. The weathered concrete wharf predates the park and provides shelter from all but the most direct onshore winds. This is where the best coastline begins. Corney Brook, a park campground and another departure option is 2 km (1.2 mi.) further north although access to the beach is over a steep embankment. Since Fishing Cove is normally a three-hour paddle, plan ahead before committing yourself. Onshore winds will rapidly build a dumping surf, and there are few good landing sites en route. Pigeon Cove is the best, although it, too, offers little shelter. Strong and sustained westerly winds—common during late summer and fall—might dictate a departure on the east, to Ingonish, side.

3. From Cape Rouge to Red Head

paddle close to the cliffs if water conditions permit, under the cormorant nests—hence the name Shag Roost—and waterfalls, if the season has been a rainy one. Keep an eye out for sea caves, particularly ones that reach more than 30 m (100 ft.) into the mountain through an unassuming entrance. The name Red Head refers to the rust-coloured granites. Nova Scotia has well over a dozen "Red Heads" but most are sandstones. The White Capes, a little further up the coast, are named for the quartz veins that have entered fissures in the granites. This bedrock was formed deep under the earth's surface and is now exposed, due to crustal uplift and erosion. Watch for black bears on the hillsides. Pigeon Cove, a large crescent-sand and cobble beach, lies between Red Head and White Capes. It gets its name from the Black Guillemot, a short, stubby sea bird with bright orange webbed feet. The guillemot is closely related to the Atlantic Puffin and to the extinct Great Auk. It nests on the bare cliff ledges.

4. Fishing Cove

This is the best and only officially sanctioned coastal camping site on this side of the park. Pigeon Cove, 3 km (2 mi.) south, offers some refuge in an emergency but little shelter from a rough sea or strong onshore winds. The narrow valley supported several families until the early part of this century, when the only way in and out was via the sea. It was abandoned before the park was established. There are campsites (with unsightly wood platforms) on the cleared hillside, fire grates with fuel wood (no open fires permitted), and an outhouse. A large stream runs through the valley, forming a pool behind the cobble bar (which is rearranged during every storm), ideal for lounging in fresh (but cold!) water. At the entrance to the cove are several sea caves. This is a scenic spot, and one of the best overnight hiking destinations in the park, so don't expect to have it to yourself.

5. Pleasant Bay

Along with Bay St. Lawrence and Dingwall, this is the most sheltered harbour on this route. Originally, it was only a shallow river entering the gulf through a gravel bar. It has since been enlarged and periodically dredged. The village was settled by the Scots and English in the 1800s and, until 1927, it was accessible only by water or a narrow footpath over the mountains. Many of the inhabitants moved here from more isolated communities, including Fishing Cove. Pleasant Bay was almost totally destroyed in

1948, when a forest fire swept the valley and the surrounding hills. Everyone had to be evacuated by sea and sent to a tent city outside Chéticamp. Today, the artificial harbour is maintained by breakwaters and regular dredging.

The shallow bay has a long, mainly sand beach below sandstone cliffs. These have been scoured by the glaciers and are overlain by thick deposits of till. The boundary between the two is abrupt. Further in the valley, the lush hardwood forest suggests a temperate climate, in spite of its northerly setting. At the northern edge of their range, Sugar maple, White ash, and Red oak follow the meandering Grand Anse River. The village has a general store, restaurants, and a motel. It is an optional departure point (a small launching fee is charged) and stopover when the surf poses problems on the other beaches. I've camped beside the breakwater when stuck.

6. Polletts Cove

Long before I ever embarked in a sea kayak or canoe I discovered this Shangri-la well beyond the reach of the car and casual wanderer. A three- to four-hour winding coastal hike leads to a dramatic confluence of river valleys, forested slopes, and hidden fields, unlike any other in the province. Although the early inhabitants have long since left, field stone foundations, root cellars, and a graveyard recount a past familiar to most of Nova Scotia's coastal areas. In the spring, cattle and sometimes horses forage unattended until the first snows push them out. Note: These creatures can take a liking to salty tents, so be forewarned. There is no sheltered landing spot in the 8 km (5 mi.) between Pleasant Bay and Pollets Cove, so make sure that the conditions are right before heading up. At Pollets Cove a broad, driftwood-dominated cobble beach invites a surf in all but the most benign conditions. Also, a large temperature difference from day to night can funnel strong land breezes down from the Highlands, and tents in the open have been flattened.

7. The Plateau

A natural adjunct to paddling along this route is the superb hiking. From Pollets Cove, a trail of sorts leads up to the barren plateau. To get there, cross to the north side of the river and follow the fields a few hundred metres above the beach. Then turn right, up the slope through the regenerating spruce, into an open wood and out onto a small field. The stone remains of a foundation will indicate that you are at the right spot. This is already a great view of the cove and the gulf, and blueberries are abundant in late summer. Continue north, into the Sugar maple woods above the field, where a blazed path first leads down and then gradually up to a steep gully. Follow the stream bed up to the top. (Caution: this section involves some scrambling over wet, slippery rock.)

North of Pollets Cove this spire of resistant conglomerate has separated from the mainland.

On a clear day you can scan the Highlands weaving down the coastline towards Pleasant Bay, and you can pick out the Magdalen Islands. This is an ideal vantage point for spotting Pilot Whales. The border of the plateau is open and rolling and offers an incredible panorama down into the Blair River gorge. Some maps indicate a trail leading from here to Meat Cove, at the very tip of the island, but it is nonexistent. A featureless melange of budworm-decimated fir, open barren, and impassable bog will soon frustrate even the hardiest hiker. However, this is the preferred habitat of moose, and we have sighted them wandering over the open terrain.

If you decide to hike, wear good footwear and bring food, drink, and emergency supplies. Carry a map and compass and give yourself a full day—it will take two to three hours just to get to the top. Be on the look out for the arrival of low clouds. They bring along lower temperatures and stronger winds, and can reduce visibility to near zero. Be wary, too, of improvising a return descent into another valley. It may take a longer and be much more difficult than you anticipate.

8. Pilot Whales

Locally known as Blackfish, they frequent the highland coastline from August to September, feeding on the seasonal squid and mackerel (dense schools travel near the surface, breaking the water in noisy unison). These are among the smallest of the toothed whales, usually under 6 m (20 ft.) but certainly massive enough to excite a paddler. I've paddled with them on over 80 per cent of my trips up this coast, and they can pass within a few feet of the boat.

9. The High Capes

This is possibly the most spectacular part of this route. This small section of an ancient Precambrian shield resembles the stark coastline of northern Scotland. Enormous bedrock buttresses border deep gullies, where fast-moving streams tumble down into the gulf, often ending in a waterfall. Rock spires, sea caves, and tortured shoals provide unending fascination and an intricate pathway for expert paddlers who weave among. For several kilometres, a safe landing in rough weather is impossible. However, on the south side of Delaney Brook, a level plateau of eroding glacial till forms an acceptable campsite, adjacent to an impressive waterfall. Patterned schists and gneisses cover the beach. It is exposed to the westerly winds, and tree cover is limited.

10. Lowland Cove

Here the Highlands descend onto younger carboniferous hills which, cleared during previous settlement, form one of the few accessible camping spots along this section of the route. A trail links to Meat Cove, a two-hour hike, and horses and cattle are sometimes pastured. The cove is fringed with steep boulder beaches, much rougher than at Pollets Cove, the result of an incessant and violent surf and the longshore currents that move any available sediment up the coast. Landing will often be difficult, and your stay may be prolonged in poor weather.

The Cape Breton Highlands are home to the largest moose population in the province.

11. Cape St. Lawrence

This is a relatively nondescript headland, marked by a navigation beacon alongside the ruins of the former light station. The gulf currents that pass into the Atlantic around this point can vary from negligible (usually) to frightening (once in a while). Approach with caution. Should circumstances dictate, you can usually land at the small cove just prior to the actual cape—easier than landing right at Lowland Cove—to await improved conditions. There is a stream and campsites.

12. The cliffs between Cape St. Lawrence and Meat Cove

These vividly demonstrate the sheer power of crustal movement.

Hundreds of metres of layered carboniferous bedrock have been folded and faulted into colourful bands that, at times, drop vertically and, at times, slide into the ocean in huge sheets. Fossils and ripple marks are embedded in the rock at Fraser Beach, which has been intruded by massive, ice-white calcite veins. Erosion has cut caves and arches. The scattered beaches are held like prisoners between the Highlands and the sea.

13. Meat Cove

This is the northernmost community in Nova Scotia. It is at the end of a winding dirt road that hugs the eroding cliff face (and has sent more than one careless driver into oblivion). It is also the first potential take out after Pleasant Bay, 33 km (20 mi.). A private campground overlooks the Cabot Strait—a departure point for a short tour of the cliffs should a southerly blow prevent the longer trip. According to one story, Meat Cove traces its name to the French occupation of Louisbourg. In the autumn, the fortress garrison would round up the woodland caribou, which still inhabited the Highlands at that time, and stampede them over the cliffs. After butchering the animals, the meat was shipped to feed the fortress inhabitants.

14. White Rock

Trapped in the surrounding igneous rocks are these massive vertical marble veins. This is the only spot along the coastline of the province where you will find marble cliffs. A small cove, set into the rock face and partially sheltered by islets, offers the last refuge before the cape.

15. Cape North

This is the northernmost point on Cape Breton Island and also one of the highest at 350 m (1,150 ft.). The coastline here is sprinkled with shoals and islets and landing is possible only in the most benign sea conditions.

16. Money Point

Here an automated light station dominates the low, treeless coastal fringe. The original classic tower was removed in order to adorn a federal museum lawn in Ottawa. A narrow, steep trail—for four-wheel drive only—leads over the mountain and down into Bay St. Lawrence. A short distance along the coast, towards Dingwall, are the scattered remains of a large grain freighter, which was driven ashore during a hurricane where you will find a sheltered camping site. However, the currents around this point and Cape North can be very strong. Note: although one side may be sheltered from the wind and relatively calm, just around the bend, pandemonium may be waiting.

17. St. Pauls Island

It lies in the Cabot Strait, 15 km (9 mi.) northeast of Cape North, and its 152 m (500 ft.) cliffs beckon on a clear day. However, I recommend avoiding the temptation. The island was known as the "graveyard of the gulf"—second only to Sable Island in the number of wrecks off its shores. The currents can be strong and unpredictable, and landing spots are few. There are no sheltered harbours. Numerous shipwrecks—one in which over eight hundred lost their lives—ring the bottom. Before 1832, and the days of life stations, survivors from a winter sinking would slowly starve to death while the mainlanders watched their signal fires, helpless as pack ice prevented a rescue attempt. A change in weather could strand you for days, if not longer, and the local fishermen are less than pleased with incompetent paddlers who end up requiring assistance.

18. Dingwall

Extensive barrier beaches have formed at the head of Aspy Bay, practically sealing off the shallow North and South Ponds. Be wary of strong currents at the outlets. One of the tiny islets in North Pond (Lead Island) is home to a large cormorant and Black-backed gull colony. Another has a tern colony. Wild oysters are plentiful. The village sits atop a large gypsum deposit, mined from 1933 to 1955, and its harbour is dredged and protected with breakwaters. In 1761, there was no harbour and the French vessel *Auguste* foundered in a futile attempt to enter the river during a fall storm; 114 lives were lost.

There is evidence that the Aspy Valley, which extends deep into the Highlands behind Dingwall, is a continuation of the Great Glen fault in northern Scotland and was formed during the Carboniferous era as the continents were moving alongside one another.

19. White Point

It is situated at the southern rim of Aspy Bay and provides a panoramic view of the Highlands. It can be reached via a short hike from the village of White Point or by kayak or canoe, when the weather is appropriate. The cobble stone coves are steep and exposed, and the currents flowing out of the bay can be very strong. A pioneer graveyard marks the point. The two islands off the tip are nesting sites for gulls and terns. Just around the point are sea caves.

The rest of the coast to Ingonish is a low relief of metamorphic and igneous bedrock, with few sheltering coves. Neil's Harbour is one. The Cabot Trail and the associated look-offs closely parallel the shoreline.

20. Ingonish Island

This is the only large island along the Highlands route, (except for St. Pauls). It is uninhabited and has an automated light station. The former lighthouse keeper's house is succumbing to the elements. The fields on the western side, where sheep once grazed, are thick with raspberry bushes and thistles and alive with the sound and smells of gulls during nesting time. Along the eastern shore of the island, sheer rock is highlighted by sea caves and "The Chimney," an impressive 30 m (100 ft.) spire, draped with cormorant droppings. Archaic native implements (7000 B.C.) have been unearthed on the island. Portuguese fishermen may have overwintered in 1521, making it one of the oldest European "settlements" on the Atlantic seaboard.

21. Ingonish

This marks the eastern entrance and administrative headquarters of the National Park. It has campgrounds, a golf course, and a variety of accommodations, which should be booked early.

22. Cape Smokey

With its 274 m (900 ft.) granite cliffs, it dominates Ingonish Bay. The mountain highway is often blocked during winter storms, isolating Ingonish from the rest of the world. The area has yet to completely recover from the effects of a major forest fire that occurred over thirty years ago.

(A) Ingonish Harbour: This is a sheltered arrival point, but be careful when entering the narrow channel. A good take out is at the beacon on the south side of the entrance. There are other possible landing spots in both the South and North Bays.

Mabou to Port Hood 6

Departure Point:
Mabou
Follow Route l9 after crossing the Canso Causeway, approximately 330 km (205 mi.) from Halifax. There are several possible launching spots near Mabou village.

Arrival Point:
Port Hood or Little Judique Harbour.

Trip Length:
Two or three days, 30 km to 40 km (19 mi. to 25 mi.).

Charts and Maps:
Topographical maps: 11 K/3,4; 11 F/13
Marine chart: Port Hood, Mabou Harbour (#4448: 18,000)
Detailed but lacking a small coastal section between them.

Route Description:
The southwest coast of Cape Breton Island is considerably different from its southeast shores. The terrain is more hilly—the Mabou Highlands rise over 305 m (1,000 ft.)—the bedrock is younger and softer with sandstones, slates, and gypsum, and there are fewer shoals. This route also has two relatively large islands—Port Hood and Henry—and, except for Margaree Island, these are the only ones along Cape Breton's entire Gulf of St. Lawrence shore. Warmer water, especially within Mabou Harbour and a temperate climate have resulted in a richer forest, with maple, ash and oak instead of spruce and fir.

Mabou Harbour is the largest inlet on this side of Cape Breton Island; otherwise the shoreline weaves around modest headlands and into broad coves. Active erosion has eaten away at the Hogs back (drumlins) and soft sedimentary stone, leaving many steep, loose cliffs. Landing spots and beaches are common. Coal seams are exposed at several locations.

This was the site of early Scottish settlement—Gaelic is still spoken by some older residents—and many of the coastal hills were cleared for pasture. Much is still farmed, dairy in particular. It is a picturesque area, but not one for those seeking serious isolation.

SAFETY CONSIDERATIONS:

This shoreline is exposed to the prevailing southwesterlies, and a fair chop can develop as the winds flow unobstructed up the Northumberland Strait. If you aren't careful, you might be faced with a surf landing on a rocky shore. The currents at the entrance to Mabou Harbour and between Henry and Port Hood Islands, can be quite strong. Elsewhere, they are minimal. The warm water, infrequent fog, and extensive beaches make this an alternative route when an Atlantic coast trip has to be cancelled due to poor weather.

POINTS OF INTEREST:

1. Mabou

It has a population of about 400. Founded by Scottish settlers in the early 1800s, it is situated within the best dairy country on the island. It has a grocery store, a couple of restaurants, and accommodation. You can even begin your tour from a historic local bed and breakfast.

2. Mabou Harbour

It is the largest and most sheltered harbour along this coastline. It is a drowned estuary that has been carved out of soft sedimentary strata. White gypsum deposits are exposed in several places along the shore. The contrasts of open harbour bordered by meandering streams, salt marsh, and high hills make this an attractive locale.

3. Tern colony

A tiny sand island near the harbour entrance is a nesting site for the Common Tern.

4. McKeens Point

The mobile sand dunes of McKeens Point would close off the harbour mouth, except for the effluent of the Mabou River system. This is a popular local beach.

5. Green Point to Mabou Mines

The shoreline consists of steep cliffs of soft conglomerate, 137 m (450 ft.), and gypsum with coal outcrops. They are rapidly eroding. Guillemots and a large colony of Great Cormorants nest on ledges. Their guano fertilizes the algae and lichens that cover the walls like abstract paintings in green, orange, and white. Hillside fields run down to the cliffs, but the gradual encroachment of summer homes has begun to taint the pastoral ambience.

6. Coal Mine Point

It was exploited from 1899–1909, during which about 60,000

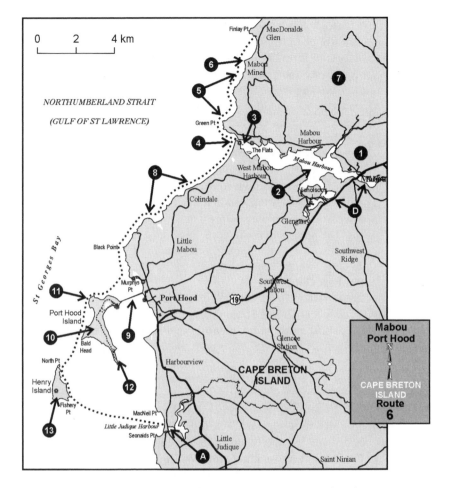

Mabou
Port Hood

N

CAPE BRETON
ISLAND
Route
6

tonnes of coal were extracted. The seams extend out under the Gulf of St. Lawrence and were mined until a tunnel was driven too close to the sea bed, and it flooded. Coal seams are exposed in the sandstones and shales along the south shore of the point. Large mounds of tailings overlook the water and railway ties extend from the cliffs.

7. Mabou Highlands

These are the remnants of an uplifted plateau which has been extensively eroded. The margins have been deeply cut, forming a series of long gorges which are covered in deciduous forest. The area is spectacular, especially under fall foliage, and is an under-rated hiking destination.

8. Hog's Back

This stretch of the route is much different from that north of the Mabou Harbour. The steep cliffs have been reduced to a drumlin topography, once referred to as Hogs Back, and there are many more landing spots. This is still farming country, but the buildings are well back from the water. There are several secluded camping sites where streams run into the gulf.

9. Breakwater

It connects Port Hood to the island of the same name and was constructed in the 1950s. Once a natural land bridge linked the two. Sandstone was used from a nearby quarry and a rough roadway was laid over top. However, only one vehicle—an oil truck—made a return crossing before a major storm washed the roadway out. The breakwater was never repaired and is gradually disintegrating. It is now exposed only during low tide. A channel dredged recently has further reduced its effectiveness.

10. Port Hood Island

It was settled in the late 1700s by Loyalists who left the newly independent United States. A large, prosperous fishing community evolved until the early part of this century, when, along with most of the other offshore islands, the Port Hood inhabitants gradually moved to the mainland for better services and opportunities. Today, there is a single year-round family who stay only as caretakers for the homes that have been sold as summer retreats. A gravel road runs the length of the island, and the old lobster cannery sits, rotting, near the wharf. Most of the island is privately owned and the owners are aloof at best and not keen on campers. The atmosphere is entirely different from the Tusket Islands, near Yarmouth, which are still used traditionally and welcome visitors.

11. Vertical Point

This striking limestone arch borders marbled cliffs with a rich chocolate brown colour. The texture of the rock in this whole area is unusual.

12. Quarried Stone

Between Portsmouth Point and the spithead is a run of cliffs that were quarried by the French for building stone during the construction of the fortress at Louisbourg. Easily accessible and of high quality, this stone was also used for a hotel in Halifax. Today, except to the trained eye, there is little to indicate this previous activity.

13. Henry Island

This was my departure point for an eventful crossing of St. Georges Bay during my 1980 circumnavigation of the province. The original inhabitants have left, but the classic white-and-red striped light tower remains, surrounded by regenerating coastal spruce. Should you plan to camp here, be discreet as it is also privately owned. Caution: the passage between Port Hood Island and Henry Island is shallow, and a strong current funnels through during flood tide.

7   THE BRAS D'OR LAKE

DEPARTURE POINT:
River Denys
Follow Route 105 (Trans Canada) after crossing the Canso Causeway. Take Exit 3 and continue to River Denys. Launch at the bridge. Approximately 310 km (192 mi.) from Halifax.

ARRIVAL POINT:
West Bay Village, or 5 km (3 mi.) sooner at the provincial beach of Malcolm Cove/MacKenzie Point. Due to the coastal road, it is possible to take out nearly anywhere along this route.

TRIP LENGTH:
Two to three days, 55 km (34 mi.).

CHARTS AND MAPS:
Topographical maps: 11/F/11,14,15
Marine chart: Bras d'Or Lake (#4279: 60,000)

ROUTE DESCRIPTION:
The Bras d'Or Lake is a unique saltwater paddling destination, different from the remaining ocean coastline in the province and also unlike any freshwater lake. It is a huge inland sea, over 1,150 km2 (444 sq. mi.), occupying much of central Cape Breton Island and linked to the Atlantic by two deep, narrow channels—the Great Bras d'Or and the St. Andrews—as well as a canal at St. Peters. The Bras d'Or has been carved from relatively soft carboniferous strata (sandstones, limestones conglomerates, gypsum, and such) that still fringes the older and more resistant highlands. Its bays and channels are elongated parallel to the ridges or uplands.

Bras d'Or Lake, (Bras d'Or means "Arm of Gold" in French, but it may originally stem from Portuguese,) is a deep basin that descends to over 180 m (590 ft.) in places. A limited exchange with the open ocean results in a negligible tidal range, and combined with the freshwater run-off from the surrounding hills, a reduced salinity—less that half that of the Atlantic. Currents are insignificant (See Safety Considerations).

The climate here is considerably more temperate, and the water warmer than along the Atlantic coast, although in the winter

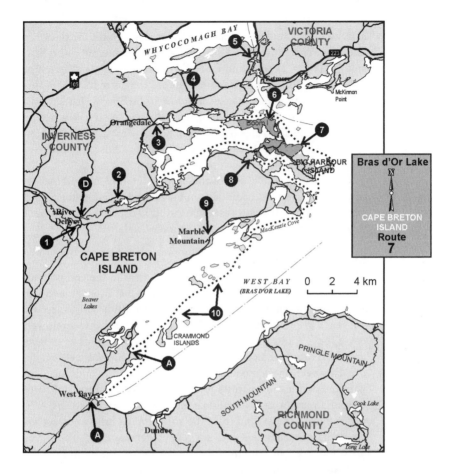

much of it freezes. Fog is uncommon. The moderate conditions have produced a rich forest cover with hardwoods predominating. In autumn, the hills are ablaze with colour. Storms erode the soft banks, undermining trees that collapse, bleached and tangled, onto a coastline devoid of a littoral zone. The liberated sand collects into innumerable narrow spits and gentle beaches, which often imprison a shallow pond. Below are the seaweeds and seashells that confirm the lake's marine nature. Above, you will sight members of the largest Bald Eagle population in the province. Good campsites are at a premium in the ubiquitous woodland, but beaches are plentiful and you don't have to worry about a flood tide washing away your domicile.

The Bras d'Or Lake is not pristine wilderness and human

activity is apparent from the moment you launch till the time you take out. The shores are a mosaic of open farmland, old fields, small villages, cabins, and meandering roads that skirt much of the lake. On the water, pleasure boats are the norm in season; this is a prime sailing destination. However, the Bras d'Or Lake still offers opportunities for paddling, especially when the weather, or your level of skill, rules out more exposed coasts. You can put in almost anywhere and poke around a pastoral landscape unique to Cape Breton Island.

The following route is one of the best on the lake, a combination of winding river and open basin, of sheltered marsh and exposed spit, of soft beach and forested island. It is a gentle environment that will take you away from the summer bustle.

SAFETY CONSIDERATIONS:

The Bras d'Or Lake offers several advantages to the coastal paddler. During summer, the water may exceed 20°C (68°F), and wet suits can be exchanged for bathing suits and snorkels. Tides and currents are negligible, and there are innumerable sheltered coves, bays, and gentle sand beaches. The water calms as soon as any wind drops, and ocean swells and dumping surf are absent.

However, these moderating factors might lull you into a dangerous complacency. In its widest sections, the Bras d'Or can exceed 15 km (9 mi.), which is a major fetch. Strong winds, arising quickly, can descend from the surrounding hills, and accelerate up narrow channels to create a considerable chop. The waves are often steep and run into one another, much different than the extended ocean pattern. Avoid long crossings. Currents, though usually slight, increase in the channels. In the narrow entrance to the lake they can exceed 10 km/hr (6 mi./hr). Freshwater streams are plentiful, but the water should be boiled or filtered prior to drinking.

POINTS OF INTEREST:
1.   Village of River Denys

It was named after the early French explorer and trader Nicolas Denys, who established a small settlement and trading post in southern Cape Breton at St. Peters in the mid 1600s. There are few houses in this isolated part of the island, but you can leave your vehicle at the general store next to the bridge, the departure point.

2. River Denys

The journey down the River Denys takes you from a lazy and winding freshwater stream into a exposed salt water basin. The initial border of dense alder bush gradually gives way to open lowland and marsh, where fields and farms still occupy the higher ground. This is an important habitat for waterfowl production and staging area for teal, American Black Duck, and Ring-necked Duck. You may also spot mink or muskrat.

3. Orangedale

This alternative departure point is a quaint pastoral village, with a historic railway museum.

4. Gillis Cove

This is the site of a federal oyster research program. The warm salt water of Bras d'Or Lake holds promise for aquaculture.

The warm water and lush vegetation belie the fact that the Bras d'Or Lakes are part of the ocean.

5. Whycocomagh Portage

The Mi'kmaq transported their canoes over the narrow Whycocomagh Portage (0.5 km) between the main body of Bras d'Or Lake and the Whycocomagh Bay.

6. Boom Island

This is an important Bald Eagle nesting site. It is a low-lying forested area with extensive marsh.

7. Malagawatch Indian Reserve

This is one of five Mi'kmaq reserves on the lake. Long before the arrival of the Europeans, Bras d'Or Lake was a centre for Mi'kmaq population and culture.

8. Canal

This early canal linked Denys Basin with Malagawatch Harbour. It can still be used as a short cut, but a bar obscures the northern entrance and a portage is also needed over the dirt road.

9. Marble Mountain

It is hardly a mountain but part of the ridge, not exceeding a height of 250 m (820 ft.), that runs the length of this shoreline. A quarry operated from 1870 to 1920 and employed over 750 people at its peak. The sheer pit face stands out and the beach is white with chips of marble and limestone. A museum in the village describes the area's history.

10. West Bay

The islands here are low, uninhabited—except for summer residences on a few—and forest covered. The trees often grow to the edge, where they are undermined by the water. Numerous sand beaches hide brackish ponds, and exposed spits stretch out into the bay. Good campsites are often difficult to find in the thick woods.

COASTAL PADDLING ROUTES
OF THE NORTH SHORE

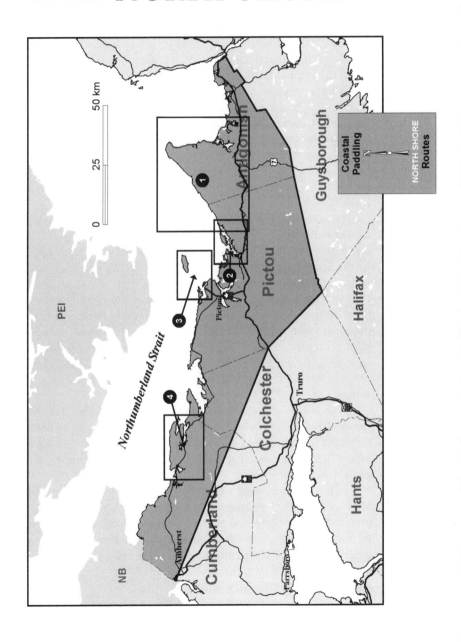

INTRODUCTION

The fog thickened and we gradually lost sight of land. The wind picked up slightly too, but we scarcely noticed it and managed the heavier swell with ease. We should have attached the spray cover as soon as we had perceived the change, but because of sloth or a false sense of security, we did not; our minds were elsewhere. When the storm did strike, we were unprepared.

A huge wave arched up in front of the canoe and crashed over Paul, drenching him and filling the canoe with several centimetres of water. How we managed to avoid the second wave and thus complete submersion in St. Georges Bay remains a mystery. We were shocked out of our daydreams and into the frightening realization that we were 17 km (11 mi.) from shore. We couldn't have picked a more inopportune time to be careless, and I was scared.

We acted quickly: Paul steadied the canoe in the heavy seas; I hauled out the nylon cover and began fastening it to the sides. It was not an easy job. The canoe was very unwieldy, made unstable by the large amount of water sloshing about the bottom, and I realized that one false move would put us under. We talked little. Only our six weeks' experience in ocean paddling saved us from being swamped. With the canoe covered, all that remained was to pump the water out. Half an hour later, that also was accomplished. But the crossing was far from over. The wind, by then at least 20 knots and rising, churned up the ocean and visibility had dropped to under a hundred metres. We were tired and wet, and wanted to rest but had to struggle on.

Five hours after the wave struck we still could not see the shore, although the fog had partially lifted and a full moon shone through the mist. It was a scene of surreal beauty. We spotted a wharf light in the distance, and it became our destination, our guide to safety.

In the early morning we finally hit the beach—twelve hours after we had left Cape Breton. By then the sky had cleared completely, the wind had died and the sea resembled a sheer black mirror. We had no idea where we were, nor did we care. All we desired then was sleep, and with our remaining strength we dragged the canoe onto the shore, unpacked our sleeping bags, and collapsed onto the warm sand.

Early the next morning the sunlight crept lazily over the marine horizon and nudged us awake. Even our exhaustion wasn't enough to keep us comfortable on the sloping sand beach, as the increasing warmth of the motionless air soaked into our bodies. The ocean was silent. Perhaps the previous night had been only a dream, but as I collected my muddled thoughts, I knew that it had been real.

Upon crossing St. Georges Bay, we left Cape Breton Island behind. We entered the Northumberland Strait—and the only period of true summer weather in our entire journey around Nova Scotia. For nearly two weeks we were bathed in warm, humid air

The sand beaches and warm water stretch uninterrupted for miles along the North Shore.

while floating over a calm and temperate sea. Dense fog gave way to bright sunshine, and bulky clothing was changed for swimsuits and snorkel gear. After numbing our toes in the Atlantic, this was a real treat.

The North Shore is one of Nova Scotia's four distinctive geological regions. It forms the southern rim of the Gulf of St. Lawrence, where it stretches from the New Brunswick border, at Baie Verte, to the tip of Cape George, and then around to the Canso Causeway. The total distance is only about 200 km (124 mi.), but this would increase substantially if we measured all the bays and inlets. Prince Edward Island shelters the area somewhat, forming the Northumberland Strait, 15 km to 30 km (9 mi. to 19 mi.) across.

Here, the coastal paddler will find some of the warmest salt water north of Virginia, certainly the warmest in this province. It can exceed 20°C (70°F) in the sheltered coves and marshes. Fog is rare in the summer. Large swells are absent and days will pass when there is barely a ripple. Be aware, though, that a steep chop will rise quickly when a strong wind funnels down the strait. The tides are modest—under 1 m (4 ft.) The currents are usually weak and travel mostly from west to east as part of the counterclockwise movement in the gulf. An exception is where the flow is constricted somewhat between Pictou Island and the mainland shore. The prevailing southwesterly winds carry a warmth and fragrance from the mainland that belies the surroundings—this is still the ocean.

This coastline is part of a large carboniferous basin that underlies the Gulf of St. Lawrence and much of northern Nova Scotia and New Brunswick. It was formed eons ago. The continents had coalesced, pushing Africa and Europe up against an early North America, and the whole region—part of a supercontinent named Pangea—was situated somewhere near the equator. Erosion from ancient mountains layered several kilometres of sediments into a landlocked basin which was intruded intermittently by sea water. Subsequent crustal uplift and a humid climate resulted in a system of deltas, estuaries, and flood plains supporting a lush ecosystem that was stable for millions of years. All these processes combined to produce the deposits of salt, limestone, gypsum, coal, and especially sandstone that now define the region.

The gentle topography of the coastal plain, which extends from Baie Verte to Merigomish Island, alternates low ridges with shallow valleys. The ridges extend into the Northumberland Strait as headlands in several places, such as Cape John and Malagash Point, with Pictou Island a remnant of one such ridge in the centre of the strait. The valleys have formed inlets and harbours where river estuaries have been flooded by a rise in sea level. Variable but ubiquitous glacial till covers the region. The soft bedrock and abundant sediment on the North Shore have produced numerous beaches, bay mouth bars, sand bars, spits, dunes, salt marshes, and mud flats. None of the original forest is left and white spruce and red maple characterize the wooded areas today. Further inland are stands of sugar maple and large areas that have been converted to blueberry barrens.

The extensive intertidal zones, formed by the very gradual slope of the sea bottom, are rich in invertebrate animals, such as clams, mussels, and marine worms. There are extensive salt marshes and eel beds in the bays. These are important waterfowl breeding and migratory staging areas. Ducks, geese, and shorebirds seldom seen elsewhere are common. Seals, dolphins, and porpoises can also be spotted.

An exception to this low-lying landscape is the cliffs that stretch from Merigomish Island around Cape George and down part way to Antigonish. East of a fault that follows the shoreline are the older and more resistant igneous and metamorphic rocks of the Antigonish Highlands.

The North Shore was frequented by the Mi'kmaq who prized the large shellfish beds. When the French first arrived, they dyked and drained many of the marshlands, where they farmed until they were expelled by the English. In 1773, a large contingent of Scots arrived and founded the town of Pictou. Settlement spread up the coastline, and today there are several communities with Scottish ancestry—in the largest is New Glasgow, population over 9,000—with a diverse economic base in farming fishing, coal and salt mining, forestry, and pulp production.

The climate along this shore is more conducive to agriculture than on most other coastal areas in the province; there is even a prosperous vineyard and wine-making industry. Increasingly important is the tourism industry which takes advantage of the sun, sand, and warm water. Along with Prince Edward Island, the North Shore has become a mecca for the vacation crowd. Some camp in tents, some bring a motor home, and others stay in cottages that crowd popular beaches. Sail and motorboats compete for water space near the resorts.

For the paddler, a little seclusion can still be found, but wilderness campsites aren't as readily spotted and don't offer the isolation you may expect along the other shores. There are also practical concerns for the paddler more attuned to the chilly and rocky Atlantic shores: sand in the meals; butter melting in the heat; and mosquitoes and horseflies. It is a dramatic change from the rugged and moody Atlantic coast, both for the beginning paddler and the experienced tripper seeking a change. So bring your snorkelling gear and beach towel and prepare to relax.

Lismore to Pomquet Harbour ⟶

1

DEPARTURE POINT:
Lismore Government Wharf
Take Exit 27 on Highway 104, east of New Glasgow and continue north on route 245. Put in at the Government Wharf in the village of Lismore. Approximately 185 km (115 mi.) from Halifax.

ARRIVAL POINT:
Pomquet Harbour. There are several take out locations in Pomquet Harbour. (Refer to the topographical map.) Antigonish Harbour, 10 km (6 mi.) sooner, is another potential exit point.

TRIP LENGTH:
Three to five days, 75 km (47 mi.).

CHARTS AND MAPS:
Topographical maps: 11/E/9; 16 11/F/12,13
Marine charts: Cape George to Pictou (#4404: 76,000); St. Georges Bay (#4462: 75,000); Antigonish Harbour (#4446: 12,000)

ROUTE DESCRIPTION:
This route contains a little of everything that the North Shore of Nova Scotia has to offer. It has the usual beaches, sand bars, dunes, and marshes that predominate much of the gulf shoreline up to the tip of Miscou Island in New Brunswick, and it has the soft sandstone from which these features are formed. However, it also has resistant highlands, with steep slopes, cliffs, and excised valleys. Precambrian bedrock alternates with a unique melange of igneous, sedimentary, and metamorphic rock. Much of this older rock was formed prior to the attachment of southern Nova Scotia, then part of an early Africa. Abundant fossils in some places are among the oldest in the province. They are closely related to the fauna from a similar time period found in Northern Europe, indicating a close connection in the distant past.

This coastline is less travelled than the rest of the North Shore, by either boat or car. There are no major population centres, except Antigonish, which is at the very end of the route, and the beaches aren't quite as prolific as they are to the west. The highway overlooks the gulf as it winds and weaves up to the "lofty" heights of Cape George, about 150 m (492 ft.) From here, you have a clear view Cape Breton and Prince Edward Island.

SAFETY CONSIDERATIONS:

Don't assume that just because the air and water temperatures are usually warmer than elsewhere in the province, you can let your guard down. Most of this route follows a linear, exposed shoreline with rocky beaches backed by steep, forested hills. Even the sand beaches are subject to heavy surf. A careless landing during rough weather can result in more than just a scratch to your expensive boat. Be cautious when entering the narrow channels at the mouth of Antigonish and Pomquet Harbours. The currents are sometimes very strong.

POINTS OF INTEREST:

1. McArras Brook

Here we leave the low topography behind as the hills edge closer to the shore. Carboniferous sandstone gives way to older sandstone, shales, conglomerates, and basalts of the Devonian era. These accumulated when the area lay within Pangea.

2. Arisaig group

From Moydart Point to Arisaig Harbour, we pass along the bluish siltstones, tan mudstones, and shelly limestone called the Arisaig group. This rock is much older than the previous strata and dates as far back as 440 million years, during the Silurian period, and is the result of sediments collecting in a shallow marine environment. It contains numerous fossils, including: trilobites (extinct for over 300 million years); brachiopods (lamp shells, very abundant in the Palaeozoic but uncommon today); pelecypods (bivalves, such as clams); cephalopods (such as squids and nautilus); and bryozoa or sea mats, among others. A good field guide to the fossils will help in identification. The fossils are more closely related to those found in Europe than from elsewhere in North America—strong evidence that a part of the European plate remained attached to North America when the supercontinent finally split apart.

3. Arisaig Point

Here highly resistant volcanic rocks, the oldest in the Arisaig area, about 450 million years old, form a natural breakwater along this otherwise linear coastline. Dark green balsatic lava flows have

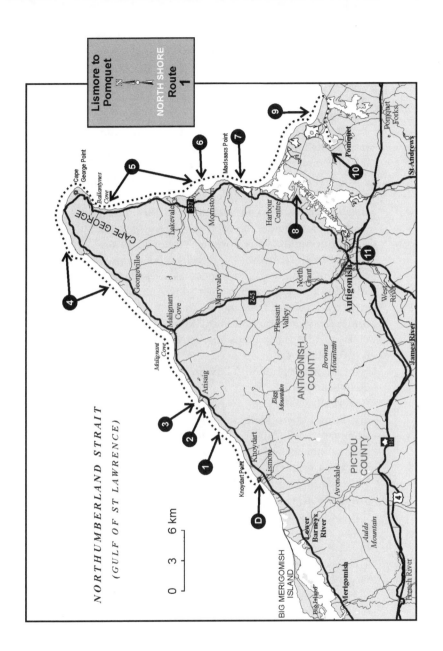

been overlain by reddish-orange rhyolitic flows, and columnar jointing is evident in the basalt. Note the red to purple layers between the basalt flows, believed to be ancient soils that developed between volcanic eruptions. Rhyolite is highly viscous lava and exhibits strong folding.

4. Shoreline between Malignant Cove and Cape George

Here is the boundary between the weaker and younger strata of the Northumberland Strait and the more resistant and older rocks of the Pictou/Antigonish Highlands. These are the highest cliffs along the North Shore and offer few good landing spots. Dense woods often run right down to the coast. Near Livingstone Cove, a thick deposit of glacial till overlies wave-cut bedrock.

5. From Ballantynes Cove to Cribbons Point

Here reddish sandstones and conglomerates predominate on a coastline of rolling hills and open fields. The highway closely parallels the water and brings the cottages and homes with it. This stretch is sheltered from the full force of the westerly winds, and brings the warm fragrance of wild flowers and hay—an unusual sensation for the coastal paddler in Nova Scotia.

6. Cribbons Point

Here we made landfall following our harrowing crossing of St. Georges Bay. The light we noticed at the time was on the Government Wharf, on a small headland marking a fault boundary. From here to McIsaac Point, there is ancient metamorphic siltstone and sandstone—the oldest on the route. Conglomerate and limestones overlie the sandstones.

7. The Crystal Cliffs

This outcrop of pink and white gypsum is 75 m (246 ft.) high. The mineral precipitated from an evaporating inland sea when this area was situated near the equator. Cormorants nest on the eroded ledges.

8. Antigonish Harbour

This is a shallow, irregular intrusion into a basin of soft sedimentary rock; a drowned estuary. From the entrance of the harbour to the town of Antigonish is about 10 km (6 mi.). Abundant sediment has formed two spits—Mahoney Beach and Dunn Beach—which, except for the channel, close off the mouth of the harbour. Exposures of gypsum and the karst type of topography can be seen around the shoreline. Be cautious when entering as the current can be strong.

9. Pomquet Beach

It consists of numerous parallel dune ridges forming a wide barrier beach across Pomquet Harbour. It is possibly the most interesting beach and dune system in the province, demonstrating complete succession from beach colonizer, to forest, to salt marsh and to lagoon. It is also an excellent example of a pro-grading dune system, one which increases in height from west to east. This results from the ocean waves entering St. Georges Bay and striking the shoreline at an angle, causing a strong longshore movement of sediment. Thus, unlike many other beaches, such as those along the east coast of Cape Breton Island, Pomquet is moving seaward.

10. Pomquet

This small village, population 510, was settled in 1761 by Acadians who had returned to the province after the Expulsion of 1755.

11. Antigonish

It is the largest town in northern Nova Scotia with a population of about 4,925 and is also the home of St. Francis Xavier University.

2

MERIGOMISH HAROUR

DEPARTURE POINT:
Merigomish
Take Exit 27 (Highway 104) and continue north along route 245 to Merigomish, 7 km (4 mi.) Put in near bridge. Approximately 175 km (109 mi.) from Halifax. There are many other potential put in sites around the harbour, including Barney's Point Campground, Savage Cove on Merigomish Island and Quarry Island.

ARRIVAL POINT:
Same as departure point.

TRIP LENGTH:
One to two days, 25 km (15 mi.).

CHARTS AND MAPS:
Topographical maps: 11 E/9, 10
Marine charts: Merigomish Harbour (#4445: 18,000)

ROUTE DESCRIPTION:
The year after I circumnavigated Nova Scotia, I left academia in Quebec and returned home. Working with test tubes in a university laboratory, while at times intellectually stimulating, was a long way from the love of the outdoors that first drew me to the science of biology. Uncertain of what direction I wanted to take, I took on the job of Voyager Director at Big Cove YMCA camp. I had never attended summer camp as a kid, but in this single season I made up for it. Although I never quite got into the campfire scene with "100 bottles of beer on the wall," I was given a free hand to set out tripping along the coast of the province with a group of teenagers.

We paddled to Prince Edward Island via Pictou Island and also undertook a voyage along the rugged Atlantic coast. However, most of the time was spent poking around the confines of Merigomish Harbour; a large, protected basin just east of New Glasgow and at the eastern limit of the soft sedimentary rock that forms the backbone of most of the province's north shore. It is protected from the Northumberland Strait by a large island of the same name, although it has been linked to the mainland by a barrier beach and road for well over a century. There is only one relatively narrow

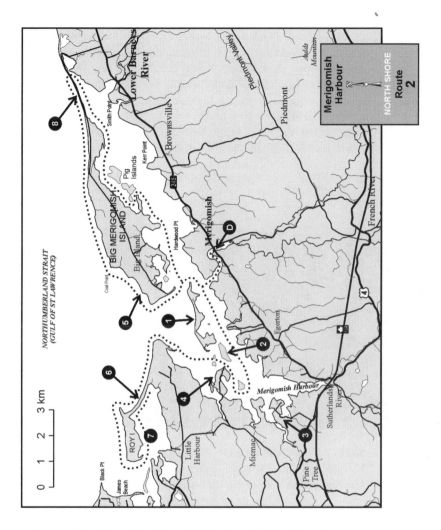

entrance 1 km (0.6 mi.) wide to the harbour. The harbour has several islands. Some are forested, others are little more than sand bars. One was farmed, another had a quarry, and another is a Mi'kmaq burial ground. Most are now uninhabited and unused.

Tongues of salt water have eaten passages into the soft bedrock fringe, and fine silt has settled, forming mud flats and salt marshes. Ducks, mink, and muskrats hide in the grasses. The surrounding scenery is a mixture of farmland, forest, and cottage development.

A few miles to the south, the Antigonish Highlands rise almost 305 m (1,000 ft.). To the north, the strait waters reach to Prince

Edward Island. The harbour is sheltered and shallow. The water temperature is among the warmest along the entire shore. Clams and mussels are abundant, and this is a good spot in which to study the biology of mud flats, beaches, and salt marshes, or to just relax and enjoy the sunshine. Outside the harbour two large, active barrier beaches contrast with the interior tranquility and attract a large vacation crowd. Melmerby Beach is a provincial park with supervised swimming. Merigomish Beach is less crowded.

Salt marshes form in the shallow upper reaches of the inlets and bays.

SAFETY CONSIDERATIONS:

Merigomish is shallow, sheltered, and warm during the summer. The threat of hypothermia isn't high in the event of an accidental capsize. You will also never be more than a kilometre from land, where roads and habitations rim the shoreline. However, the southwest-northeast lay of the harbour is aligned with the prevailing wind direction (i.e., from the southwest) and a 15 km (9 mi.) fetch is certainly enough room for some serious chop. If you don't pay attention to what the wind is doing, you could end up stuck at one end of the harbour.

The harbour entrance deserves special attention. It is crisscrossed with channels and sand bars scarcely noticeable on the surface, but they affect the speed and direction of the currents entering and leaving. Add the possibility of an opposing wind from the strait stirring things up even more, and extreme caution is advised when heading out. Note wind and current direction and scan the entrance for whitecaps and standing waves.

Once outside, the adjacent linear coastline offers no sheltered landing, and expect a dumping surf in the event of a strong onshore wind. Tidal rips and erratic wave patterns aren't restricted to the harbour mouth and will sometimes also characterize the sandbars off the beaches. These can be great places to practise if you know what you are doing but should to be avoided by the novice paddler.

POINTS OF INTEREST:

1. Olding Island
This is the largest island in the harbour, about 3 km (2 mi.), and the only one to have had a farm. It has long since been abandoned, with coastal spruce reclaiming the fields on the western end. The island has a few forests, hills—drumlins left from an ice sheet that covered much of this area with glacial till—sand spits, and a small salt marsh.

2. Indian Island
Part of a Mi'kmaq reserve, it has a small chapel and a burial ground.

3. Big Cove YMCA summer camp.

4. Quarry Island
Now linked to the mainland by a causeway, it derives its name from a gypsum quarry, an indication that the basin was once part of an evaporating sea.

5. Merigomish Island
A small band of coal is exposed in the sandstone cliffs near the end of Merigomish Island.

6. Melmerby Beach
This is one of the most popular beaches in the province and part of the provincial park system. It is a thin barrier beach connecting Roy Island with Kings Head and has progressively become narrower due to sand removal, until its protection in 1966. Abundant sediment just offshore has been deposited as a series of shifting bars. It has supervised swimming in season.

7. Little Harbour
This is a picturesque basin and very shallow at low water.

8. Barrier Beach
It connects Merigomish Island to the mainland. The remains of a sea wall protects the exposed roadway. It is less than a 100 m (328 ft.) wide at the narrowest point and an easy portage.

3

PICTOU ISLAND

DEPARTURE POINT:
Caribou Harbour
Follow Route 106 to the Prince Edward Island ferry terminal at Caribou Harbour. Take Pictou Island Ferry exit and put in at the concrete slip. Parking is available at the adjacent terminal. Approximately 175 km (109 mi.) from Halifax. Alternative departure point: Caribou Provincial Park, 2 km (1 mi.) east of Caribou Harbour.

ARRIVAL POINT:
Same as departure points.

TRIP LENGTH:
Two days, 35 km (22 mi.). Pictou Island is about 8 km (5 mi.) from Caribou.

CHARTS AND MAPS:
Topographical maps: 11/E/10, 15
Marine charts: Cape George to Pictou (#4404: 76,000)

ROUTE DESCRIPTION:
Pictou Island, opposite the town of the same name, is the largest island in the Northumberland Strait. It lies about one-third of the distance between Nova Scotia and Prince Edward Island, just east of the ferry route that funnels droves of visitors to the "Land of Anne" during the summer months.

As a child, I, too, would travel this passage to our cottage on Prince Edward Island's North Shore, often pondering the mysteries of Pictou Island as we passed it in the distance. However, my first visit to Pictou Island was in 1981, as the Voyageur Director at Big Cove, a YMCA summer camp in Merigomish Harbour. For one of our "expeditions" we decided to cross the Northumberland Strait to Prince Edward Island in a flotilla of canoes. With fine weather and warm waters, we reached Pictou Island in five hours. We had left the North Shore at Roy Island, a distance of 16 km (10 mi.).

The following day a strong wind grounded us, so we set out on foot to explore this secluded isle and, as it turned out, to take a step back in time.

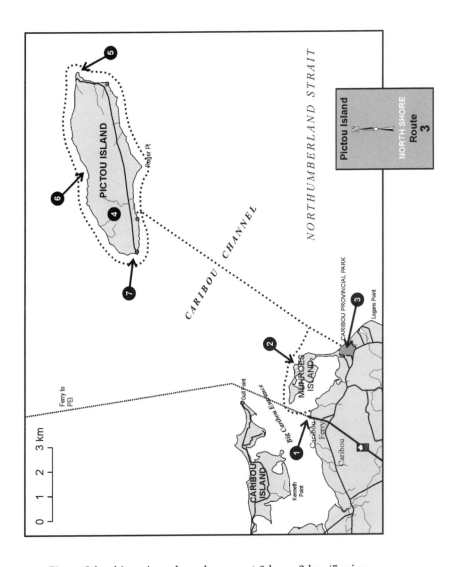

Pictou Island is a cigar-shaped remnant 8 km x 2 km (5 mi. x 1 mi.) of a carboniferous sandstone ridge that once sat in the middle of the strait. In many ways, it resembles Prince Edward Island: gentle beaches, sand dunes, soft cliffs, open field, coniferous forest, and rustic century homesteads. Only the salt marshes and deep inlets are absent.

Pictou Island hasn't been spared the inexorable erosion of its soft bedrock, but fortunately it has been spared the more recent wave of coastal development. It remains a quiet, pastoral isle steeped in an ambience of earlier and more prosperous days, an idyllic haven in which to while away a few precious summer moments.

SAFETY CONSIDERATIONS:

In winter much of the Gulf of St. Lawrence freezes and thick pack ice is usually jammed onto the North Shore by the prevailing north winds. Ice-breaking ferries are needed to maintain the link with Prince Edward Island. The arrival of spring is delayed, and even when the melt finally arrives, and the lobster fishermen can set their traps, the Northumberland Strait waters remain cold sometimes well into June. For a time they are even colder than the Atlantic. However, the shallow waters also warm up rapidly and from mid-July until the end of August, and often well into September, the strait is remarkably temperate for these latitudes. Water temperatures can exceed 20°C (68°F), whereas along the Atlantic they usually remain below 15°C (60°F) and in the Bay of Fundy they can dip as low as 5°C (40°F). Warm continental air adds to this vacation climate which, along with the extensive beaches, makes this such a popular holiday destination. Dry suits are not standard equipment! Instead, bring your mask, snorkel, and beach towel.

Unfortunately, this description of benign conditions, emphasized in the tourism literature, may lead paddlers to lower their guard. There are dangers inherent to all coastal paddling, and you ignore them at your own peril. The strait waters are usually less demanding, but an 8 km (5 mi.) paddle from the mainland is not without its risks. Winds may be absent for days, but they arise rapidly, funnelling down the long Northumberland fetch. It takes little time for a major chop to develop, especially when opposing the currents—2 km/hr (1 mi./hr) is common more around the tip of Pictou Island.

Check the weather forecast before departure. The conditions usually don't change within minutes, but they could in the two to three hours it takes to reach the island. Be prepared to alter your plans. Use the "ferry"—a modified fishing boat—if necessary. It leaves early in the morning and returns late in the afternoon, although not every day. If the weather dictates, an alternative to a paddle is a hike around the island—a day-long trek. Plan your return to coincide with the ferry departure, in case a paddle back to the mainland isn't practical. The island has phone service should you wish to call someone to confirm your arrival, but you will just have to knock on someone's door to use a phone.

Special Caution: When navigating Caribou Harbour avoid the ferry traffic. These large boats move faster than you may think and create a considerable wake. Even if they spot you in their path they probably won't be able to avoid you in time. Be wary, too, of pleasure and fishing boats. They are also common inhabitants of the harbour and won't be on the look out for inconspicuous canoes or kayaks.

More than anything else, sand beaches define the Northumberland Strait.

POINTS OF INTEREST:

1. Ferry terminals

The terminal for one of the car ferries linking Prince Edward Island with the mainland is situated in Caribou Harbour. The other link to Prince Edward Island is at Cape Tormentine, New Brunswick, where the Confederation Bridge crossing the strait was completed in May 1997. Caribou Harbour is sheltered by Caribou and Doctor Islands and is quite shallow. The ferries don't have much room to manoeuvre. They run at least once an hour, so observe the channel markers and be sure to keep clear of the boats. The Pictou Island ferry departs to the right of the main terminal.

2. Doctor Island

Uninhabited and mostly forest-covered, with sheltered lagoons, salt marsh, and sand spits, this island has recently been acquired for a natural park. When I passed this way during my circumnavigation in 1980, a narrow channel separated it from the mainland (still marked on some maps). Since then, a strong storm has closed it.

3. Caribou Provincial Campground

This is an unserviced park 3 km (2 mi.) from the ferry terminal. No showers and only pit toilets. It is an excellent base from which to explore the surrounding area and for departure to Pictou Island.

4. Pictou Island

It was settled in the early 1800s by Scottish immigrants—many from the Isle of Mull off Scotland's west coast. By 1823 it had a population of fifty-nine. In 1887, there were twenty-seven farms and nearly four hundred residents, making this one of Nova Scotia's largest island communities. As recently as sixty years ago, a fish packing plant on the north side employed thirty workers. However, the island was often cut off—with no sheltered harbours or coves, vessels often couldn't land, even in summer. In winter, the thick pack ice isolated the inhabitants for up to four months. It became more difficult to make a living, and emigration had begun by the end of the nineteenth century. Today, although it is still used as a lobster fishing base, summer residency is the norm. In 1994, only thirty stayed year-round.

Pictou Island descends gradually into the sea over regenerating fields, dunes, and the sand beaches that stretch along much of its southern shore. A narrow gravel road runs the entire length and is bordered by well-maintained, stately century homesteads alongside disintegrating houses. White spruce is retaking fields once grazed by cattle and sheep. A recent livestock count yielded one horse and one donkey. Rabbits are common, pursued by red foxes and possibly coyotes. White-tailed deer are also sometimes seen, but a swim from the mainland is challenging.

There are no services on the island (i.e., accommodation or stores) so bring all your supplies with you, including fresh water, although you can probably get refills from one of the residents. Any electricity is supplied by the wind, the sun, or gas generators. A telephone cable has been laid, but with no pay phones, you will have to knock on a resident's door to find one. Mail is delivered twice a week by plane, using the road as a landing strip. Except for a small area around each light beacon, the island is privately owned; there are no official campgrounds, but beach camping is permitted. Otherwise ask permission.

5. Seal Point

This is the extreme eastern end of the island and appropriately named. Each time I've been here, regardless of the season, I have been in the company of seals. The loose cliffs of sand and mud are continually eroding, undermining the spruce forest. Dark sandstone accretions, resembling petrified cow paddies, stand out in the washed reddish bedrock at the base. The island sandstone creeps along just below the surface, for several hundred metres before finally dipping down into the strait. When the current crosses these shoals it can become quite agitated, especially at low tide and against the wind. Caution is advised. However, in midsummer with the warm water, it can also be a great place to practice advanced techniques. Once across the shoals, the sea again calms down.

Just to the south of Seal Point and at the end of the road, a breakwater shelters a sandy beach. Several cabins in various states of disrepair are used by fishermen during the spring lobster season.

6. The northern shoreline of Pictou Island

A mostly boulder/sand beach borders eroding cliffs and dense woods. One exceptional sand beach (indicated by the arrow on the map) occupies the centre of the island, far from the "developed" south coast, and is an excellent campsite. Other than a narrow road near the western end, above the "harbour", the north coast is difficult to reach. Even the trails marked on older topographical maps are now overgrown.

7. West Point

This is also an area where caution is advised. The shoals are not as pronounced as at Seal Point, but currents can create a fair chop next to shore. Fern fossils are found in the sandstone below the banks, the upper edge of which are lined with swallow burrows. Massive pieces of cast iron—parts of the former light tower—are found in the field below the present beacon.

4

Wallace River to Pugwash River

DEPARTURE POINT:

Middleboro Bridge (Wallace River)
At Exit 11 on Highway 104 continue north on Route 4 to Wentworth Centre. Follow Route 307 (8 km, 5 mi.) to turn off on left leading to bridge. Parking space by bridge. Approximately 155 km (97 mi.) from Halifax.

Note: There are several considerations here: Since this initial section of the Wallace River route (4 km) is non-tidal, it is only passable when the flow is sufficiently high, usually only in spring or fall, or during a wet summer. Other departure options include the next bridge (further north on Route 368) and putting in here at high tide. At other times you can depart at the causeway, crossing Wallace Bay at the Nature Wildlife Area (a channel reaches here during all but the lowest tides).

ARRIVAL POINT:

There are several take out spots depending upon where you begin and the length of your trip. Other than Wallace Bay they include Pugwash and Conns Mills (Pugwash River). Since the Pugwash River is tidal right up to Conns Mills, and it is important to time your arrival (or departure, should you decide to leave from here) with the full tide. There are not many places elsewhere on the upper portion of the river where you can access the highway.

TRIP LENGTH:

Two to three days, 60 km (37.5 mi.)
This route can be broken down into several segments that lend themselves to day long and part day trips. For example, you might paddle the Pugwash one day, followed by a trip on the Wallace the next. There are a number of put in/take out spots where the highways meet the water and a glance at the topo maps will offer suggestions (once again take account of the tides).

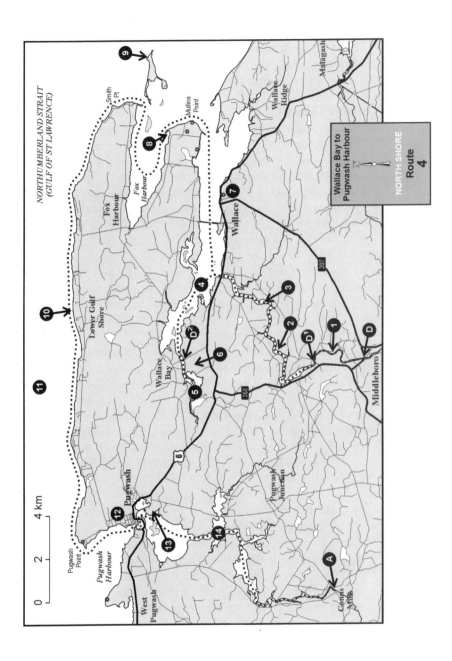

Charts and Maps:
Topographical maps: 11/E/13,14
Marine charts: None at a useful scale

Route Description:
Much of this route is inland but the rivers are tidal and, as such, constitute (at least in my mind) coastal waters. The scenery and ambience is distinctly different than most of the other routes described in this guide (including the others on the North Shore). Meandering streams, lush deciduous woods, salt marshes, inland birdlife are all part of this salt water intrusion into the summer life of the province. The waters are warm, tranquil, and at odds with the rugged nature of the Atlantic coastline only a couple of hours away. The striking topography of other coastal regions may be diluted but this is an ideal domain for beginners and families with young children—or for those who are looking for some relaxing poking around when there isn't the time for an extended tour.

Safety Considerations:
Safety considerations here pertain more to pleasure boat traffic, (which may not be on the lookout for low-profile kayaks) than to any specific paddling dangers. The main channels are buoyed so always note where the larger craft are likely to travel. If you follow the section along the exposed Northumberland shoreline, be aware that significant surf can develop with an onshore wind. A major up side is the water temperature in the rivers and estuaries, which are even warmer in the summer than in the Strait (and can exceed 20°C (68°F).

Points of Interest:
1. Upper Wallace River
Although the Wallace River extends back inland well beyond Wentworth, this is the only section of our route that is not tidal. Therefore, the freshwater flow must be sufficient to ensure passage—and, even then, you may sometimes scrape the bottom (so be forewarned, those with expensive boats and weak stomachs). However, paddling this stretch is well worth the occasional scratch. The winding stream is funneled by faults of layered sandstone (from the early Carboniferous period—over 350 million years ago) that texture the exposed cliffs. Bird life is plentiful (I spotted a couple of pileated woodpeckers the last trip) and bank

swallows have built their nests in the edges of the small floodplain. The forest of white pine, red oak, and hemlock is broken by the occasional field, which spills onto the river's edge. During autumn you not only have coloured foliage but also overhanging apple trees, with fruit that can be picked from the boat.

2.   Lower Wallace River

Shortly downstream of the bridge (an alternative departure point), the Wallace River is tidal and almost uniform in width (about 150 m) and until it empties into Wallace Harbour. However, the current is so gentle that paddling is easy, even against the flow. Of more concern would be a strong sea breeze which, from the north, would funnel up the river (although in summer the prevailing southwesterlies will be at your back). The river continues to bend about the natural faults in the sedimentary bedrock and is relatively secluded, with a mixed deciduous/ conifer forest lining much of the banks. A campsite will not be hard to find. When the tide is low, salt marshes emerge and narrow the channel.

3.   Wallace Bridge

This branch line of the Canadian National Railway was abandoned many years ago and, for much of its length, has been transformed into a segment of the Trans-Canada Hiking trail. The classic stone and steel bridge has been refinished and overlain with a

Apple picking in the fall along the Wallace River.

wooden pathway. The round pillar on the east bank supported the span that would have been rotated when a ship came up the river (although they would have been unable to continue much further up the shallow waterway).

4. Wallace Harbour

This shallow harbour is sheltered from the Northumberland Strait by its narrow entrance. However, the low profile of the surrounding land does little to block any wind. The most interesting parts are the salt marshes that border the narrowing passage, running east into Wallace Harbour.

5. Wallace Bay National Wildlife Area

Established in 1980 under the Canadian Wildlife Act (following years of work by Ducks Unlimited to control the water flow) these wetlands have long been important waterfowl migration and breeding grounds and it is a great spot to view birdlife. If time allows you should stop at the causeway and follow the trail built and maintained by the Wallace Area Development Association (6). This path will take you along the dikes and through several distinct habitats: salt marsh, freshwater marsh, abandoned fields, hardwood stands and conifer woods—with a chance to spot the associated birdlife (e.g., ducks, hawks, warblers, red-winged blackbirds, thrush, woodpeckers, chickadees, nuthatches, among many others).

7. Wallace

This modest fishing and farming community was once the site of quarries where sandstones were cut for both building and grinding purposes. Specific sandstones were needed. For sharpening tools, the grains had to be of a uniform size. They also needed to be cemented together such that they would gradually come off when rubbed against the steel. For construction purposes, fine sandstone that could be cut without splitting, in any direction (hence the name freestone) was required. The Wallace quarries had both kinds. The provincial legislature building in Halifax was built with Wallace sandstone.

8. Fox Harbour Park

This provincial day use park is a good departure/arrival point. At low tide, large areas of Fox Harbour are exposed sand and mud, and there are many shoals around Oak Island.

9. Quarry Point

Sandstone was once cut from these cliffs.

10. Gulf Shore Camping Park

This shoreline is part of a resistant sandstone ridge. It is mostly private and a steady stream of cottages will dissuade the wilderness camper. This campground is the only one available.

11. Northumberland Shore
This relatively linear coastline is bordered by low sandstone cliffs and plenty of beach. Forest cover is limited, most of it cut down—initially for farms and more recently for the cottages that extend almost uninterrupted from Wallace Harbour to Pugwash Harbour. It is exposed to any winds coming in off the strait as there are no protective islands and few indentations in which to take shelter. However, landing is easy on the extensive sand beaches (providing that you do so before any significant surf builds) and the highway is not far.

12. Pugwash
This small town offers accommodation (some border the water), gas stations, craft shops, and grocery stores.

13. Salt mines
Early in the Carboniferous period (about 350 million years ago), the earth's continents were moving together to form one major supercontinent. An area that covers the present day Gulf of St. Lawrence and beyond was a subsiding basin that received sediment from the surrounding highlands. Incursions of the sea flooded the huge basin intermittently. This area was near the equator at the time and the climate was hot. When the sea was cut off the water evaporated and the dissolved salts eventually precipitated out. First to come out of sea water was the calcium carbonate, then the anhydrate and gypsum (when 3/4 of the water was evaporated) and then the sodium chloride (when 9/10 of the water was gone). Over time, and after repeated incursions of the sea, huge plains of salt hundreds of feet thick were deposited. This is the source of the salt mines where, since 1956, millions of tons of this rock salt have been removed from the huge caverns, some as much as 250 meters underground. All the road salt that we use in the province during the winter comes from here.

14. Pugwash River
The river is tidal up to Conn Mills and has vast areas of marsh and mud at low water. Several irregular coves give the lower regions a dendridic appearance. Much of the shoreline is still forested but during the last couple of decades the ubiquitous summer cottage has also made inroads here.

A Equipment Checklists

The following is a selection of equipment that I have found useful at one time or another during a coastal paddling trip. Some of it is indispensable (the boat and paddle, of course) and some I have rarely, if ever, used (an EPIRB, for example). What you bring will depend upon several factors, including the location and duration of your trip, the time of year and temperature of the water, your level of expertise, and the thickness of your wallet. I have **noted with an asterisk** the items that I consider essential for a day-long summer outing in sheltered water. You may decide to add to these, and you will eventually develop your own list to fit your particular needs.

BOAT AND ACCESSORIES:
*Kayak or canoe (properly outfitted, with floatation)
*Paddles (including spare)
*Spray skirt (spray deck for canoe, optional)
*Bailing device (pump, scoop, sponge)
*Signalling device :
    Audio: whistle, air horn
    Visual: flares, day and night
*Life vest, PFD
*Compass
*Topographical maps/marine charts
*Knife (keep it sharp and accessible)
*Water bottle and snack bag
*Thermos (or means to make hot drink)
*Bivouac sack (or means to make shelter)
*Tow line:
    (necessary with a group, and 15 m to fulfil the CG standard)
*Self-rescue method, if alone:
    (Eskimo roll or re-entry technique)
AM/FM radio;
VHF radio/cellular phone;
EPIRB (emergency position indicating radio beacon)
*Repair kit:
    (appropriate to your craft)

The Canadian Coast Guard has always had a list of minimum requirements for canoes/kayaks and updated the list in 1999:

Paddle
Buoyancy aid (to fit the paddler—previously it didn't need to fit)
Signalling device
Bailing device
Heaving line (15 metres of floating rope)

Note: There has been much controversy surrounding the last item which I consider a misguided and possibly dangerous addition. Although it is important to have a towing system in a group (and the knowledge of how to use it!), having a simple rope breeds a false sense of security—and can be a potential recipe for disaster if it is improperly stored or used by an inexperienced paddler.

CAMPING GEAR:

Tent (capable of withstanding heavy wind and rain)
Ground sheet
Sleeping bag (three-season), pad
*Day pack
Clothing/equipment packs (waterproofing system)
Flashlight/batteries
Lighter/matches
Bow saw and hatchet
*Small shovel
Extra rope

COOKING GEAR:

Stove and fuel
Grill
Foil
Frying pan, spatula
Pots, plates, cups, cutlery
Can/bottle opener
Coffee pot
Dish soap, scouring pad, drying towel

CLOTHING:

Paddling:
*Footwear (sneakers, Tevi sandals, neoprene booties when cold)
Wet suit (farmer john) or dry suit
Paddling jacket (waterproof)
*Poggies, mittens, or gloves
*Hats (for sun and cold)
Sunglasses
*Change of clothing

General:
Extra footwear
Long pants (fleece, nylon)
Shorts or swim trunks
Underwear, undershirts
Shirt
Sweater (fleece)
Windbreaker
Rain jacket/pants

APPENDIX A (continued)

MISCELLANEOUS
PERSONAL:

Toilet articles (toilet paper,
   towel/face cloth, soap,
   toothbrush and toothpaste)
Camera equipment and film
Binoculars
Sun screen, lip balm
Bug repellent
Needle/thread
Watch/clock (with alarm)
Fishing line, lures
Field guides
Novel
Pen and paper

Kits

REPAIR KIT

It is prudent to assume that you will need to occasionally make repairs. You may put a hole in your kayak, snap a rudder cable, lose a footrest, or rip your tent. I've experienced all these and much more. The following are some of the items that I stock in my kit, with an emphasis on materials and tools that will help you to improvise a repair.

Tools:
Screwdriver (multi-bits)
Pliers/vice grips or Leatherman
Trauma scissors
Utility knife/extra blades
Small file
Whet stone

Materials for Attaching and Patching:
Duct tape
Shoe glue
Epoxy resin
Sikaflex (elastic adhesive)
Vinyl adhesive (tents)
Large elastics
Assortment of stainless steel nuts, bolts, and washers
Extra steel cable (if kayak has a rudder)
Bungie cord
Fastex buckles with webbing
Deckline anchors/hardware
Twine and rope
Tent patch
Needle and thread (sail maker's needles)

Miscellaneous:
Extra batteries
Extra footrest
Lighter
Extra tent pole and joiner; pegs

Appendix B (continued)

Emergency/First Aid Kits

Accidents can happen on a coastal paddling trip, and outside help may be some time in coming. Therefore, you should be prepared, as much as reasonably possible, for that eventuality. What you bring and how you prepare yourself will depend on when and where you travel. However, bring a kit along even on a day-long outing. Someone in your group should have appropriate first aid experience.

A. Abbreviated Kit:

This should be modest in size and weight, waterproof, and attached to your person or within easy reach in the event of a capsize. Mine includes the following items: day flare, night flare, lighter or waterproof matches and fire starter, knife, space blanket, chocolate or candy, Leatherman tool, tape and bandages, pain tablets.

B. Standard Kit:

This should contain various medicines, bandages, and other materials needed to cope with a variety of potential wilderness emergencies. It should be compact, accessible, and waterproof. Refer to a wilderness first aid manual for suggested contents. Better still, participate in a good wilderness first aid course.

Tours, Courses, Rentals, Sales

Coastal paddling is a relatively new sport in eastern Canada. However, businesses catering to participants have grown considerably since publication of the first edition of this guide. Operators are now found throughout the province and the following are some of those presently active in sea kayaking in Nova Scotia. Although all have been in business for at least two years, this listing does not necessarily indicate an endorsement.

OUTFITTERS

AquaAcadie Adventures*
64 Coolen's Road
Shad Bay, NS • B3T 2B7
(902) 852-5322
**www3.ns.sympatico.ca
/aquaventures**
Day-long and overnight guided tours

**Cape Breton Sea
Coast Adventures**
Wreck Cove,
RR#1 Englishtown, NS
B0C 1H0
(902) 929-2800
1-877-929-2800
**www.members.tripod
.com/adventure_4u**
Full and half day guided trips. Rentals.
Accommodations

**Crescent Beach
Kayak Tours**
RR#1, LaHave
Crescent Beach, NS
B0R 1C0
(902) 688-2806
**www.outdoorsns.com
/crescent**
Full and half day guided trips.

Coastal Adventures*
PO Box 77
Tangier, NS • B0J 3H0
(902) 772-2774;
1-877-404-2774
**www.coastaladventures
.com**
Eastern Canada's most experienced coastal paddling operation. Day-long, weekend, and extended sea kayaking tours throughout Atlantic Canada. Courses for beginners and advanced paddlers, leading to certification in the BCU, the CRCA and AECSKO. Naturalist led and outfitted trips. Rentals.
Accommodation.

APPENDIX C (continued)

Hinterland Adventures*
54 Gates Lane
Weymouth, NS • B0W 3T0
(902) 837-4092;
1-800-378-8177
**www.outdoorns
.com/hinterland**
Day-long and overnight
guided trips. Rentals.

Isle Madame Paddling Adventures
P.O. Box 228
Arichat, NS • B0E 1A0
(902) 226-9371
**www.islemadame
.com/waterandsky**
Full and half day guided
trips. Rentals

Kayak Cape Breton
RR2
West Bay, NS • B0E 3K0
(902) 535-3060
**www.destination-ns
.com/brasdor/kayak**
Full and half day guided
trips. Accommodations.
Rentals.

Mahone Bay Adventures*
618 Main Street
Mahone Bay, NS • B0J 2E0
(902) 624-6632
**http://fox.nstn
.ca/~ seakayak/**
Full and half day guided
trips. Rentals.

North River Kayak Tours*
RR#4
Baddeck, NS • B0E 1B0
(902) 929-2628
**www.chatsubo
.com/nrktours**
Day-long and overnight
guided trips. Rentals

Rossignol Surf and Kayak
216 Main Street
Liverpool, NS • B0T 1K0
(902) 683-2530
**www.outdoorns
.com/surfshop/**
Day-long and overnight
guided trips. Rentals

SeaSun Kayak
St Marys Boat Club
12649 Fairfield Rd
Halifax, NS • B3J 3A5
www.ventured.com
(902) 471-2732;
1-888-338-3688
Day-long and overnight
guided trips. Rentals.

Seaclusion Kayak Adventures
1270 Argyle Sound Road
Box 33, West Pubnico, NS
B0W 3S0
(902) 762-2191
Day-long and overnight
guided trips

Shoreline Adventures
RR#4 Harbour Centre
Antigonish, NS • B2G 2L2
(902) 863-5958
**www3.ns.smypatico
.ca/shoreline.adv/**
Full and half day guided
trips. Rentals

Member of the Association of Eastern Canadian Sea Kayaking Outfitters

STORES

Old Creel Canoe & Kayak
1700 Portobello Road
Waverley, NS • B0N 2S0
(902) 860-1938;
1-888-875-1800
Sea kayaks and accessories.

Ron's Army Navy
714 Windmill Road
Dartmouth, NS • B3B 1C2
(902) 468-7667
Sea kayaks and accessories.
General camping
equipment

The Trail Shop
6210 Quinpool Road
Halifax, NS • B3L 1A3
(902) 423-8736
www.trailshop.com
Sea kayaks and accessories.
Topographical maps.
General camping
equipment

KAYAK BUILDING

Whynot Boats
Box 1074
Wolfville, NS • B0P 1X0
(902) 542-3244
**www.valleyweb
.com/whynot**
Offers courses in building
wooden kayaks

CLUBS AND ASSOCIATIONS

**Association of Eastern
Canadian Sea Kayaking
Outfitters**
RR#1, Carling Bay Road
Nobel, Ontario
P0G 1G0
www.aecsko.on.ca
Member guidelines for sea
kayaking guides, tours and
rentals.

**Canadian Recreational
Canoeing Association**
P.O. Box 398
Merrickville, Ontario
K0G 1N0
(613) 269-2910
www.crca.ca
The CRCA has developed
a national sea kayaking
program.

NS Coastal Water Trail
c/o Sue Browne
seatrail@istar.ca
Organisation developing a
provincial paddling trail.

South Shore Paddlers
**www.angelfire
.com/md/paddler**
Local club active in both
inland and coastal paddling

MARINE CHARTS
AND TOPOGRAPHICAL MAPS

TOPOGRAPHICAL MAPS:

These can be purchased at many outdoor stores, such as the Trail Shop, or at the Nova Scotia Government Bookstore. They cost approximately $13.00 plus tax. For mail order and to obtain an index contact the Canada Map Office, Department of Energy, Mines and Resources, Ottawa, ON, K1A 0E9. (613) 952-7000.

MARINE CHARTS:

Most marine supply stores carry copies of the regional charts. They cost about $20 plus tax. For mail order and Index 1: Atlantic Coast contact Hydrographic Chart Distribution Office, Department of Fisheries and Oceans, PO Box 8080, Ottawa, ON, K1G 3H6. (613)998-4931.

CANOE WATERWAY MAPS:

The Shubenacadie Canal and River System maps are available from Land Registration and Information Service, Box 310 Amherst, NS, B4H 3Z5. (902) 667-7231.

GEOLOGY MAP:

The *Geological Highway Map of Nova Scotia* illustrates the earth history of the province in considerable detail, not just that along the highways. It is quite helpful to the coastal paddler interested in the topic. It can be purchased from the Nova Scotia Government Bookstore or the Nova Scotia Museum of Natural History located at 1747 Summer St., Halifax, NS, B3H 3A6 or phone (902) 424-7353.

RELATED READING ⟋◢⟍

Coastal paddling has seen an information explosion in the past decade. Almost all outdoor publications have covered it, some, especially paddling magazines, include regular features, and at least three magazines are devoted exclusively to sea kayaking. There are also several newsletters and numerous books on the subject. The following lists a few of those publications that I have found useful.

MAGAZINES:

Atlantic Coastal Kayaker
PO Box 520, Ipswich, MA, 01938. US $20/10 issues. This magazine contains information on places to paddle, safety, instruction, and clubs of interest to east coast paddlers (mainly the eastern seaboard of the US).

Canoe and Kayak
PO Box 3418, Kirkland, WA, 98083. US $21/6 issues. Mainly dedicated to river and lake paddling but with increasing coverage of sea kayaking.

Explore
Suite 420, 301-14th Street, N.W. Calgary, AB, T2N 2A1. $27/8 issues. This Canadian outdoor adventure magazine continues to improve in quality and has expanded beyond its western roots to now cover the entire country. Every issue contains at least one article of interest to a coastal paddler.

Kanawa
C/O CRCA, P.O. Box 398, Merrickville, Ontario, K0G 1N0. $20/4 issues. This is the voice of the Canadian Recreational Canoeing Association and contains information on recreational paddling in Canada, including frequent articles on sea kayaking.

APPENDIX E (continued)

Paddler
PO Box 697
Fallbrook, CA, 92028. US $15/6 issues. This 1991 fusion of Canoesport Journal, River Runner, Ocean Kayak News, and Paddler (Canadian version) is, as the origin implies, an attempt to cover most paddle sports.

Sea Kayaker
6327 Seaview Avenue, Seattle, WA, 98107. US $24/6 issues. The best North American magazine specializing in sea kayaking. Excellent quality. Articles on all aspects of the sport, including in-depth destination pieces, analysis of technique, and equipment evaluations.

Wave-Length
RR#1, Site 17, C-49, Gabriola Island, BC, V0R 1X0. $17/6 issues. This sea kayaking magazine frequently has articles of interest beyond its base of the west coast.

GUIDES AND MANUALS:

Bowyer, Peter J.,Ed. *Where the Wind Blows*. Minister of Public Works and Government Services, Canada, 1995.
Excellent description of the components defining the weather off our Atlantic coast. It incorporates and expands upon four earlier publications and includes chapters on the wind, sea state, fog, storms, and weather forecasting.

Burch, David. *Fundamentals of Kayak Navigation*. Chester, CT: The Globe Pequot Press, 1999.
A profusely illustrated, well-written account of all aspects of navigation involving sea kayaks. Applies equally well to coastal canoeing. The only book of its kind that you will need.

Rowe, Ray, Ed. *Canoeing Handbook*. London, England: The Chameleon Press Limited, 1989.
The Official Handbook of the British Canoe Union. It contains detailed information on all aspects on canoeing, which in British lingo usually means kayaking, both inland and coastal. They even have a chapter written by Bill Mason on reading white water.

Of particular interest are the comprehensive chapters on design and selection of equipment, construction materials and methods, and basic paddling strokes. This is the best all-round reference book on the sport.

Dowd, John. *Sea Kayaking—A Manual for Long Distance Touring*. Seattle, WA: University of Washington Press.
Revised and updated version of the 1983 classic touring manual. Covers all aspects of expedition paddling with an emphasis on double kayaks.

Foster, Nigel. *Nigel Foster's Sea Kayaking*. Old Saybrook, CT: The Globe Pequot Press, 1998.
One of the premier practioners of the sport, he addresses weather, tides, currents, charts, and the handling of heavy surf. Step-by-step descriptions accompanied by excellent photos make this one of the best manuals in the sport.

Hutchinson, Derek. C. *Eskimo Rolling*. Old Saybrook, CT: The Globe Pequot Press, 1999.
Describes many different Eskimo roll techniques, well illustrated with drawings and anecdotes.

Hutchinson, Derek C. *Expedition Kayaking*. Old Saybrook. CT: The Globe Pequot Press, 1999.
Caters to the North American market. This manual emphasizes the equipment and techniques of single boats. Hutchinson has a preference for narrow beam "Greenland" style boats. An interesting read but with some chapters irrelevant to our waters.

Seidman, David. *The Essential Sea Kayaker*. Camden, ME: International Marine Publishing, 1992.
This is a well-written and illustrated introduction to sea kayaking for the North American paddler. The author is a self-professed novice and approaches the topic from that perspective.

NATURAL HISTORY:

Bascom, Willard. *Waves and Beaches*. New York: Anchor Books, 1980.
The classic book (now out of print) describing how waves and beaches behave under all kinds of conditions.

APPENDIX E (continued)

Berrill, M. and D. Berrill. *The North Atlantic Coast*. San Francisco: Sierra Club Books, 1981.
> The single most useful reference for a paddler on the flora and fauna and the ecology of Nova Scotia's coastline. More than a field guide, this book is full of details on how the various components of the coastal ecosystem interact.

Browne, Sue and Davis, Derek. S., eds. *The Natural History of Nova Scotia*. Halifax: Nimbus Publishing Ltd and the Nova Scotia Museum, 1996.
> This two-volume, spiral-bound reference work is often dry and technical (not for casual reading). However, it contains a wealth of information on the province's natural history not readily available elsewhere.

Foster, Nigel. *Sea Kayaking*. Old Saybrook. CT: The Globe Pequot Press, 1998.
> This guide to the sport is a notch above the rest. It is well written and illustrated by someone who is both an prominent paddler and an excellent communicator.

Fox, William, T. *At The Sea's Edge*. Englewood Cliffs, NY: Prentice-Hall, 1983.
> Describes the physical processes, coastal landforms, and marine ecology, with reference to various coastlines throughout the world. Good general reference.

Gibson, Merritt. *Summer Nature Notes for Nova Scotian Seashores*. Hantsport, NS: Lancelot Press, 1987.
> Useful companion to *The North Atlantic Coast*, with more detailed information on the life forms specifically populating our coastline.

Gosner, Kenneth L. *A Field Guide to the Atlantic Seashore*. Boston: Houghton Mifflin Company, 1979.
> Profusely illustrated, with detailed descriptions of the creatures you will encounter along our seashore. Common seaweeds are included; shore plants are not.

Roland, Albert, E., revised by Zinck, Marian. *Roland's Flora of Nova Scotia*. Halifax: Nimbus Publishing and the Nova Scotia Museum, 1998.

This recent, two-volume revision of the *Flora of Nova Scotia* is not something you would ordinarily pack for your paddling trip (although I sometimes make an exception) but is our major reference work to the plants of the province.

Roland, Albert, E. 1982. *Geological Background and Physiography of Nova Scotia*. Halifax: The Nova Scotian Institute of Science.

Detailed resource for those wishing to understand the origin and evolution of our coastal landforms. Includes many specific examples.

Thurston, Harry. *Tidal Life—A Natural History of the Bay of Fundy*. Halifax. Nimbus Publishing, 1990.

Illustrated by Stephen Homer, this is a well-written overview of the diverse nature of the Bay of Fundy.

Tufts, Robie, W. *Birds of Nova Scotia*. Halifax: Nimbus Publishing and the Nova Scotia Museum, 1986.

This revised classic includes paintings, descriptions, and anecdotes on all our native bird species. Ideal companion to a field guide.

HUMAN HISTORY:

Campbell, G. G., ed. *Castaway on Cape Breton*. Wreck Cove, Cape Breton Island: Breton Books, 1991.

Two fascinating accounts of early shipwrecks on Cape Breton Island: Ensign Prenties' Narrative, 1780, and Samuel Burrows' Narrative, 1823.

Day, Frank Parker. *Rockbound*. Toronto: University of Toronto Press, 1973.

This tale of life on the offshore islands of Nova Scotia during the early part of this century was based on the author's visit to the Tancooks. It is one of the few novels with a theme of early island life. His detailed and often unflattering portrayal of the local fishermen (based on actual individuals) raised the ire of the locals. It is worth a read.

APPENDIX E (*continued*)

Hatchard, Keith, A. *The Two Atlantics*. Hantsport, NS: Lancelot Press, 1981.
   The true story of the shipwreck of the SS *Atlantic* at Prospect, NS on April 1, 1973. Five-hundred-and-thirty-five passengers and crew (mostly woman and children) died in the greatest maritime disaster on the east coast of North America.

Mitcham, Allison. 1984. *Offshore Islands of Nova Scotia and New Brunswick*. Hantsport, NS: Lancelot Press; Paradise or Purgatory (1986); and Island Keepers (1989) are all by Allison Mitcham.
   They describe the history of many of the main offshore islands in the Maritimes. These are the best easily available sources for such information.

Stephens, David, E. *Lighthouses of Nova Scotia*. Hantsport, NS: Lancelot Press, 1973.
   A general introduction to lighthouses in the province from a time when most were still manned. Stories and descriptions of several South Shore lights are included—Sambro, Cape Roseway, Cape Sable Island, Seal Island, and Cape Forchu.

Miscellaneous:
Daniel, Linda. *Kayak Cookery*. Chester, CT: The Globe Pequot Press, 1997.
   Useful recipes designed for the limited space available in sea kayaks.

Isaac, Jeff and Goth, Peter. *The Outward Bound Wilderness First-Aid Handbook*. Vancouver: Greystone Books, 1991.
   This comprehensive guide was produced for Outward Bound and also used by Wilderness Medical Associates. It addresses the specific and unique first-aid needs for Canadians who frequent remote areas. It is well written and illustrated.

Starkell, Don, and Wilkens, Charles, ed. *Paddle to the Amazon*. Toronto: McClelland and Stewart, 1986.
   Thrilling tale of the longest canoe voyage ever undertaken. Includes large sections of coastal waters.